SENTINEL

AN AMERICAN SON

Marco Rubio served in the Florida House of Representatives from 2000 to 2008 and was elected to the U.S. Senate in 2010. His committee assignments currently include Commerce, Science, and Transportation; Foreign Relations; Intelligence; and Small Business and Entrepreneurship. He and his wife, Jeanette, have four young children and live in West Miami.

AN AMERICAN SON

A Memoir

MARCO RUBIO

Sentinel

SENTINEL
Published by the Penguin Group
Penguin Group (USA) Inc., 375 Hudson Street,
New York, New York 10014, USA

USA | Canada | UK | Ireland | Australia | New Zealand | India | South Africa | China
Penguin Books Ltd, Registered Offices:
80 Strand, London WC2R 0RL, England
For more information about the Penguin Group visit penguin.com

First published in the United States of America by Sentinel,
a member of Penguin Group (USA) Inc., 2012
This paperback edition with a new epilogue published 2013

THE LIBRARY OF CONGRESS HAS CATALOGED THE HARDCOVER EDITION AS FOLLOWS:
Rubio, Marco, 1971–
An American son : a memoir / Marco Rubio.
p. cm.
ISBN 978-1-59523-094-2 (hc.)
ISBN 978-1-59523-101-7 (pbk.)
1. Rubio, Marco, 1971– 2. Senators—United States—Biography. 3. United States.
Congress. Senate—Biography. 4. United States—Politics and government—2009–
5. Legislators—Florida—Biography. 6. Florida—Politics and government—1951–
7. Cuban Americans—Florida—Biography. 8. Florida—Biography. I. Title.
E901.l.R83A3 2012
328.73'092—dc23
[B]   2012014788

Printed in the United States of America
10 9 8 7 6 5 4 3 2 1

Set in Minion Pro
Designed by Daniel Lagin

Penguin is committed to publishing works of quality and integrity. In that spirit, we are proud
to offer this book to our readers; however, the story, the experiences, and the words are the
author's alone.

To the memory of my father and grandfather,
who I wish were here to read this book.

Contents

An American Son

CHAPTER 1

November 2, 2010

"WE'RE CALLING IT FOR YOU."

At exactly eight p.m. eastern time, Brendan Farrington, an Associated Press reporter, turned to me and spoke those words.

Seconds later, the AP report flashed simultaneously on multiple television screens. Fox News called the election as well, confirming the consensus that I would be the new senator from Florida. After all these years of watching elections, it felt a little surreal to see my name with the words "projected winner" underneath my picture. But there it was right in front of me: "Projected Winner: Marco Rubio."

The next few minutes were a blur. I shook some hands. I kissed my wife, Jeanette, and was whisked away to a separate room to field phone calls. The entire day—the entire two years of my life before that night—culminated in a flurry of congratulations, handshakes and hugs. In the midst of the celebration, I felt a tug on my jacket and saw my eight-year-old daughter, Daniella, looking up at me. "Daddy, did you win?" she asked. "Yeah, I won," I answered. "No one told me," she complained as I bent to hold her in my arms.

My family later told me I had seemed like someone else. The man bounding up the steps to the stage, grinning and waving from the podium, was attentive and expansive. That man, the gregarious public man, didn't appear in their company very often. He didn't live at our house.

The husband, father and brother they knew had been a remote figure in their lives over the last two years, a tired and distracted candidate who came home only to seek relief from the pressures of a demanding campaign. The perfect strangers whose votes I hoped to earn, who shook my hand and told me about their lives, got the best part of me. My family got what I had left, which wasn't much. In the intimacy of family life, I was quiet and withdrawn, and resisted attempts to pull me into conversations about the campaign, although my mind rarely concentrated on anything else.

I had imagined election night many times during the campaign, on good days and harder ones. I had pictured all of it: the people, the place, the sounds, the shared feelings of pride, relief, exhilaration. Even on days when I did not believe it would happen, on a long drive home from a fund-raiser where we had collected a few hundred dollars or after another poll had me thirty points behind the sitting governor of my own party, I would envision this night for encouragement. I would put on my iPod earphones, listen to my guilty pleasure, hip-hop, close my eyes and see it. And here it was, at last, no more vivid in reality than it had been in my imagination.

We were at the Biltmore Hotel in Coral Gables. I had grown up less than two miles from the Mediterranean-style landmark nestled between large banyan trees and lush golf courses. We live a short drive from it today.

The Biltmore had once boasted the world's largest swimming pool. The hotel had been the tallest structure in Florida when it opened in 1926, and in its long and colorful history it has welcomed as guests royalty and movie stars, politicians and mobsters. A famous gangster had been murdered there.

My high school friends and I had snuck onto the resort's golf course at night; its gazebos offered the perfect hiding spot for underage beer drinking. When I practiced law, I would meet clients for breakfast or lunch in its ground-floor café. As a city commissioner and later a state legislator, I attended dozens of fund-raisers and other political events in its suites and ballrooms. And in November of 2006, as the incoming speaker of the Florida House, I had waited for election results in there. Jeanette and I had been married two blocks from the Biltmore and had spent our wedding night in a room on the seventh floor. There isn't another place in the world I would rather have held what I expected would be my victory celebration.

I had good reason to be confident. Every recent public poll confirmed that I held a commanding lead. Our own tracking polls offered as good or better news. The Republican turnout in absentee ballots and early voting had given me a comfortable cushion. But as the day progressed, I couldn't shake the uneasy feeling the race would be closer than expected and I might end up on the wrong side of a historic upset.

In the open-air courtyard on the west side of the hotel, workers set up an elevated stage and placed a podium in the center, in front of a row of American and Florida state flags. Family, friends, supporters and spectators congregated in the courtyard throughout the afternoon and into the evening. Behind them stood a large riser for television cameras and media crews from around the country and the world, providing an unrestricted view of the podium where I would deliver my speech.

On the ground floor beneath the ballroom, campaign staff gathered in an improvised war room. They stared at laptops and television screens, worked their phones and chatted nervously about the weather and turnout in this or that county.

Around half past six in the evening, my twenty-four-year-old nephew Orlando, or Landy as we call him, picked us up in a rented minivan and drove us to the Biltmore. As soon as we arrived I was briskly escorted to the war room, where aides were still sitting in front of their laptops and holding their phones, waiting for news of final turnout numbers. Numerous televisions sat in the middle of the room tuned to the broadcast and cable networks that would soon begin reporting election results. Most polls in Florida close at seven p.m. eastern time, except in the Panhandle, which is in the central time zone. The polls there close an hour later, so the media refrains from projecting winners until then.

A little before eight o'clock, Brendan Farrington took a phone call. I knew from the look on his face it was important. Over a year earlier, Brendan had traveled with me on a campaign swing through the Panhandle. We were halfway through the first day's drive when a source called to tell him I was about to drop out of the Senate race.

I had all but convinced myself to quit. I had discussed getting out with several people whose discretion I trusted. I was badly trailing Governor Crist in popular support and fund-raising. Even if I were to get a little traction eventually and start to close the gap in the polls, he would have raised more than enough money to bury me in negative advertising, and I wouldn't have anywhere near enough to respond. I feared he would so tarnish my reputation that I would have a hard time finding a job after the primary and would never hold another elective office.

I felt trapped. I was bound by a sense of obligation to my supporters, the people who believed in me when no one else did, and I didn't want to disappoint them. Some of them had risked a great deal when they had crossed a sitting Republican governor by endorsing me. I had received, as had some of my prominent supporters, subtle and not so subtle threats that we were jeopardizing our future by continuing in a hopeless cause. Family and friends urged me to remain in the race. But others assessed the race as I had, as unwinnable, and agreed I should give serious consideration to making my exit. I experienced a feeling I had never had before, a sense that I was incapable of changing my circumstances, that self-reliance wasn't enough, that my industry, my convictions and my determination couldn't overcome the challenges I faced.

I had wrestled with my predicament for some time and had nearly reached the point of making the difficult decision to swallow my pride, abandon the reasons that had encouraged me to enter the race and withdraw.

But when Brendan hung up and asked me whether his source was accurate, I got angry.

I felt certain the call had come from someone in Governor Crist's campaign who decided to disclose the sensitive information to force my hand. They were trying to muscle me out of the race again, and I didn't like it. I turned to Brendan, and with a firm resolve I did not actually feel, categorically denied I would be dropping out of the race, not now or ever. I crossed the bridge and burned it behind me. There was no way back and no way out but forward.

On election night, as I watched Brendan take another phone call, glance at his watch and frown, I began to feel uneasy. Would the AP report the exit polls showed a much closer race than the polling had predicted? Worse, would they report that Governor Crist was on the verge of pulling off one of the greatest comeback victories in Florida political history?

No, they wouldn't. After a couple of minutes, Brendan turned to me and delivered his news. They were calling the election for me.

And that was that.

The first call came from former president George W. Bush, who joked I had won despite his brother Jeb's help. Then came concession calls from my opponents. Congressman Kendrick Meek called first. Our relationship had always been respectful, and during the campaign I came to admire him a great deal. When Crist decided to run as an independent, Meek's campaign was doomed, and he knew it. He kept plugging away, though, fighting for his convictions and supporters. I often shared with Jeanette that I didn't know how he found the strength to keep going. Even after I had become the front-runner, there were days when I felt I didn't have the energy for another rally, another speech, another fund-raiser. Every poll had Meek in third place. But he had the fortitude and character to persevere to the end.

Governor Crist called next. It's no secret that ours had been a bitter race, and I was often angered by some of the governor's attacks. He had gotten personal at times and I had taken it personally. But, unexpectedly, I felt empathy for him now.

As our campaign rejoiced in our success, Crist's camp suffered intense disappointment. I was mindful that only four years earlier he had been elected governor and must have felt the same joy I was experiencing now. And as heady as the experience of an election victory is, I had enough sense to know that fortunes can change quickly in politics. One day I might be on the other end of such a call. Exulting in my opponent's defeat suddenly seemed an arrogant and foolish temptation.

We had arranged with the Crist and Meek campaigns for their candidates to address their supporters before I addressed mine. The networks would cut away from their remarks the moment we took the stage, and after a long and arduous campaign they deserved to be heard in full. I used the time to sketch an outline of the points I wanted to make in my speech. In the final days of the campaign, I couldn't bring myself to write a victory speech. I worried I was getting ahead of myself, and might still lose the election. If that happened, I would have wasted valuable campaign time laboring over a speech I would never give. I also felt that, were I to win, my supporters would be so happy with the victory that my speech wouldn't matter. If I lost, no one would be watching.

A little after nine o'clock, it was time for me to take the stage. Jeanette and our children joined me in the hallway and we proceeded to a holding area next to the walkway that led to the stage. I reached into my wallet and removed a note of encouragement Jeanette had written for me during some of the campaign's darkest days.

Jeanette didn't enjoy politics. She had no desire to be a senator's wife. The life she wanted was the life she had not had as a child. She wanted a father for her children who came home for dinner every night, a husband who left his work behind when he was at home and who shared in the responsibilities of running a household. My political career had deprived her of the settled, predictable family life she longed for. I had never been able to get the balance right between my career and my personal life. When I thought I would lose, the only thought that consoled me was the prospect of giving my family the attention they deserved. Now, as I read her note again, I recognized my election meant a normal life would continue to elude us. It wasn't fair to her, and I knew it. As I prepared to make my first speech as Florida's newly elected senator, I was acutely conscious of the great debt I owed her.

Former governor Jeb Bush reached the end of his introduction, and we got the signal to make our way down a roped-off corridor to the stage. Just before we reached it, I spotted a group of senior citizens from a local senior center. I didn't know any of them personally, but I knew their stories. They were Cuban exiles of my parents' and grandparents' generation who had come to this country a decade or more before I was born. The young tend to forget that their parents were once young, too, and had dreams for their lives, dreams that were not so different from our own.

These exiles left their home and came to a foreign place where most would never achieve the dreams of their youth. They lost them to an accident of history. Most believed they would return home someday. They never would. They would accept their loss, and devote themselves to giving their sacrifice a purpose. Their children and grandchildren would never suffer what they had suffered. They would do things their parents could not do. They would live their own dreams in a country that believed in them.

My success and the success of anyone from my generation is deeply personal to them. It affirms that their lives have had purpose and meaning. As they near the end of their lives, they ask themselves the question we all ask in the end: What was it all for? Did we matter? Their children, a generation privileged by their sacrifices, were their answer. Yes, they mattered. Our children are the mark they made in the world.

It took me years to understand this—years of knocking on doors and visiting senior centers, listening to the stories of a generation of exiles, stories of loss and struggle and hope and faith in the promise of their sacrifice.

I knew them. I knew what they had given and what they had achieved. I knew the members of my generation were the beneficiaries of their sacrifices. I knew how the trauma of exile—disbelief, guilt, a sense of loss—had shaped their lives and my own. I knew that their love born of gratitude for the country that had welcomed them and encouraged their aspirations, and the loss that had brought them here, had made them vigilant in their watch for anything they thought could threaten America and the great promise of freedom that had rescued them.

This is the culture that shaped my youth, and the community that had elected me to the West Miami City Commission and then the state legislature. Politics permeates every aspect of life in Miami's Cuban American community. It is impossible to be apolitical in a community of exiles. Their passion enveloped me very early in my life, a life that would have turned out very differently without their influence.

My family and I took the stage together. I went up first, with Jeanette and the kids right behind me. I pulled together the notes I had scribbled down and looked up at the press riser. I had been told to expect more than two hundred credentialed members of the press to attend our event, and now I saw the cameras. Every spot on the riser was taken. It was then that it hit me. I was about to speak to the largest audience I had ever addressed in my life.

Through much of the speech I could feel the bustle of the kids behind me. From the corner of my eye, I saw Jeanette holding our squirming three-year-old son, Dominick, who had lost patience with the whole spectacle. At one point he walked up to me, and almost unconsciously I gently pushed him back toward his mother while I continued my speech. It was a metaphor for our life. I was in the spotlight doing my thing, and Jeanette was in the background making it possible for me to do it, dealing with the reality of four small children while I got all the attention and acclaim.

I spoke for less than twenty minutes. The speech was well received by my supporters, but I wasn't pleased with it. I felt my thoughts had been disjointed and unorganized, and I regretted not saying a few words in Spanish for people watching on the Spanish-language networks. I couldn't get a feel for what I wanted to say. I wanted people to know I had run because I believed our nation was headed in the wrong direction in a hurry, a direction that would diminish our country if not reversed, and I believed our party had been complicit in this calamity. I entered the race because I didn't see anyone else running who would do something about it. And I stayed in the race because I believed that if my opponent won he would support the policies that had set us on this disastrous course.

But the campaign had become so much more to me than that—so much more than politics. I had discovered so much about myself, about the people I loved and who loved me, about the community I was raised in, about my country and my faith. I didn't have the words or time to give voice to all the thoughts that filled my heart and mind that night as I struggled to express my gratitude.

The campaign had tested me, and taught me lessons about myself that I needed to recognize but had not been ready to learn. I learned about my weaknesses and insecurities, my inattentiveness to important details, my impatience with people whose opinions I didn't share—my flaws had been exposed for all to see and had humbled me. I learned so much about the people who loved me, and the great generosity with which they expressed it. I came to appreciate far better than I had before how everything I have attained in my life has come from the support and sacrifices of others, from my parents, my community, my wife and children, and from the privilege of being an American. And I knew again the presence of the real and living God, who uses everything we want and everything we fear to lead us to Him. A speech cannot give adequate thanks to all that love, to all who made me who I am and who I yet hope to be. This book is my attempt to pay them all belated tribute.

I wasn't sure where we were supposed to go after I finished my remarks. I turned to Jeanette and asked her, "What do we do now?" Then the confetti cannons went off. Tiny bits of paper started falling from the sky. At one point, so much confetti was falling, I couldn't see the crowd. The kids loved it. It's funny how the mind works. All I could think of was how long it would take to clean it all up.

I looked to my left and saw my mother coming up the steps to the stage. She turned eighty that day. My election had brought her joy on her birthday, and I choked up with gratitude. She had once dreamed of becoming an actress, but spent her working life mostly as a maid. Absent from the celebration was my father. He had lost a short battle with lung cancer less than two months earlier. He hadn't lived long enough to see me elected to the

Senate, although he died believing I would be. He had wanted to be a business owner, to be his own boss, but instead had settled for work as a bartender. My parents relinquished their ambitions without resentment to make a comfortable and stable home for their children. They couldn't give us everything we wanted, but they made certain we had everything we needed. We were children of privilege: secure, happy and loved.

My maternal grandfather, whose dignity and courage and wisdom had been an inspiration to me when I was a boy, was gone, too. It would have meant a great deal to him and my father to have been there. It would also have meant a great deal to me. But I felt their presence, and I will always feel it as I live the life they made possible for me.

Their lives, too, were stories of loss and hope and love. Those stories, the preface to my own, began on a Caribbean island little more than two hundred miles from where I stood that night as a newly elected United States senator with debts to pay.

CHAPTER 2

Storyteller

PEDRO VÍCTOR GARCÍA, MY MATERNAL GRANDFATHER, was born in the Cuban province of Villa Clara on January 31, 1899, the same month and year Spanish forces left. Much of the country lay in ruins, and a provisional American military authority governed the island.

My great-grandparents had emigrated from Spain. They were land-owners and farmers in the small rural community of Jicotea, in the northern part of the province. My great-grandmother Ramona García was a petite woman, but what she lacked in size she made up for in personality. She was the independent, outspoken matriarch of her household, which included seventeen children from her relationship with my great-grandfather Carlos Pérez and at least three children from a previous relationship. She is said to have been a stern but loving mother, who demanded formal courtesy and respect from her children. For reasons no one in the family remembers, she didn't marry my great-grandfather until shortly before his death.

Carlos Pérez was a quiet and simple man, a hard worker who left the raising of his children entirely in the capable hands of their mother, while he made a comfortable livelihood for the family. American capital dominated Cuban agriculture after the Spanish left. The American military authority controlled Cuba's currency. American monopolies owned 25 percent of the country's best farmland, buying properties at bargain prices from farmers who couldn't afford to maintain them. Carlos had refused to sell, and farmed his own land.

Cubans held their first official elections the year after my grandfather was born. The results were a defeat for supporters of annexation to the United States. The United States military subsequently withdrew from Cuba in 1902, and the president of the new Cuban republic was sworn into office. Cuba was independent at last, and the Cuban people were eager to make the most of their hard-won freedom.

My great-grandparents modestly prospered in the new Cuba. They never became wealthy, but achieved a respectable self-sufficiency that relied on the labor of the entire family. As soon as they were physically able, my grandfather's siblings worked beside their father in the fields rather than attend school. Most of the rural population was illiterate.

My grandfather was the only one of his brothers and sisters to receive an education. He was stricken by polio when he was a small boy, which left one of his legs permanently damaged. His disability prevented him from working in the fields, and with nothing productive for him to do at home, my great-grandparents sent him to school.

He thrived. He loved to read, especially history, and he acquired a love of learning he would cherish until the end of his life. The knowledge he attained prepared him to make a living with his head rather than his hands, and to escape the physical toil that was the common fate of children with his background. It made him ambitious for professional and social status. It informed his political beliefs and patriotism, the way he looked at history and the way he lived his life.

He was part of the first generation of free Cubans, and he was heavily influenced by the writings of José Martí, the Cuban statesman, poet and journalist who gave his life to the cause of Cuban independence. My grandfather was usually deliberate and soft-spoken when he talked, but his voice would raise an octave when he spoke of Martí. He came of age as the republic came of age, and its principles were ingrained in his psyche. The ideals of political and intellectual independence shaped more than his political philosophy. They were the essence of his personality—the insistent individualist, who made his own way in the world. After his parents married and his father died, he was advised to adopt his father's surname to acquire a share of the inheritance. He refused, and kept his mother's maiden name.

Many years later, he would make a pupil of me, and impart his ideals, his love of learning and his self-regard.

He became a telegraph operator and climbed the ranks of the railroad business. He was an intelligent and ambitious young man, with a good, steady income and a bright future. He often traveled for business, and he met Dominga Rodríguez, my grandmother, at a festival in the city of Cabaiguán. She was one of seven children born to Nicolás Rodríguez and Beatriz Chiroldes. She had been raised in poverty and had finished her formal education after the sixth grade. Despite the differences in my grandparents' backgrounds, they fell in love and married in April 1920, when my grandfather was twenty-one years old and my grandmother was just shy of her seventeenth birthday. One year later, she gave birth to their first daughter, my aunt Olga.

They enjoyed financial security and a large home with servants and nannies. They welcomed another daughter, Elda, in 1922, and then a third, Orlanda, in 1924. Tragedy struck them eight months later, when Orlanda died of meningitis. Two years later, a fourth daughter, Irma, was born.

But by the time their fifth daughter, Dolores, was born, their fortunes had turned. First, the railroad line demoted my grandfather in favor of someone who had better connections; then, later, he was dismissed permanently. There wasn't much work available for someone with a physical disability, and their situation had become dire by the time their sixth daughter, my mother, Oriales García, was born on November 2, 1930.

My grandfather took any work he could find. They lost their house and moved into a tiny, one-room home, which my grandmother kept clean and tidy. "Just because we're poor," she told her daughters, "it doesn't mean we have to live like pigs." She taught her daughters to help with household chores. She made their clothes, handing down dresses and shoes from one child to the next. They bore their misfortune with dignity.

My grandfather walked with a cane, and often lost his balance. He would come home from work with scrapes on his knees from the falls he suffered on long walks to and from jobs. My mother helped my grandmother treat his injuries with herbs and other natural remedies. She was the baby in the family at the time, and was very close to both her parents. The physical pain my grandfather suffered for their sake distressed her terribly. But no one in her family ever went to bed hungry—my grandfather made sure of it, no matter what he had to endure.

He eventually found work at a tobacco mill. It wasn't a glamorous job, but it allowed him to do the things he most loved: read and learn. He was responsible for keeping the workers' minds occupied so they wouldn't become restless with the drudgery of rolling cigars. Each morning he began by reading newspapers aloud as if he were a radio news broadcaster. When he finished the papers, he read novels to them, taking care to accentuate in his speech and manner the drama and emotions of the stories. The job didn't pay well, but it didn't take a physical toll on him, either, and he enjoyed it. He became a skillful storyteller, and used his education to share knowledge with his illiterate but captive audience. I think he was proud of that, and never lost the skills or the desire to employ them for the entertainment and education of others.

I imagine when he lost his job at the railroad line he must have been close to despair, though he never conceded it to me. He was a proud man then and always. How defeated he must have felt to lose everything: profession, standard of living, distinction, every aspiration he had. To fear he wouldn't be able to feed, house or clothe his family. To see his dreams disappear overnight, never to return again. Education was considered a privilege in Cuba then; to have an education and then lose all opportunities to make good use of it must have been heartbreaking. I don't know if I could recover from it, or bear it with the austere dignity my grandfather possessed.

The experience taught my grandfather that anything in life can be taken from you. He never lost his spartan realism. In time, he would lose his country. And he would suffer the consequences of that, too, with dignity, though whenever he discussed the subject he would show anger and other emotions he normally restrained. He never raised his voice with his children or grandchildren unless the conversation turned to the country he had loved and lost.

They had two more daughters, my aunts Adria and Magdalena. They were now a family of nine living in a one-room house with a dirt floor. My grandmother assumed almost all the parenting responsibilities as my grandfather spent days away from home looking for work that would put food on their table.

My mother recalls the humiliation she and her sisters endured. Their parents gave them dolls made of Coke bottles dressed with rags, while other girls, who had "real" dolls, laughed at them. She used to sit outside a neighbor's house, listening at the window as their daughter played the piano, and dreamed of taking piano lessons herself. The girl's mother discovered her one afternoon, insulted her and chased her away.

As soon as my mother and her sisters were old enough, they had to work outside their home. They handed over their paychecks to my grandmother, who used the money to buy food and other necessities. Three of the older girls found jobs in a home in Havana where nuns cared for abandoned children. They soon determined that job prospects were better in the nation's capital, and convinced my grandparents to move. In 1940, the family packed their few belongings, said good-bye to Cabaiguán and moved to Havana.

They moved into a *solar*, a low-income housing complex that typically consisted of one large building surrounding an open courtyard. Several families would live in the building's apartments, which were very small and without a private bathroom. No one knows how or when he learned the trade, but my grandfather began repairing shoes outside the *solar*.

My mother found work as a cashier in a store called La Casa de los Uno, Dos y Tres Centavos (The One, Two and Three Cent Store). Like her sisters, she gave all her earnings to her mother, and kept nothing for herself. The job was menial and unrewarding. But it would change her life forever, when one morning a young man with an even sadder story walked into the store.

CHAPTER 3

Boy from the Streets

MY PATERNAL GRANDFATHER, ANTONIO RUBIO, WAS ORIG-
inally from the Pinar del Río province at the western end of the island. He was fourteen when he lost his parents, Dionisio Rubio and
Concepción Pazos, in some sort of tragedy, the details of which are lost to
history. He was left in the care of relatives. After his older sister, Pura,
moved to Havana, Antonio ran away. He wandered the country alone, at
one point spending nights in an abandoned canoe. Eventually he reached
Havana, and was reunited with his sister.

He worked odd jobs in the capital, where he met and married my
grandmother, Eloisa Reina. My grandmother was born and raised in Havana and had six siblings. I know virtually nothing else about her family
history except that her father, Rafael, was born in Spain.

My paternal grandparents didn't have their first child until 1920, when
my grandfather was in his midthirties and my grandmother in her late
twenties. Their first child, I learned from my aunt Georgina, died at birth;
my father never spoke of it. Antonio (Papo) was the next of seven more
children, followed by Emilio, Eloisa (Nena) and Concepción (Concha).
Mario Rubio, my father, was next, born on October 29, 1926, followed by
another sister and brother, Georgina and Alberto.

The family lived in a house on Tenerife Street in Havana. When my father was a boy, there were usually six children at home. My grandfather's sister never married or had children of her own, so my grandparents let her care for Nena much of the time. My grandparents ran a catering business, preparing breakfast and dinner for the workers at a nearby cigar factory. My grandmother cooked the meals, and my grandfather delivered them.

My grandfather liked to joke and tease his family, and my father inherited his playful character and clear blue eyes. My grandmother, who suffered from tuberculosis much of her life, is remembered as being more conservative and reserved. She had the stronger personality of the two, and was the disciplinarian.

The family lived simply but comfortably in a large house by contemporary urban Cuban standards, and their children were content and well cared for. My father shared only general recollections of his early childhood, mostly scenes of playing at home with his siblings and holidays spent with relatives. They often held the family's Christmas Eve dinner at their home. My grandmother would roast a pig that had been slaughtered and hung to dry the night before, and serve a traditional Cuban *lechón*.

The good times came to an abrupt end when the cigar factory closed its doors, and the catering business lost its only client. The family was forced to leave their home and move in with relatives. Eventually the family moved into a boardinghouse in their old neighborhood.

My grandfather would struggle the rest of his life to support the family, working as a vendor selling coffee and cookies on the street corners of Havana and any other jobs he could find. My father was only eight years old when he had to quit school to work. Though his formal education had ended, he would teach himself to read and write, a testament to his natural intelligence, discipline and work ethic.

My grandmother's health began to deteriorate rapidly from the physical strain of giving birth to eight children and the emotional strain caused by their poverty. In 1935, on her forty-second birthday, she passed away from pneumonia. My father was four days shy of his ninth birthday. They held her wake in the common living room of the boardinghouse, and buried her in a small ossuary my grandfather had purchased in Havana's Colón Cemetery.

My grandfather was left to care for seven devastated children, the oldest just sixteen and the youngest four. He became deeply depressed after his wife's death, and was never the same man again. He worked the streets all day, leaving the kids to fend for themselves. Nena moved in with her aunt permanently, and the rest of the children remained with their father in a single bedroom at the boardinghouse.

They were hard times, and food was scarce. When she was nine, my aunt Georgina went to work as a maid for a Spanish family, who let her bring their leftovers home. But many nights, my father and his siblings went to bed hungry. None of the kids ever complained. "When you grow up hungry," Georgina recalled, "you learn not to ask." My father's memory of not having enough to eat might explain why, rather than chastise us, he would always get up from the table and bring us something else to eat when we refused to eat the meal my mother had prepared. He never wanted us to go to bed hungry, even if it meant spoiling us.

My father found his first steady employment at a bodega near the boardinghouse, where he had often watched the shop's Spanish owner and his customers play dominoes. One day he found a wallet on the ground and asked the men if any of them had lost it. One of the customers accused my father of stealing it. The owner came to his defense, and scolded his accuser. Rather than scream at him, he told his customer, you should give him a reward. Chastened, the other man offered him a small reward, but my father refused it. Impressed by his character, the shop owner offered him a job on the spot, busing tables in the bodega's small cafeteria. My father was only nine years old, and would earn his own living for the next seventy years. The job didn't last long; the owner fired him when he caught him eating a chocolate bar without asking permission.

A few years after his wife died, my grandfather began a relationship with a woman named Dolores Cardín. She lived with her children in her own home, and my grandfather moved in with them. My father and his brothers, Papo and Emilio, remained at the boardinghouse. My grandfather and Dolores never married, but they had a son, and remained together for the rest of my grandfather's life.

My father rarely discussed Dolores with us. On the few occasions he mentioned her, he did so very matter-of-factly, without giving much weight to her role in his life. We know from my mother and aunt that she was very unkind to him and his siblings. Her own children took precedence over the motherless Rubios. She made them feel like outcasts in their father's home. Five years after my grandmother died, my father was living on his own. He was just fourteen years old.

My father never resented his father for bringing Dolores into their lives and, according to my aunt, he never criticized her. He visited his father, and occasionally spent the night. Naturally, he must have wondered why his father hadn't insisted on keeping his children with him. What else could a fourteen-year-old boy abandoned by his father have felt but that he was unloved and unwanted?

My father was a humble man, and a cheerful one. I never saw him betray bitterness or resentment toward anyone. He had learned to cope with adversity as a boy and conceal his emotions. Some people who bear painful memories in silence appear aloof and unfeeling. My father was just the opposite: he was kind, considerate and friendly to almost everyone he met.

I never saw the scars he hid. The evidence of his pain wasn't apparent in the things he said, but in all the things he left unsaid. Yet his behavior often hinted at the insecurities hidden beneath his stoicism. If he felt he was being made fun of, he could get easily offended.

I learned much of what I know of his childhood from my aunt and my mother. It wasn't until shortly before his eightieth birthday that he finally shared some stories from his boyhood with my sister Veronica—stories my mother said he had never shared with her.

He remained on good terms with his father during his teens, but he never lived with him again. My father lived on the streets and was raised by the streets, as his father had been. He became a man without a very good example of what a man should be, and eventually became the father he had never had. He was nineteen years old when his father contracted pneumonia and died. After that, he was truly on his own.

Working as a street vendor, my father searched for opportunities to get ahead. In 1947, twenty-one years old and looking for a little excitement, he joined an ill-fated military plot to overthrow Dominican dictator Rafael Trujillo, known as the Cayo Confites Expedition. Twelve hundred men were detained by the Cuban navy before they reached the Dominican Republic. A young law student, Fidel Castro, had joined the plot as well, although I don't believe my father met him.

When the commotion over the expedition subsided, he found work as a security guard in a cafeteria. He lived in a storage room in the back of the cafeteria with several young coworkers, and slept on wooden crates.

Later that year the cafeteria was purchased by the store next door, La Casa de los Uno, Dos y Tres Centavos. The new owners kept my father on, and allowed him to continue sleeping in the storage room. He met a girl there, one of the cashiers, Oriales García, and they started dating. My mother bragged to her sisters that her new boyfriend looked like the famous film star Tyrone Power. Less than a year after they met, they married on April 28, 1949, in a small civil ceremony attended by close friends and my mother's family. My father was twenty-two, my mother eighteen.

My mother's parents embraced their new son-in-law as one of their own, and for the first time since his mother died, he experienced the happiness of a loving family life. The newlyweds moved into a small apartment of their own, and continued working in the store where they had met. A year later, my older brother, Mario Víctor Rubio, was born.

My father worked hard to provide for his family on his meager salary as a security guard. He tried desperately to improve their circumstances, but these were difficult times in Cuba, and opportunities for a kid from the streets were scarce. He took a correspondence course to learn how to repair televisions and radios, but he struggled because he still had a very limited reading ability. By all accounts, he had a wonderful singing voice, and was especially fond of singing tango. He got an audition for a popular radio talent show, but his nerves got the better of him. After three failed attempts to hit a high note, he got the hook. My mother also loved to perform, and dreamed of becoming an actress. She competed in several talent competitions, and won one of them. But both of their personal aspirations gave way to the immediate needs of providing for their child.

With no education and no connections, my father's prospects for escaping a life of poverty were poor. They were even worse after he injured his leg by stepping into a hole while playing baseball with friends. The injury caused severe nerve damage, and he would walk with a limp for the rest of his life.

One of my mother's sisters, Dolores, or Lola as she was known, had emigrated to the United States, and reported back that jobs were plentiful there. On May 27, 1956, seven years after they had married, my parents and their son left Cuba for America. It cost around five hundred dollars at the time to bring someone to the United States. Each family member who arrived in the States paid for the next member to come, and soon my grandparents and most of the family had emigrated. Their timing was fortuitous. That same year, Fidel Castro was busy making camp in the Sierra Maestra Mountains, where he would begin his revolution against the dictatorship of Fulgencio Batista.

While Cuba descended into violence in the revolution that would eventually replace the corrupt Batista dictatorship with Castro's communist dictatorship, the United States enjoyed a period of unprecedented growth and prosperity. My family moved first to New York, where my father took whatever small day jobs he could find. The New York winter proved too much for my mother, though, and the following year they moved to Miami, where both my parents found steady work in an assembly plant that built aluminum lawn chairs. My mother still has a visible scar from an accident she suffered at the plant when machinery tore her thumbnail from the root.

They had very little money, but they had the will to improve their circumstances and the confidence they were in the right place to do it. Life in the United States wasn't easy for my parents, but it was better than the alternative.

By the end of the 1950s, my father had begun training as a bar boy, a bartender's assistant, and was hired by the Roney Plaza Hotel in Miami Beach. But his real dream was to own his own business. Between 1958 and 1965 he opened a succession of small businesses, including a vegetable stand, a dry cleaning store, a discount store and a small supermarket. My mother claims my father never had much of a business mind—he was too generous, she said, and often gave items away to customers who couldn't afford them. The businesses all failed, and at some point—we can never be quite sure when—he gave up his dream, deciding instead to provide the best living he could for his family by working in the employ of others.

He worked hard at the hotel bar and was promoted to bartender in 1959. Yet the family was discouraged by the business failures, and they missed Cuba. My grandfather, too, had hated the cold in New York, and his attempt to establish a shoe repair business in Miami had failed. So after the fall of Batista, he returned to Cuba. He intended to stay there for the rest of his life even though his wife and daughters were still in the United States. The immigrant experience is seldom an instantly successful one. In the beginning it's usually a tale of hardship, menial labor, sacrifice, scrimping and heartache for the country and family you left behind. My parents' and grandparents' experience was no different, and like many Cuban Americans, they believed they might one day return home.

My sister Barbara was born in the early summer of 1959. By the end of that year my parents began to contemplate doing what my grandfather had already decided to do, return permanently to Cuba. Early on there were few signs that Cuba would soon join the Soviet Bloc. On a visit to the United States in April 1959, Fidel Castro professed his belief in democracy and denied being a communist. He even wore a medal with the image of the Virgin Mary. At the time he was a hero to many working-class Cubans.

In the summer of 1960, my father and my brother, Mario, took a ferry to Cuba so they could bring my father's car, which he wanted to show off to his family. My mother and Barbara flew to Havana and met them there. They wanted to see the new Cuba and explore giving life on the island another try. But during their visit they began to comprehend the direction of Castro's revolution.

Castro's criticism of the United States had begun to severely damage relations between the two countries. While claiming he wasn't a communist, he was nationalizing oil companies and commercial real estate. He expropriated sugar refineries as well, and began receiving economic and military assistance from the Soviets. When my parents arrived in Cuba, my father's brother Emilio warned him against returning permanently. The regime was imprisoning thousands of dissidents, he explained; opposition newspapers had been shuttered, and the regime controlled all radio and television stations. Better to stay in the States, Emilio said, at least for another year.

My father heeded my uncle's advice. He never returned to Cuba, nor did he ever see his siblings, Emilio, Antonio and Concha, again. But my mother would return one last time.

In March 1961, my mother returned to Havana to care for her father, who had tripped while boarding a bus and broken his one good leg. She stayed with him for nearly a month while he healed. It was clear during her visit that events in Cuba were going from bad to worse. The entire family wanted my grandfather to go back to Miami. She pleaded with my grandfather to return, and he finally consented.

Cuba had changed radically by then, and travel privileges were curtailed.

When she attempted to board her return flight to Miami, she encountered the scare of her life. Because she had been born in the United States, my sister, only two at the time, could leave Cuba. But my brother and my mother would not be allowed to leave, she was told. She was ordered to leave the airport, and to consider Cuba her home from now on. Though frightened, she refused to accept the decree. She returned each day for several days, pleading that her husband was in Miami, and she couldn't remain in Cuba without him. Finally, one of the guards took pity on her, instructing her to come back the next day and get in his line. When she did, he waved her through, and she boarded a flight for Miami. The experience scared her so badly she never went back to Cuba again.

The CIA-supported Bay of Pigs invasion began the following month. In December, Castro declared he was a Marxist-Leninist, and the United States broke off diplomatic relations. In early 1962, the United States imposed a near-total economic embargo against Cuba, and by October the Cuban Missile Crisis had begun. I've always been immensely grateful to my uncle Emilio for warning my parents when he did. Had he hesitated, I might have lived a very different life.

With a return to Cuba now an impossibility, my parents devoted themselves to making their life in America work. My father continued working as a bartender at the Roney Plaza, and eventually became one of the hotel's head bartenders. But my parents were always on the lookout for a place where the grass appeared greener, and they became restless whenever their prospects for advancement seemed uncertain. In the summer of 1964 they moved the family to Los Angeles in search of better opportunities in the fast-growing city; they moved into a small and dingy apartment where my brother slept on a recliner. Yet my father could find only odd jobs, and after just a few weeks, they tried Las Vegas next. The only employment he was offered was as bar boy, so by the end of the summer the family returned to Miami, where my father got back his job at the Roney Plaza.

My father was a very generous man who made sacrifices all his life, not only for us, but for anyone who needed his help. My aunt Georgina recalled for me how he treated one of his coworkers who had been fired for drinking on the job. He visited my father at work and complained he had been offered a new job, but couldn't accept it because he didn't have suitable shoes to wear. My father refused to give him money because he suspected he would use it to buy liquor. Instead, he met his friend outside the hotel after work, removed his own shoes and gave them to him. Walking home shoeless would have been more than an inconvenience to him. He wore a leg brace, and was embarrassed by it—we rarely saw him barefoot even around the house. He owned only two pairs of shoes: one for wearing in public, the other for wearing at home.

I don't remember him ever buying anything for himself. He drove a red 1973 Chevrolet Impala for twenty years. He wore a Seiko watch until the day he died, even though its gold plating had worn off long before. Every item of clothing he wore had been purchased for him by my mother or given to him as a gift. He wasn't perfect, but I've never met another person in my life as selfless as my father.

Life was changing in the States. The civil rights movement was reaching its zenith. America was increasingly involved in Vietnam, and the war's unpopularity, particularly among the young, helped cause the social upheavals that gave the decade its reputation for radicalism. The changes demanded by social activists in the baby boomer generation, who weren't content to be an exact replica of the preceding generation, would affect the values of every institution in America—education, lifestyles, laws, relations between the sexes, entertainment.

Acculturation is never an easy process for immigrants, but it must have been all the more daunting when American mores seemed to be changing overnight. My parents were conservative by nature and in their politics. America was their haven. They had never expected the United States to be beset by so much turmoil, much as they hadn't expected that the Castro regime would prevent them from living in Cuba again. But they raised their children to respect their new country, and the conservative values they held dear.

My parents bought their first house in 1966, in Miami. All my mother's sisters were now living in the United States, with her parents living in a nearby apartment building. In 1967, my grandmother suffered a fatal heart attack in her sleep. She was sixty-four years old, the beloved matriarch of the García family. Her sudden death devastated my grandfather and mother, and was a crushing blow to my father as well. She had treated him as her son, and he had loved her as his mother.

The nation's political and social unrest dominated the news in 1968.

But after a decade of struggles, my parents had come to achieve some relative stability. My brother, Mario, was the quarterback of the local high school football team. My sister Barbara was enrolled in ballet lessons, and my mother doted on her like a little doll. After high school, my brother enlisted in the army, serving as a Green Beret in the 7th Special Forces Group, stationed at Fort Bragg. My parents couldn't afford to send him to college, but after he completed his service in 1971, he used the GI Bill to finish his education.

By the start of the new decade, my parents had much to be grateful for. Although he had failed at business, through hard work my father had achieved enough financial security that my mother, who had worked as a cashier at the Crown Hotel, could now consider staying at home. My father was forty-five and my mother was forty-one, an age when they could expect my brother, who would soon marry, to give them grandchildren. In October of 1970, my parents learned that a new member of the Rubio family was indeed on the way. But it was not my brother's wife who was expecting.

I was born on May 28, 1971. My younger sister, Veronica, was born the following year. My mother and father were starting over again as parents in the country they now called home.

My parents had lived in America for nearly two decades. It was clear that Cuba had become a thoroughly totalitarian state, and would likely remain so for some time. They had endured many disappointments, and their lives would never be easy. But slowly and surely they made a better life for our family than they had had as children, or could have ever been possible for them in Cuba. Three of their children were born Americans. Mario had naturalized after returning from the army. And in 1975, they, too, became citizens of the United States.

CHAPTER 4

Early Childhood

M Y EARLIEST MEMORIES ARE OF MY FAMILY'S HOME IN Coral Gate, a neighborhood west of Little Havana. I remember playing with my sister on an aluminum swing set my father had built in the backyard, and a dome-shaped monkey bar–type contraption he added later. We had a screened porch large enough for me to ride around in on my tricycle.

A sunroom in the rear of the house doubled as our playroom. My father installed an indoor gate system so when my mother had things to do around the house, she could put us in the sunroom and not worry about us wandering off. He also converted our garage into a bedroom for my grandfather, who would live with us for much of the remainder of his life. His arrival at Coral Gate began one of the most influential relationships in my life.

We lived just down the street from St. Raymond Catholic Church, where every Saturday evening I would attend Mass with my mother. I can still recall her complaining when I would drop the kneeler on her shin and leave her with bruises. I had a habit as a child of playacting scenes from experiences that had made an impression on me. When I came home from the movies or some other entertainment I would stage repeat performances. After returning home from Mass, I would sometimes wrap myself in a sheet and pretend to be a priest, re-creating that day's service.

Barbara, my older sister, still lived at home. She was in high school and employed in her first job. She seemed so mature and smart to me, and I was fascinated by her. I would wake up early just so I could join her for breakfast. She had the same thing every morning: *café con leche*—Cuban coffee with heated milk—and a square piece of toast my mother placed on top of the cup. It looked like a graduation cap. Barbara worked in a T-shirt shop on Coral Gables' "Miracle Mile." I woke up one night to find at the foot of my bed a T-shirt with the shark from the movie *Jaws* ironed on the front of it. It was my favorite shirt.

Around my fourth birthday my parents became concerned about my legs, as my knees were turned inward. They took me to an orthopedic specialist who prescribed the use of leg braces. Every morning my mother would struggle to strap them onto my legs. The braces were cumbersome and restrictive, and I hated them. I begged her not to put them on me. When that failed, I physically resisted her, bending and kicking my legs.

She eventually devised a trick to encourage my cooperation. Whenever I refused to wear my braces, our phone would ring. My mother would answer it, then hand the receiver to me. It was Don Shula, head coach of the Miami Dolphins. "Marco," he'd say, "you have to wear your braces if you're going to play for me someday." I would eagerly comply. Years later it would occur to me that Coach Shula didn't have a Cuban accent, and the voice on the telephone had been my father's, who had taken time from work to call me and impersonate one of my childhood heroes.

Happily, after I had worn the braces for a year with little progress to show for the effort, my parents took me to a new doctor. He instructed my parents to stop using the braces and assured them I would outgrow the condition soon enough, which I did.

My earliest Christmas memories are also from our years in the Coral Gate house. One Christmas Eve in particular still stands out. Veronica and I had gone to bed for the night. I woke up for some reason and made my way to the living room, where I discovered my father and my sister's boyfriend and future husband, Orlando, assembling a bicycle. You would have thought I'd walked in on two burglars. After a frantic attempt to cover up the evidence, my father and Orlando explained they had both been using the bathroom when Santa Claus had arrived and delivered our presents. It sounded plausible to me, and I went back to bed happy that Santa had made it to our house and been so generous.

These are most of the memories I have from our time in Coral Gate. They're just a few scattered snapshots of the earliest years of my life. But I remember them affectionately as part of the pervasive sense of well-being I had throughout my childhood. I always felt I lived a charmed, happy life, with limitless possibilities there for the taking. Security, comfort, confidence and happiness were the gifts my parents gave Veronica and me.

My parents had been very young when Mario was born. My grandmother Dominga had cared for him while my parents were at work. She picked him up from school, and made his dinner. My parents usually came home late from work, sometimes just before Mario's bedtime. During that period my father often worked on the weekends and holidays. After my sister Barbara was born my parents, especially my mother, were able to devote more time to their children, though not as much as they wished. They rarely had the money to take Mario and Barbara on vacation. It wasn't deliberate neglect, nor was it a failure of love. They cherished their children and did all they could for them. But the remorse they felt for not having had more time to spare for their older children, especially Mario, drove their almost obsessive determination to be more attentive to their younger children.

Ours was a privileged childhood. I know that now. I think I knew it even then. We were the center and purpose of our parents' lives; our happiness was their only concern. Unlike when my older siblings growing up, my father was often at home on the weekends and holidays. He earned enough to allow my mother to stay home with us during our early childhood years, and to buy us toys and take us on occasional vacations. My parents deferred buying all but the most basic comforts for themselves so we could enjoy all the entertainments they could afford; they had no hobbies of their own. They rarely made us do things we didn't want to do, and they carefully shielded us from every disturbance and anxiety in their own lives.

It's a great blessing for a child to know he is so well loved. We had little money growing up, but Veronica and I had everything we needed, and a lot that we merely wanted. That sense of stability and security can give a child all the confidence necessary to become an accomplished adult. I've never lived a day when I wasn't sure I was loved, nor have I been in circumstances when I haven't believed I could make my life whatever I wanted it to be.

But it can spoil you, too. When you grow up as the central occupation of others and are accustomed to an inordinate amount of attention, you will very likely struggle as an adult, as I have, to learn to subordinate your own desires to the needs of others—a quality indispensible to a mature and lasting happiness. Mario had left home by the time I was born, and Barbara would stay in Miami when we moved to Las Vegas in 1979. We were a small household when I was growing up—just Veronica and me, our parents and my grandfather. The trade-offs, the deference and the self-denial that are the habits of peaceful coexistence in large families were never imposed on us. We've had to learn them as adults, and it has not been an easy endeavor.

When Veronica and I were very young, five and six years old, my parents would take us to the nearby International House of Pancakes on Sunday mornings. We loved the pancakes, and I was an avid collector of the little NFL football helmet magnets IHOP sold at the time. Moments after we placed our orders, I would begin complaining about the time it took to get our meals. "I'm starving, Papí. Where's the food? Why's it taking so long?" Instead of correcting me and urging me to be more patient, my father would become agitated as well, and begin pestering the waitress for our food. I struggle with impatience to this day, and when I exhibit the weakness at a restaurant or in some other public place, my wife will remind me that I am behaving like that six-year-old at IHOP.

Shortly before my fifth birthday, my father was approached by the manager of the hotel where he worked with an interesting opportunity. He offered him a job managing Toledo Plaza, an apartment complex in a working-class Cuban neighborhood near the airport. The job came with a rent-free apartment, a salary comparable to his earnings at the Roney Plaza and a promise my father could continue bartending on weekends for extra money. He accepted.

My parents sold our Coral Gate house and moved into three apartments on the ground floor of Toledo Plaza. The first unit served as the building's front office, where my parents worked, as well as a storage room. Veronica and I spent a lot of time in the storage room, playing hide-and-seek among the furniture and equipment kept there. The second and third units were our home. My father opened the walls to combine them into one apartment. Our playroom, my bedroom and Barbara's bedroom were in the first unit; the living room, kitchen, Veronica's bedroom and my parents' bedroom were in the second. All three units had sliding glass doors that opened onto a large lawn in the apartment complex's center courtyard, which became our backyard.

The yard had two large palm trees standing a few yards apart. My father bolted the ends of a metal pipe to each tree, then drilled holes in it for metal hooks from which he hung two swings. The yard was a paradise in my imagination. It served as the football field where I pretended to be Bob Griese leading the Miami Dolphins to another victory, and as Gotham City, where I fought crime as Batman.

We had a great life at Toledo Plaza. I was in the first grade at Henry M. Flagler Elementary, and had plenty of friends. My father worked where we lived. He dropped us off at school every morning and picked us up in the afternoon. My mom helped in the office, but was always home with us. Because my father was the building manager, we had the run of the place, and we made the most of it. I was in thrall to the first of my two abiding temporal passions: football and politics.

I was football crazy. I still am, but with a somewhat more restrained and mature appreciation for the sport than I had as a kid, when I thought it was the most important thing in my life. I loved the Dolphins. I loved Don Shula, who was hired as the Dolphins' head coach the year before I was born and almost immediately turned around the team's fortunes. I loved the unselfish, thoughtful and heroic play of the great Bob Griese, who quarterbacked the Dolphins throughout the seventies, led them through an undefeated season and to three consecutive Super Bowls, winning two of them. And later, I would love Dan Marino, whose dazzling performances would ease the heartache Bob Griese's retirement had caused me. My father took me to my first Dolphins game in 1977. They beat the Seattle Seahawks and I was delirious with joy.

My obsession with football originated in my admiration for my brother. I never lived with Mario, yet he lived in our lives as a legend in the tales my father would tell about his exploits at Miami High.

He had played varsity football in high school in the late 1960s, having attained some acclaim as the first Cuban American to play quarterback for the Miami Stingarees. Miami High was a perennial football powerhouse in those days, and their games in the Orange Bowl often drew crowds of over twenty thousand fans. My father's interest in the game began when his son was the star quarterback for the school. Dad sat proudly in the stands at Mario's games, beaming whenever the announcer described a play by Mario Rubio. After each game my father would meet Mario in the stadium's parking lot, holding a Cuban sandwich he'd brought for him, and he would smile as he watched his son, the young, handsome quarterback, hold court amid a circle of adoring girls vying for his attention.

Everyone in my family became football fans, except my grandfather, always the individualist. He told me he thought it was a vulgar and pointless game, and if anyone ever tackled him the way they did in football games, he would punch the tackler in the nose. He loved baseball, which he had played as a boy despite his disability. The elegant symmetry of baseball gave it purpose, he insisted, and beauty.

I grew up listening to my father's stories about Mario's exploits on the football field. I kept a picture of him wearing his football jersey in my room, and l imagined myself leading Miami High as quarterback—another Rubio at the helm, and a worthy successor to the famous Mario, my brother.

Life was good. Then suddenly everything changed. My father's employers sold Toledo Plaza to new owners. Their representatives appeared at the front office one morning without warning. They changed the locks to the office, informed my father his services were no longer needed and asked him to vacate our apartment within seven days. Virtually overnight, my parents had lost their livelihood and our home. We had nowhere to go since we had sold our other house. And my father had given up his bartending job at the Roney Plaza.

I am a father and provider now, and can appreciate how worried my parents must have been over their sudden misfortune. While we were a little upset over the disruption of our happy lives at Toledo Plaza, Veronica and I were oblivious to the fears that must have troubled my parents at the time. They were exceedingly careful not to betray the slightest trace of anxiety in our presence. We never noticed a worried look on their faces or overheard a single word of concern in whispered conversations between them. My only vivid recollection of the entire experience was the day the moving truck arrived to collect our belongings.

My parents were worried, of course—I'm sure they were devastated to have their world turned upside down in one moment. But things turned around for them fairly quickly. My father found a new job managing an apartment building in Hialeah. After a short stint in a rental home, we found a house right across the backyard from my aunt Adria's house, where my cousin Manny, who was only two years older than me, was my new neighbor.

The house had a big yard that reminded me of the yard at Toledo Plaza. Plus it had an extra room, so my grandfather, who had been living with my aunt since we didn't have room for him at Toledo Plaza, could move in with us again. We lived across the street from my new school, Kensington Park, where Manny was a student.

Not long after we moved, I had a severe attack of stomach pains. It wasn't the first time. When we were still living in Toledo Plaza, Barbara and Orlando had taken me to the movies, and I consumed a large box of Cracker Jacks. Within hours I was doubled over in excruciating pain. That night my father took me to the emergency room. My parents blamed the episode on the Cracker Jacks and forbade me to eat them again. This time, though, there had been no sugary snacks involved. The pain set in suddenly, and the only way to find relief was to bend into a fetal position. I made another trip to the emergency room. When the next attack occurred, the pain was more severe and nothing relieved it. The emergency room doctor, unable to diagnose my condition, suggested I might be faking it. Without speaking a word in response, my father lifted me from the examination table, carried me in his arms out of the ER and drove directly to Variety Children's Hospital in central Dade County.

A few hours later, the examining physician informed my parents that I was suffering from intestinal intussusception, a serious but treatable condition. If treated promptly, the prognosis was excellent. If left untreated, it could cause severe complications, even death. Only surgery would correct the problem permanently. My abdomen would have to be opened and the affected area resected. After surgery, I would be fed through a tube for three days, and would need to spend another week to ten days in recovery. As the doctor explained the procedure, Barbara began to cry. I don't remember my mother's reaction, but I do remember my father's. He told me he would promise to give up smoking in exchange for God seeing me safely through surgery. I learned later he had returned to the other hospital and searched for the doctor who had claimed I was faking the ailment, intending to give him a piece of his mind.

I was operated on the next day. Those first few days after surgery weren't particularly comfortable, but I was released from the hospital in less than two weeks and was back at school within the month.

For a few months all was well, or as well as could be expected, until my father lost his job managing the apartment building in Hialeah. The owners had hired a management company to maintain the place at a lower cost. My dad went to work for Adria's husband, my uncle Manolito, who owned a small house-painting business. He would have preferred to work as a bartender again, but by the late seventies the tourist industry in Miami Beach was in decline, and the hotels weren't hiring. While he was grateful for the work Manolito gave him, my father knew it wasn't a long-term solution to our troubles.

The city of Miami was entering a difficult period in its history. By 1978, it was experiencing a rapid, significant increase in murders and other violent crimes. Cocaine traffickers had begun using Miami as the primary point of entry into the United States and as the distribution center for their highly lucrative trade. As rival gangs and dealers began competing for territory and business, they commonly employed violence to settle their disputes.

We weren't directly affected by the increase in crime, but it was one more concern added to my parents' growing fears that their changed circumstances would rob them of their hard-won security. The disco-centered social scene in Miami, which they considered a decadent lifestyle for young people, was yet another worry. Their predicament felt more serious than a temporary setback in a tough economic time. They worried my mother would have to go back to work and my father would again work weekends and holidays. They would have neither the time nor the resources to provide us a better childhood than they had given my brother and older sister.

It was never in my parents' nature to become paralyzed or stymied by fear. They acted decisively, even precipitously, whenever they felt their aspirations threatened. A quarter century before, they had reacted to a stagnant economy and growing violence and instability in Cuba, leaving their family and the only world they knew to follow my aunt Lola to Miami. They believed emigration was the only course that would allow them to give their infant son a decent chance in life.

Now they concluded Miami no longer promised a better life for their children, and they would have to leave home again. They looked for a place with better job opportunities, better living standards at a more affordable cost and a more wholesome environment for children. Then they packed our belongings and followed Lola, once again, to Las Vegas.

CHAPTER 5

A Brand-new Life

L AS VEGAS IS NOT OFTEN THE FIRST PLACE THAT COMES to mind for people looking to raise their children in a wholesome environment. Yet in many respects it would prove to be the family-friendly community my parents hoped it would be. It was a smaller city in those days, with 160,000 inhabitants, and about a half million people in the metropolitan area. Today, metropolitan Las Vegas is nearly four times as populous. Of course, it was the established capital of the gaming industry, with the less than wholesome reputation its nickname, Sin City, implied. But while it had many big-city amenities and vices, beyond the Strip, Vegas in the late seventies felt like a small town compared to Miami.

My aunt Lola and her husband, Armando, had moved with their children to Vegas in the early seventies. Armando was employed at the Sands Hotel as a room service waiter, and made a good living. Lola often promoted the quality of life in their new city to her Miami relatives, and two more of my mother's sisters, my aunts Irma and Elda, moved there, too.

Las Vegas would offer the security and community values my parents sought, but our life there began discouragingly. My parents made the decision to move in the fall of 1978. The following January, my father traveled alone to Vegas to find a job and a home for us, promising to return soon to collect us. Almost five months would pass before he could keep his promise.

Unlike in Miami, hotels were flourishing in Vegas and jobs were abundant. But it was a heavily unionized industry that didn't welcome outsiders looking for work in anything but entry-level positions. My father was fifty-two years old, with twenty years of bartending experience and excellent references. The hotels were hiring younger bartenders and promoting employees who had worked in junior positions.

He stayed in a spare bedroom in Aunt Irma and Uncle Enrique's house. Day after dispiriting day he searched for work with no success. By the end of January, he was desperate and considered returning to Miami, when Enrique tipped him off to a possible opportunity at a new hotel.

Enrique worked in the maintenance department of the California Hotel. The owners were about to open an Old West–themed resort hotel, Sam's Town, in Sunrise Manor, a Vegas suburb. My father applied for a bartending job there, and was offered a position as a bar back, a bartender's assistant, with the promise he would be considered for a bartending job in the future. He took it. With two young children and a wife waiting in Miami for him, he wasn't in a position to turn down a job, even one that didn't pay enough to allow us to join him.

He went from being a top bartender on Miami Beach to being an assistant to a twenty-one-year-old bartender just out of school. He lugged supplies from the storeroom to the bar. He cleaned glasses, disposed of empty bottles and mopped the floor behind the bar. When the bartender got an order for a drink he didn't know how to make, he would ask my father to make it. Sometimes he shared his tips with my dad; sometimes he didn't. It was a humbling experience for a proud man. Fortunately, after a few months in the job, he was offered a better-paying position as a bartender in the hotel's room service department.

My father's absence was difficult for me, especially so when I saw my friends enjoying time with their fathers. I missed him a great deal. In the days before cell phones, e-mail and Skype, long-distance phone calls were very expensive. He could afford just one brief call a week on Sundays. Veronica and I wrote to him a few times, and sent him pictures. I know now how fortunate I was to have parents who were married and a constant presence in my life except during this one temporary separation. As upsetting as it was at the time, my experience seems trivial compared to the deprivation of children whose parents are deceased, divorced or disinterested in

their lives. Nor was my separation from my father as extended and worrying as the experience of children whose fathers or mothers serve overseas
in the military. But when I encounter children in such circumstances, I
remember how painful my separation from my father was, and how difficult it was for me to understand it.

My father came home near the end of May 1979, just in time for my
eighth birthday, which we celebrated with a surprise trip to the Kennedy
Space Center. Later that summer, we said our good-byes and left for Las
Vegas. My sister Barbara had decided to stay in Miami. She was nineteen,
working and had been dating her future husband, Orlando, for four years.
Her decision terribly upset my parents, especially my mother. When Barbara was growing up, before Veronica and I were born, my father worked
late nights, and my brother was a socially active teenager and seldom at
home. Barbara and my mother were often alone together in the house, and
they became very close. The thought of leaving Barbara behind, alone, terrified my mother. Her decision was the subject of a very heated disagree-
ment between them. If Orlando truly loved her, my mother argued, he
would marry her now or follow us to Las Vegas. But more than her relationship with Orlando kept my sister in Miami. All her friends lived there. It
was her home. And as painful as the separation would be, she would not
change her mind.

There was no turning back for my parents, though. In early June,
dressed in a brown suit and tie, I boarded a plane with Veronica and my
parents, and flew west to our brand-new life in fascinatingly strange Las
Vegas.

My first impressions of the place were of its striking physical qualities:
the sun-glazed reddish brown mountains surrounding the Vegas Valley
that looked like painted cardboard scenery; the blast of hot air that rushed
us as we emerged from the airport, so unlike the still, humid heat of Miami.
It was all alien and intriguing to me.

Strange, too, were the complicated relationships between my mother's
sisters, which I was exposed to soon after we arrived. We lived with Aunt
Irma and Uncle Enrique for our first two months in Las Vegas.

Irma was the fourth of my mother's sisters, and in childhood she had
been the most generous and protective sibling. My mother recalls Irma
often taking the blame and the punishment for her sisters' misbehavior.

On a few occasions, when my mother or another of her sisters found themselves on the wrong end of my grandmother's belt, Irma had jumped between them and taken the lashes herself.

But Irma's compassion was one facet of a sensitive nature that could make her touchy and querulous over the slightest injury, intended or not. Irma viewed Lola as a rival for our affection, and she had wanted my parents to buy a house near hers. When my father informed us he had purchased a home three blocks from my aunt Lola's house, Irma was not pleased.

Our new home at 3104 East Lava Avenue was situated on the corner of a U-shaped cul-de-sac in a working-class neighborhood in North Las Vegas. The one-story house had three bedrooms, two bathrooms and a curved driveway with a covered carport. The front yard had a single tree in its center. Sliding glass doors led to a covered porch and a small backyard enclosed by a wooden palisade fence. In my child's imagination, the fence served as the walls of an Old West fort. The semicircular driveway was an Olympic speed track for roller skating. The low-traffic street became a football field with a tall street lamp marking the goal line, and sidewalks indicating the sidelines.

We quickly made friends with the five Thiriot boys, who lived directly across the street from us. Their father worked for the Clark County juvenile justice office, and their mother stayed at home. The Thiriots were members of the nearby Mormon Church and had become friends with Lola's family. They were a close-knit and lively family who were always doing things together. They represented the kind of safe, respectable family life my parents wanted for us.

Veronica and I began our new life in earnest in September 1979, when we entered second and third grade at C. C. Ronnow Elementary School. Our new school was only a few blocks from our house, close enough that we could walk there every day with the Thiriots and other neighborhood kids, while my mother trailed a few steps behind us. In Miami, our schoolmates had all been like us, the sons and daughters of Cuban exiles. But C. C. Ronnow had an ethnically diverse student body. We went to school with white, non-Hispanic kids like the Thiriots, with African American students who were bused in from a neighborhood several miles away and with Hispanic children, mostly of Mexican descent, as well. At first, it was an unfamiliar environment, but one we quickly adapted to and enjoyed.

After we finished our homework in the afternoon, we went outdoors to play with the Thiriots. Our games were the kind of innocent activities my parents imagined would occupy us in our new surroundings. Sometimes we pretended to be settlers defending our frontier fort from an Indian attack. Other times we pretended our neighborhood was a country called Ingraham, named for the cross street next to our house. The four older Thiriots and I were soldiers in Ingraham's army, Veronica was our queen and the youngest Thiriot, only an infant at the time, was heir to the throne.

My parents, especially my mother, attributed the neighborhood's wholesomeness to the influence of the Mormon Church. The neighborhood church sponsored a Cub Scout pack, father-and-son camping trips, and various other family activities.

Mormons are encouraged by the church to recruit converts to the faith, and almost as soon as we moved to the neighborhood, Lola started converting us. Her son, Moses, discussed the church's teachings with me.

I had been baptized in the Catholic Church, and when I was very young had regularly attended Mass with my mother. But ours had not been a very Catholic home for some time. By the time I had entered grade school, weekly Mass was no longer part of our family routine, and I had yet to receive the Church's sacraments that were granted to children my age.

I don't believe my mother ever really understood Mormon theology, but her intense desire to be part of a community with upstanding values and caring, cohesive families made her an eager convert. My mother, Veronica and I were baptized into the Church of Jesus Christ of Latter-Day Saints, and began attending Sunday services at the church next door to my school.

Sunday services lasted the entire morning. They began at nine o'clock with a general assembly of the entire congregation, where we would sing hymns. Our bishop would deliver a sermon, and then members were encouraged to give personal testimony before the entire assembly. Following the testimonies, the children left to attend Sunday school, and the men and women divided into separate meetings. My mother attended meetings of the Relief Society, the church's official women's auxiliary. We usually returned home a little after noon.

I liked Sunday services. I got to wear my best clothes and see school friends who attended our church. Later, as I became even more obsessed with football, I would complain about having to spend the entire morning in church, because televised East Coast NFL games would have already started before we got home. Otherwise I enjoyed the lifestyle our church encouraged. I joined the Cub Scout pack the church sponsored. I went with my friends to watch their fathers play intramural basketball games on the church's basketball court. I attended daylong parades, where children dressed as early church pioneers and reenacted their journey to the West. I went with my uncle Armando on father-and-son camping trips to an estate Howard Hughes had bequeathed to the church. My father, who was embarrassed by his injured leg and the brace he had to wear, did not accompany me.

My father never really embraced Mormonism. He wasn't particularly religious, and he was skeptical about the church's teachings. I saw him pray only once. Mormon fathers are considered the spiritual heads of their households, and one evening not long after we had joined the church, my mother asked my father to lead the family in prayer. He had spoken for only a few moments, thanking God for his children and family, when he broke down and was unable to continue. He left the table and tried to compose himself. His tears shocked Veronica and me. We had never seen him cry before, and would only see him cry again on one other occasion. My mother tried to explain to us why he had suddenly become distraught. She told us his childhood had been a very sad one. His mother had died when he was a very young boy. His father had moved in with a woman who had mistreated him. He had never known a happy family life in Cuba, she explained, and he had cried that night in gratitude for the blessing of having one now.

Some of the church's rules were difficult for my parents, especially my father, to abide by. The LDS health code, the "Word of Wisdom," banned the use of tobacco. My dad had been a smoker since he was a boy of thirteen and working in the streets of Havana. He'd tried to quit several times but never succeeded, and eventually lung cancer and emphysema would claim his life. The church also strictly prohibited the consumption of alcohol. I never saw my parents consume anything more than an occasional glass of beer or wine, and we never kept spirits at home. But my father was a bartender, and while the church didn't object to one of its members working in that occupation, it considered liquor poison, which could have bothered my father with feelings of remorse for making a living by dispensing it. It certainly bothered me, and I admonished him for trading in the sinful substance, urging him to find other work. He ignored my tactlessness. Both my parents loved Cuban coffee, a staple in Cuban households, and could never permanently give it up in compliance with the church's prohibition of caffeine consumption, although they did discourage us from drinking Coca-Cola.

These proscriptions and his doubts about Mormon theology were the reasons my father remained somewhat detached from the life of our church. Nevertheless, out of deference to my mother, he didn't object to our church membership, and did what he could to support our spiritual growth in our new faith. In the summer of 1980, he took us on a family vacation to Utah, where we visited important LDS sites in Provo and Salt Lake City. Although we visited the famous Mormon temple in Salt Lake City, we didn't enter it. To enter a Mormon temple, you have to have been a member of a Mormon church for at least a year and been deemed worthy of the privilege by receiving a "temple recommend" from your bishop and stake president following interviews with each of them to confirm your adherence to the church's teachings. We would remain members of the church for just three years, and my father's lukewarm embrace of Mormonism deterred us from applying for an interview.

In contrast to my parents, I immersed myself in LDS theology, and understood it as well as an eight-year-old mind can. Although my school grades were never impressive, I was a voracious reader, and I studied church literature and other sources of information to learn all I could about the church's teachings.

All in all, the Mormon Church provided the sound moral structure my mother had wanted for us, and a circle of friends from stable, God-fearing families. When we left the church a few years later, mostly at my instigation, we did so with gratitude for its considerable contribution to our happiness in those years.

I began playing Pop Warner football that fall for the Caesars Palace Gladiators. I played quarterback that first year. The following year, I played on the defensive line for the International Brotherhood of Electrical Workers Sooners. I wasn't happy about the change in position, my father even less so. He suspected the coaches were favoring their own kids when assigning positions. In truth, I wasn't a very good quarterback, and never would be.

When football season was finished for the year, I looked for new pastimes to occupy my time. Veronica was the star student in our house. I was the avid reader with an aptitude for self-education. I borrowed books from the school library, and devoured magazines and newspapers for information about religion, the military, farming and other subjects that one time or another came under my enthusiastic scrutiny. After the wedding of Prince Charles and Lady Diana, I became fascinated with royalty, and made a study of the great European monarchies. I would never become proficient at math and science, and my school grades ranged from mediocre to poor. But my reading comprehension and vocabulary and knowledge of history and politics were the skills that would save me from a lifetime of underachieving. On Christmas of 1982, my parents gave me what I still consider the best present I ever received: a complete set of *World Book* encyclopedias. I still have them.

In addition to my *World Book*s, newspaper subscriptions and trips to the library, I had an invaluable living research guide in my home, who encouraged my amateur scholarship. My grandfather loved history and politics as much as I did, and was far more knowledgeable about them. He became my tutor, my companion and close friend and one of the great influences in my life. But for his encouragement, I think my life would have turned out very differently than it has.

CHAPTER 6

Papá

MY COUSINS CALLED HIM OUR *ABUELO*—GRANDFATHER— but Veronica and I, imitating our parents, called him Papá. He lived with us for all but the winter months, when Vegas became too cold for him and he returned to Miami to stay with my aunt Adria's family. He woke up early every morning, and dressed in a suit unless the day was very warm, when he would substitute a Cuban guayabera for the suit. Three times a day, after breakfast, lunch and dinner, he retired to our small front porch, sat in an aluminum chair and smoked one of his three daily cigars. I would sit at his feet, some days for hours.

He was very slender, and never had much of an appetite. He was taller than he appeared when he walked with his cane. His hair was thin on top and thick on the sides, and he had a pronounced bump on the back of his head, where he had been struck by a rock his brother had thrown at him when they were boys. He had narrow eyes, which made him look slightly Asian, an ethnic heritage he occasionally falsely claimed. Despite his stooped posture and slight frame, he had a very dignified air about him, a stateliness in his dress and manner, which seemed to be a conscious effort to appear cultured and successful.

Papá was proud of his education, and resentful that his against-the-odds rise to middle-class prosperity in Cuba had been lost to the depredations of others. He was an adherent of the "great man" school of history, and admired historical figures whose will and accomplishments had singularly influenced their times. He believed the United States was destined to be the defender of human progress, the only power capable of preventing tyranny from dominating the world. He revered Franklin Roosevelt and Harry Truman. He had detested communism even before Castro came to power. He accused John F. Kennedy of betraying the Cuban exiles who had fought at the Bay of Pigs, but loved Bobby Kennedy for plotting to kill Castro. And despite his Latin heritage, he strongly supported Britain's military expedition to recover the Falkland Islands. He told me he thought Margaret Thatcher should have ordered an invasion of Argentina itself.

He had few hobbies in his later years. He liked to play bingo at the casinos. He smoked his cigars. He read voraciously, and never stopped trying to master English. And he talked to us, especially to me.

Our relationship was more than a natural family attachment. I think we recognized and respected each other as fellow autodidacts. He was the son of farmers whose love of newspapers and history books helped him rise above the low station to which he had been born. I was the grandson whose enthusiasm for learning wasn't apparent in school but was obvious to him.

The summers of my Vegas childhood were carefree. I went to a public swimming pool around midday. Veronica and I watched reruns of sitcoms in the late afternoons. When the temperature dropped a little, we went outside to play with neighborhood friends until dark. But two hours or more of each morning were dedicated to Papá's tutorials. Before he consented to answer my questions on the subject that preoccupied me at the moment, he had me read to him from a copy of *Diario Las Américas*, the Spanish-language daily newspaper published in Miami that our relatives mailed to us. He would have already read the paper by then, but insisted I read it to him again so I would learn to speak his native language correctly.

He nodded to indicate when I had read enough, and he was ready to expound on any issue I cared to raise. My questions were often related to some fanciful ambition I had at the time. When I told him I wanted to be a farmer, he recounted his childhood on his family's farm: the crops they had raised; the care and feeding of the animals they had kept; the harsh nature of the work and the meager living it provided; the tools and techniques they had employed to overcome the challenges of weather, climate and soil.

When I shared that I was interested in the military, he discussed how

American soldiers had helped liberate Cuba from the Spanish and Europe from the Nazis. He chronicled the history of the conflicts. He explained their causes, the politics that had led to them, influenced their direction and been shaped by their conclusion. He recounted the actions and motives of the wars' central figures. He described important battles, and commended the virtues of the military leaders who had won them; Generals MacArthur and Patton were his favorites.

When I boasted I would someday lead an army of exiles to overthrow Fidel Castro and become president of a free Cuba, he narrated the life of José Martí and the heroics of the Mambises, who had won Cuba's independence. He identified the virtues and flaws of postindependence leaders such as Carlos Prío Socarrás, Ramón Grau and Eduardo Chibás.

Papá seemed to know something about almost everything, or everything that interested me anyway. He was a gifted storyteller, the talent he had learned as a cigar factory lector. His accounts were exciting and forceful, rich in imagery and telling anecdotes. They held me spellbound.

My interest in politics began around the time we moved to Vegas, and by 1980 politics was a preoccupation second only to football. Two events had captured my attention that year: Senator Edward Kennedy's challenge to President Carter for the Democratic presidential nomination and the Iran hostage crisis. I was a Kennedy supporter. With rapt attention I watched the Democratic convention in New York, and was crushed by the outcome of what seemed an excruciatingly slow delegate count that gave the nomination to President Carter. I was inspired by Senator Kennedy's concession speech.

My grandfather didn't admire either of them. Ronald Reagan was his man. He despised President Carter because of the Iran hostage crisis, a humiliation Papá seemed to feel personally. America must be a strong country, he constantly preached, or the world would succumb to darkness, and a strong country requires a strong leader. He thought the world didn't respect or fear Carter. He was weak, he said, and other countries preyed on his weakness. That's why the Soviets had invaded Afghanistan and the Iranians had seized our embassy. He blamed the failed attempt to rescue the hostages on cuts to defense spending Carter had made. Ronald Reagan would restore our strength, he assured me. He would confront communism. Our allies would follow him and our enemies would respect him.

When Reagan was elected and Iran released our hostages on his inauguration, Papá made certain to point out to me that it confirmed everything he had been telling me. Reagan had barely been sworn into office, and our enemies were already capitulating to him. Reagan's election and my grandfather's allegiance to him were defining influences on me politically. I've been a Republican ever since. More than just help me develop a political identity, my grandfather instilled in me the importance of strong leadership and conviction. He urged me to study and learn but, more important, to do something useful with the knowledge I acquired.

I wrote a paper in the fifth grade praising President Reagan for restoring the U.S. military after it had been demoralized and allowed to decay in the years before his presidency. I recently found it in a red suitcase that had belonged to my grandfather, and still contains some of his possessions.

Papá was an unwavering supporter of President Reagan for the remainder of his life. He loved Reagan's anti-Soviet and prodemocracy rhetoric, and he staunchly defended the more controversial Reagan policies. I particularly remember his outspoken support for Reagan's development of the MX missile, and support for the Contras in Nicaragua and the government of El Salvador.

My grandfather's talks weren't always about history or current events. Neither were they scrupulously objective. He wasn't an admirer of our new church. He was never a religious man, although I know he believed in God, and openly acknowledged Him. But I never saw him attend any religious service except on the single occasion when he agreed to accompany us to Sunday services at the Mormon Church. After we came home and ate lunch, he went to smoke his cigar on the porch and I followed him. I asked him what he had thought of the services, and he told me he would never go back because he hadn't seen a single African American in attendance. He wasn't entirely accurate. There was a biracial family in the congregation at the time. But the argument didn't impress my grandfather, and true to his word, he kept his distance from our church.

He could be quite sharp in his criticism of people, even people close to him, of whose behavior he disapproved. He frequently found fault with some of my Miami cousins who he believed lacked direction and ambition. When the Culinary Workers Union staged a strike at my father's place of employment, which my father, as a member of the union, was obliged to join, he told my father he hoped Reagan would fire them all as he did the striking air traffic controllers.

For reasons he never shared with me, Papá didn't like my friends, the Thiriots. When they called the house and asked for me, he would hang up the phone. When they came to the door, he would tell them I wasn't at home. Some of my behavior frustrated him. He couldn't abide my passion for football and resented my refusal to play baseball. He loved Tommy Lasorda and the LA Dodgers and was hurt when I wouldn't agree to watch their games with him.

He had odd quirks. He liked to call my sister by an invented nickname that scrambled the letters of her name, "Canirove." He constantly drummed his knuckles on a table or the arm of a chair in a specific and unvarying rhythmic pattern, a tic I now possess. He claimed to be part Chinese, which he was not. He boasted he was directly related to José Martí, whom he slightly resembled, but who is not, according to any known records, one of our ancestors. In his last years, he insisted he was born an American citizen around the turn of the century in Tampa, Florida, where Martí had lived in exile for a time. We kept an old Universal weight-lifting machine that I used to train for football in the rec room in our house that also served as his bedroom. He frequently complained that the contraption wasted electricity. When I explained that it didn't use electricity, he ignored me.

My father liked to tease my grandfather about little things, his quirks and some of his opinions. Most of it was good-natured kidding, and it didn't anger my grandfather. It might have annoyed him a little at times, but he never showed it. "Okay, Mario. Whatever you say, Mario," was usually the only response he would give. My mother, on the other hand, would get angry at my father. She thought his teasing was disrespectful, and would scold him for it.

My father probably shared my grandfather's political views, but he rarely discussed politics with my grandfather or with me when I was young, or with anyone as far as I know. He was consumed by the business of making a living and raising his children, and showed little interest in much else. He shared the family's antipathy to communism and visceral dislike for talk about redistributing wealth. Like my grandfather, he believed such schemes led only to entrenching the power of the regime at the expense of the powerless, who lost jobs and opportunities because their employers had fled the regime that had confiscated their property.

My father and grandfather were different in many respects. They had different personalities, and neither was given to effusive expressions of affection. But they loved each other. My grandfather admired how committed my father was to our family, how hard he worked to give us a decent home, how carefully he protected us. To my father, the young refugee from an unhappy home, my grandfather and grandmother were his first experience with two loving parents since his mother had died.

My father regarded Papá as his father. Papá lived with or near us for most of his life in the United States. My father never complained about having to support him. Every house he owned had a room for my grandfather. My father never considered buying a house that couldn't accommodate his father-in-law. The second and last time I saw my father cry was when Papá died.

My grandfather was my mentor and my closest boyhood friend. I learned at his feet, relied on his counsel and craved his respect. I still do. He constantly urged me to study hard and go to college. He wanted Veronica and me to live accomplished lives when we grew up. He wanted us to have not just jobs, but distinguished careers that would give our lives purpose and the social status he had always wanted for himself. He would scold me for performing poorly in school, but he never let me believe I was incapable of being successful. He knew I could be, and he helped me prepare for it. His dreams for us were his legacy.

He taught me many things, but none more important than the conviction that I must not waste the opportunities my parents had sacrificed to give us and our country made available to us. I've always believed, even when I was an inattentive and undisciplined student, that the time would arrive for me to become serious and do something important with my life, and I would be ready for it. I believed it because Papá taught me to believe it. And that, more than the wealth of knowledge he shared with me, more than the epics of history he evoked so powerfully for me, more than his opinions and passions and eccentricities, has made all the difference in the world to me.

CHAPTER 7

Growing Up Vegas

B Y THE TIME I ENTERED THE SIXTH GRADE, I WAS ACCUS-
tomed to living in an ethnically diverse community, unlike the Cuban
enclave where we had lived in Miami. Las Vegas was no longer a peculiar-
looking desert town. It was my home. I was comfortable and happy there.
I had no reason to feel otherwise.

Our neighborhood was predominantly white. Along with our neighbors
from Mexico, we were one of the few Hispanic families who lived there. But
I went to school, played football and became friends with African American
and Mexican American kids. I had felt part of a majority in Miami; I was a
minority of a minority in Vegas. Yet I rarely felt out of place in the community that had, for the most part, welcomed us warmly. I was a Vegas kid, and
content to be one, even after my first exposure to racial prejudice.

In the summer of 1981 an older kid in the neighborhood became upset
with me for reasons I no longer recall. His name was Bruce. One day he
came by and started kicking and breaking the wooden fence in our backyard. My mother heard the ruckus, and came outside to confront him.
Bruce told her we were trash, and she should take us on her boat back to
where we had come from. I had no idea what he was talking about. My
mother didn't swim. She was terrified of the water and, as far as I knew, had
never been on a boat in her life. My parents later explained to me he had
been referring to the Mariel boatlift, which had occurred the year before,

when Castro had emptied jails and mental wards and sent their inhabitants to Miami, along with many genuine political refugees.

My parents told me later I shouldn't blame Bruce for his behavior. He must have watched the news about the boatlift with his parents and overheard them make racist remarks about Cubans, which he then repeated to us. My mother told me I should feel sorry for him—that he had problems I didn't have, that it was his parents' fault he behaved the way he did. Bruce's parents worked at a hotel casino, and they often stayed to gamble after work late into the night, leaving Bruce to fend for himself. A few weeks after the incident, he came to our door and asked for something to eat. My father drove him to Burger King and bought him dinner.

Las Vegas structured its public school system differently than other cities. Sixth grade was considered a bridge year between elementary school and junior high, and students attended a "sixth-grade center," a separate, one-year school that prepared us for junior high. In 1982, I enrolled in Quannah McCall, a sixth-grade center in a predominantly black neighborhood. African American students had been bused to the elementary school in my neighborhood. Now I was bused to my new school in their neighborhood. It seemed fair to me, and the newness of the experience had more to do with the distinction of being a sixth grader than the unfamiliar neighborhood where it was located.

I began my third season in Pop Warner football that year. I still wanted to play quarterback, but my father and I knew I wouldn't be allowed to play the position if I stayed with the Sooners. My dad asked that I be allowed to play for another team, and I joined the Cavaliers, sponsored by the Young Electric Sign Company. Not long after the season began, my father became convinced the coaches' sons got more playing time than others. He didn't know enough about football to coach it, but he volunteered to be the team's equipment manager in the hope that his official role with the team would encourage the coaches to give me more playing time at the quarterback position.

The kids I played with on the Cavaliers were from a different neighborhood than the kids I had played with on the Sooners. I was one of a few non–African Americans on my team. Yet we seemed to fit in better with the Cavaliers. The parents of my new teammates were friendlier to my father than the Sooners parents had been, and he seemed more comfortable with them. I'm not really sure why that was. My dad was older than most of the other fathers, and maybe his age or accent had been more of a social barrier to the Sooners parents than it was to the Cavaliers parents. When I played for the Sooners, the parents often hosted casual get-togethers at their homes after the games. We had never been invited. After Cavaliers games, the parents hung around the field for a while, drinking beer and joking with each other, and my father was welcome in their company. He joined and eventually led an effort to collect money to give as cash prizes to players who scored touchdowns or made the hardest tackles.

My teammates on the Cavaliers had an edge to them. They were tougher and more intense than the kids who played for the Sooners. Their aggressive play and attitude took me aback at first, but I adapted to it. By midseason, I had the same attitude and approach to the game.

I got to play quarterback, sharing time at the position with a kid named Larry Cook. Larry was a better athlete and a better player. When I came on the field, he shifted to running back. My job was to hand him the football and let him run, which he did very well. My dad liked Larry. He promised to buy him a Burger King Whopper after the game for every touchdown he scored, and was astonished that Larry could consume two Whoppers in one sitting.

Larry and I became friends. Most of the friends I made at my new school were black. In order to fit in with my new social circle, I started listening to R&B music. I watched *Soul Train* on Saturday mornings, and became a big Michael Jackson fan. By the end of sixth grade, I had begun enjoying a new kind of music, rap, and I've been listening to it ever since. My white friends liked hard rock acts—Van Halen, Ozzy Osbourne and others. I didn't care for that kind of music anymore, and they didn't care for my preferences, Afrika Bambaataa and Grandmaster Flash.

I was exposed to something else I had been unfamiliar with before sixth grade: inner-city gang violence. Street gangs from LA were expanding to other cities, and spin-off gangs from the infamous Bloods and Crips appeared in my friends' neighborhood. It wasn't a problem at school, but I could see it distressed my friends. They often told me they had to be careful not to wear blue or red clothes, which were gang colors and could be mistaken as a sign they were affiliated with one gang and a target for the violent enmity of the other. Some of my friends had brothers who had joined gangs and been hurt in a fight or jailed. Every afternoon I took the bus home to my peaceful neighborhood, while my friends returned to their increasingly violent one.

We had a pool party for my twelfth birthday. My uncle Aurelio, Elda's husband, had given us an aboveground pool his family no longer used, and my father had reassembled it in our backyard. I invited friends from the neighborhood and my old school as well as some of my black friends from sixth grade and the Cavaliers. Everyone seemed to have a good time— I certainly did. But I later learned that several friends from the same family were no longer allowed to come to our house. They told me their parents would let them play with us outside but had forbidden them to enter our house again because we had entertained black kids there, and they didn't want their kids making friends with them. I was mystified and irritated.

It was an eventful time in my life—a new school, new football team, new friends, new music and new interests. I soon had a new church, too. I had kept in touch with a friend from elementary school, a Catholic, though not a very devout one. Yet his religious identity piqued my curiosity about my former faith, and early in 1983 I began a new research project. I read about the Church in my *World Book*. I checked out books on Catholicism from the school library. I pestered my mother about her religious upbringing. During Easter Week of 1983, when the most sacred traditions of the Catholic liturgy are on display and a papal Mass is broadcast on television, I made up my mind. I wanted to be a Catholic again.

The depth of our commitment to the Mormon Church hadn't progressed beyond attending Sunday services and social functions. My father had never felt comfortable there, and my mother had mostly joined the Mormon Church because she believed it was a safe and welcoming place for her children that would make us happy. So my parents posed no objection when I argued we should return to the Catholic Church, and in the spring of 1983 Veronica and I enrolled in CCD, the Catholic Church's religious instruction program.

My aunt Lola was upset, as was her entire family. I think Lola's family suspected my aunt Irma, a vocal critic of Mormonism, of convincing us to return to Catholicism. But it had really just been my decision. We left the Mormon Church with nothing but admiration for the place that had been our first spiritual home in Las Vegas, and had been so generous to us. I still feel that way.

I've often remarked that my parents couldn't give us everything we wanted, but they made sure we always had everything we needed. And when they could afford to give us more, they did. When Veronica and I were old enough to be at home alone or with only my grandfather to supervise us, my mother started working again. She got a job as a maid on the casino floor of the Imperial Palace Hotel. My father was doing well in his bartending job at Sam's Town. They made a good living between their two salaries and my dad's tips. It was not enough to support a lavish lifestyle, of course, but enough to afford a few extras. When I asked my parents to let Veronica and me attend the local Catholic school instead of the public junior high school, they agreed. The tuition at St. Christopher Catholic School was a stretch for them financially, but, as always, they wanted us to be happy.

Yet, from the start, I was anything but happy there. We had to wear uniforms, which I didn't like. The schoolwork was much more demanding, which I really didn't like. My biggest problem with the school, though, was its location directly across the street from J. D. Smith, the junior high I would have attended, and where every day I watched my friends from sixth grade and football come and go.

After one week at St. Christopher, I demanded my parents take me out of the school and enroll me at J. D. Smith. I made up all kinds of phony excuses. I told my parents the teachers were mean and the other kids didn't like us. Our priest told them to ignore me. My whims shouldn't override their judgment. I was a child and needed to obey them. But I made life unbearable in our house, and within a week, my parents had relented. I cringe today when I remember how selfishly I behaved.

I could be an insufferably demanding kid at times. I'm ashamed of it now, and I regret my parents so often gave in to me. I know they did it out of love, and it did make me happy in the moment, which they so badly wanted me to be. But they weren't doing me a favor in the long run. I can still be selfish with my time and attention, even though I have children. But Jeanette won't indulge my bad behavior as my parents had. She lets me know instantly when I am shirking my most important responsibility. I think I might have become a difficult person to like had I married someone else.

My football season that year was brief. The Cavaliers and the Sooners had decided to merge that summer, and became a Pop Warner dream team: a collection of the most talented players from two of the best teams in the area. I badly wanted to make the team, and the head coach of the new team was Coach Atkins, my former coach. I worried for weeks he wouldn't select me because I had left the Sooners when he hadn't let me play quarterback. So I was thrilled when he called in mid-July to tell me I had made the team.

The team had a great year. Me, not so much. After playing the best game I had ever played in Pop Warner, I broke my leg the next week in practice. I missed the rest of the season, including our victory in the city championship game.

We planned to spend the last two weeks of 1983 in Miami, and Barbara bought us tickets to the Dolphins' last regular-season game against the New York Jets. I was overjoyed to see the Dolphins break open a close game to defeat the Jets and finish the regular season with a 12-4 record. I was sure they would make the Super Bowl. My father bought me one of those foam "We're Number 1" hands at the game. I still have it.

We celebrated a traditional Cuban *Nochebuena* that Christmas Eve with Barbara and Orlando at their new house in a rural part of Dade County. Their house was small, but had an acre of land. Orlando was from a *guajiro* family, a Cuban term for country folk. He and his family slaughtered a pig, and on the morning of Christmas Eve they set it over a pit filled with charcoal and covered with palm fronds, where it would slowly roast for the entire day. The pig was carved and served at nine o'clock that night, along with black beans and rice and boiled cassava, a traditional holiday feast in rural Cuba.

That Christmas is my fondest childhood memory. It had been a long time since I had seen my parents so happy. My father had felt transported to his childhood in the years before his mother died. My mother was nearly overcome with emotion as she spent her first Christmas in five years with Barbara. And my grandfather was as close to our family's rural Cuban heritage as he had been since his boyhood. Only Veronica has unpleasant memories of it. She had been appalled to see a pig killed and butchered, and terrified when Orlando chased her around the house with the pig's head.

Our Christmas in Miami reawakened my affection for the city and the Cuban culture so prevalent there. But I returned to the familiar, pleasurable routines of my life in Las Vegas with little reason to wish I lived any-where else.

I became interested in girls that year and started to care about my appearance. I was popular at school, and had an increasingly active social life. My schoolwork suffered for it, of course, but I managed to get by making the minimum effort necessary. Life was great—and then it wasn't.

In April 1984, the Culinary Workers Union went on strike. I went with my father to the union hall, where several hundred workers rallied on the eve of the strike. The strike became my new obsession. The strikers set up camp in a desert field across the street from Sam's Town and took turns walking shifts on the picket line. I helped make their signs. When the hotel management sent one of their security staff to videotape the picketers, I held a sign in front of his camera to block his view.

I never grasped all the issues involved, but understood generally that the strikers were just asking to be treated fairly. They had worked hard to help make the hotels profitable, and were entitled to better compensation and benefits. I was excited to be part of the cause and join forces with striking workers from many hotels. At the height of the strike, it seemed all the kids at my school had a parent on the picket line. I became a committed union activist. I got to spend time with my father. I thought it was nothing but fun.

Initially, the financial strain on my parents was modest. They had set aside a little money in anticipation of the strike, and the union paid the strikers small sums from a strike fund. But it wasn't much, and we had to live frugally. We couldn't go to the movies or restaurants or roller skating. I remember going to the union hall with my dad to pick up government surplus cheese and peanut butter. Everyone assumed the strike would last only a few days or weeks before management would come to their senses and settle. As the weeks wore on, I began to notice the worry etched on my father's face. I remained, however, happily committed to the cause.

My father was older than most of the strikers. I remember watching him ride in a jeep with a younger striker. Bouncing along over the hills near our desert camp with a serious look on his face, he seemed so old and out of place there. Eventually, our small savings were gone and the union checks stopped coming. My parents had to dip into the modest college fund they had started for us. Many of the hotels settled with their workers.

But Sam's Town wouldn't. Every day, the camp became less crowded and the picket line thinner as more strikers gave up. We denounced them as "scabs" when they crossed our line on their way back to work.

The excitement and euphoria of the strike's early days gave way to anger and bitterness. One day, a confrontation between strikers and returning workers turned violent, and my father stopped taking me to the camp. Not long after, he informed me he was going back to work. I accused him of selling out and called him a scab. It hurt him, and I'm ashamed of it. He had had no choice.

He returned to work for a smaller salary and fewer benefits. All the good bartending shifts had been taken by new bartenders hired during the strike, and his tips were smaller. To this day, Sam's Town remains a non-union hotel.

My grandfather usually went back to Miami right after Thanksgiving and returned early in the spring. He didn't come back to us until the end of May that year. I had missed him terribly, and when we met him at the airport, I knew instantly something was wrong. He had always managed the trip on his own, but this time my uncle Manolito had traveled with him. He needed a wheelchair to get from the plane to the airport exit. He looked much older and tired.

Papá had suffered from bladder cancer for years, and the disease had progressed significantly that winter. Veronica and I had never been told he was ill, and neither had he. His daughters had kept the diagnosis from him for fear he would become depressed and rapidly decline. He knew something was wrong with him now, and despite his weakened condition, and protests from his daughters in Miami, he insisted on coming back to Vegas. He wanted to be at home with his daughter Oria and his son-in-law Mario and with Veronica and me, his favorite grandchildren.

He complained of back pains, and asked my mother, and sometimes Veronica or me, to rub Ben-Gay on his back. He didn't smoke as many cigars or sit on the front porch as often. My parents told us he was sick but would get well, and in other respects he seemed normal to me. He still loved for me to sit with him and pick his brain. He still hated football and wanted to watch the Dodgers games. Ronald Reagan was still his hero.

One morning that August, just as I was waking up, I heard a thud outside my bedroom door. I heard my mother scream, and I bolted from my bed to see what had happened. I found Papá on the floor in the hallway, where he had fallen on his way to the bathroom.

We helped him to his feet and back to his bed. He was clearly in excruciating pain. We called the paramedics, who took him in an ambulance to the hospital. I went with him to translate for him. When we arrived at the hospital, he was taken immediately to the X-ray room. As the technicians maneuvered him into the right position for the X-ray, he cried out in pain so loudly and pitiably it terrified me.

The adults began to arrive not long after, and within an hour a doctor informed us Papá had broken his hip, which didn't sound so bad to me. I had broken my leg not long ago, and I was fine now. I thought they would put him in a cast, send him home with us, and within a few weeks he would be back to normal. My parents explained to me he would have to stay at the hospital because his hip required surgery to repair. Still, I wasn't too concerned. I began to make plans for his rehabilitation. I would put him on a regimen of diet supplements and help him do daily exercises on the Universal that he believed was wasting electricity.

He passed his first night in the hospital uneventfully. The next morning my parents dropped Veronica and me off at the hospital on their way to work. They were worried he would become frustrated by the language barrier at the hospital, and wanted us there to translate for him. We were alone with him for much of the day. We made a point to talk with him about things we would normally talk about with him. We watched TV with him. I remember watching the *Brady Bunch* episode when the Brady parents put a pay phone in their kitchen to discourage the kids from spending too much time on the phone. We tried to make him feel everything was as normal as possible under the circumstances. Late in the afternoon, he began to change. He complained of ants on the ceiling and spiderwebs around him. He thought the hospital sprinklers were cockroaches. We thought he was being funny, and laughed at him.

Irma and Enrique arrived after work around six in the evening, carrying a thermos of Cuban coffee. Papá asked Irma for a sip. Right after she gave him one, he began to have difficulty breathing. We called a nurse, who, after consulting with a doctor, put him on an IV. I know now it was a morphine drip, and that the hospital staff was easing him toward his death and not, as I had believed, treating his injury.

He began to slip into unconsciousness. I knew something was wrong, so I grabbed his hand and told him I loved him. I swore I would study hard. I would do something with my life and make him proud. He squeezed my hand to let me know he had heard me. He took his last labored breath less than twenty-four hours later.

He was buried in Miami next to my grandmother Dominga in a joint plot Papá had purchased for them before I was born. We couldn't afford to travel to Miami for his burial because of the financial difficulties we were in after the strike. But we had a viewing ceremony at the funeral home in Las Vegas where his body was prepared. When I approached him, I was taken aback because he looked so different to me. I had never seen a dead person before then. My mother cried, and called his name repeatedly. She kept touching him and sobbing. Near the end of the viewing, as everyone got up to leave, my father, who had avoided the viewing stand the entire night, approached it to say his final good-bye. Then he broke down and wept inconsolably, and begged my grandfather's forgiveness for the times he had teased him.

I didn't keep the promise I made to my grandfather on his deathbed, not for a long while anyway. His death had a pronounced and debilitating effect on me. I was miserably unhappy and stopped caring about things that had been important to me. I quit Pop Warner. What little interest I had shown in schoolwork disappeared. I still went to class, but I didn't participate in discussions, and all my assignments went ignored. I failed my exams, and didn't care. I didn't want to do anything besides socialize with my friends, flirt with girls and follow the Miami Dolphins.

With Papá gone, Veronica and I were alone at home when my parents were at work. I would wander the neighborhood or ride my bike alone or visit friends' homes, leaving Veronica behind. We were supposed to make our First Communion that Christmas, after preparing for the sacrament during Sunday catechism classes throughout the fall. I refused to attend them because they conflicted with Sunday NFL games. My parents persuaded our parish priest to instruct us personally on Wednesday nights. I reacted to Papá's death by becoming more selfish, more irresponsible, more of a brat. I'm ashamed of that, and I think he would have been ashamed of me, too. In retrospect, I was a child struggling with my grief, and my parents, also grieving, might not have realized how distraught I was.

My parents watched these developments with increasing alarm. I was spending more of my time with friends they didn't know from families they knew nothing about. I was bringing Fs home from school. They began to have doubts about Las Vegas, too. They wanted us to go to college, but most of my cousins had gone to work at the hotels right out of high school. It was hard to convince them that college was necessary when they could make $40,000 in their first year of employment. My parents didn't want that life for us. That was their life, the life they had to live so we could live a better one. Vegas no longer seemed like a safe, wholesome environment for us.

My sister Barbara had met her husband in high school. I would soon be in high school, and had already become preoccupied with girls. They worried I might develop a serious relationship with someone and I would never want to leave Las Vegas, just as Barbara had refused to leave Miami. Our family would be divided forever. Just after Thanksgiving in 1984, my parents made their decision.

That summer, almost six years to the day since we had arrived in Vegas, my mother, Veronica and I boarded a flight to Miami, while my father and Uncle Manolito drove a U-Haul truck across the country with all our belongings and our two dogs, Max and Marie, towing our '73 Chevy Impala behind them. My parents returned to a city and culture they knew well and loved. After a failed attempt to convince my parents to stay in Vegas, I became excited to be moving back to Miami—the city where my Dolphins played, the city filled with people like us, the exciting city I saw on *Miami Vice*. But I was a fourteen-year-old kid from the West, and accustomed to living in a desert town, among people of various backgrounds and ethnicities. I would have to learn how to make Miami my home again.

CHAPTER 8

Back to Miami

WHAT I REMEMBER MOST ABOUT MY FIRST DAY BACK IN Miami is the thunderstorm. I had never seen so much rain fall so hard and fast. Aunt Adria picked us up at the airport, and as we drove west on the Dolphin Expressway to Barbara's house, hail began to hit the windshield. It rained all the next day, and the day after that. Miami summers follow a simple pattern. Sun and muggy heat in the morning give way to showers and thunderstorms in the afternoon. I wasn't in the desert anymore.

We stayed with Barbara until my father rejoined us the day before the Fourth of July. Adria had found a home for us in West Miami. My folks had already signed a contract to buy it, and they closed on it soon after my dad arrived. It had three bedrooms and a small family room in the back. Its biggest appeal was the garage that had been converted into an efficiency apartment. An eighty-one-year-old Cuban lady, Encarnación, and her even older husband rented it. I liked the idea of having elderly renters in our home. It reminded me of living with Papá.

I was zoned to attend ninth grade at West Miami Junior High School, but I had my heart set on attending Miami Senior High School, and playing football there as my brother had. I enrolled in summer school there to prepare for ninth grade. I was excited as I walked for the first time through the school's arched entryway, and imagined my brother walking there a decade and a half earlier. It took only a few minutes for me to realize it was unlike any school I had attended, and I wasn't likely to fit in.

All the students were Hispanic. But theirs wasn't the Hispanic culture I'd become accustomed to growing up among Mexican kids in Las Vegas. And while they could speak English, they spoke only Spanish with one another, and in an accent that was unfamiliar to me. It didn't sound like the Cuban-accented Spanish our parents and grandparents spoke. It was an accent of their own, a Miami accent, and they used slang of their own device as well. They dressed in designs I had never seen before.

I spoke Spanish very well. I spoke it exclusively at home. But I had never spoken Spanish with my friends at school, not even with Mexican American kids I grew up with in Las Vegas. At Miami High, they laughed at my "American" accent. I dressed in Las Vegas casual—polo shirt, jeans and Reebok shoes. They called me a "gringo," a term I had never been called before. In fact, in Las Vegas, because we were Hispanic everyone assumed we were Mexican. It was a massive culture shock. It lasted one day. When I got home that afternoon, I told my parents Miami High wasn't anything like they had described it to me, and I wouldn't be going back.

My dad painted houses with my uncle Manolito until Barbara found him a bartending job at a new hotel, the Mayfair House in Coconut Grove. Our new house didn't have air-conditioning, so he installed a few ceiling fans and told us they would have to do for the time being. I spent a miserable summer suffering from the muggy Miami heat.

The only good thing about being back in Miami was that it was home to my beloved Dolphins. Every morning that first summer I walked three blocks to a convenience store and bought the *Miami Herald* for its Dolphins-dominated sports page. I returned in the afternoon to buy the *Miami News*. In the evenings, I watched all three local news sports segments.

I wanted to attend every Dolphins home game, and needed money to buy the tickets. Barbara and Orlando owned seven Samoyed dogs, a beautiful breed with long white hair that was hard to keep clean. They paid me ten dollars a week for each dog I washed, and I used my earnings to buy tickets to all eight regular-season home games in 1985.

West Miami Junior High didn't have a football team, so I had to find a Pop Warner team. I joined the Tamiami Colts, who played at Tamiami Park. They were a great team. The coaches had recruited the best players

from several competing parks, and put together a team that went undefeated that season and won the city championship. I played outside line-
backer. I wasn't a standout, but I had fun. Winning is fun.

The Colts were the only social activity I had that year. I didn't like West
Miami Junior High any better than I had liked Miami High. It was every
bit the culture shock Miami High had been. Again, the student body was
almost entirely Hispanic. Veronica adjusted quickly to our new circumstances. I did not. The few friendships I managed to form effectively ended
when the bell rang at the end of the school day. When football season
ended, I had virtually nothing to do after school. I became an afternoon
recluse, and spent almost all my time alone. I pined for my friends in Vegas,
and wondered what they were doing.

When I finished ninth grade, I was glad to put the experience behind
me. I hoped I would fit in better at South Miami High, and from my first day
there I knew I would. I made the South Miami Cobras' junior varsity team.
Half my teammates were African Americans, and, at the time, I was more
comfortable in their company than with my fellow Cubans. There was real
tension between the black and Hispanic players, something I had not experienced in Las Vegas. They didn't socialize off the field, and even on the field
they huddled in separate groups.

Unhappily, my first football season in South Miami came to an abrupt
end before it began. I dislocated my shoulder during a preseason practice,
and it took eight weeks to heal. Pain from the injury still bothers me from
time to time.

Even without football, I found it easier to make friends at South Miami
than at West Miami Junior High. I socialized mostly with my African
American teammates. We spent most of our time "cracking," sitting around
cracking jokes at another's expense. It usually took the form of a contest
between two students who traded insults back and forth until the winner
was decided by acclamation of the audience. My father was always teasing
people. The practice had rubbed off on me, and I was good at "cracking." I
was happy to have finally found a social circle in Miami. It was the first
time I had felt at home since we had moved back.

Socially and geographically, Miami is a deeply segregated city. When
school finished for the day, my black friends returned to their homes in a
South Miami neighborhood known as "the Creek," and I went home to

West Miami. After school, I was every bit the loner I had been the previous year.

Football came to my rescue, as it often did. In May 1987, when I tried out for the varsity team during spring practices, I did well, but it was clear I wouldn't be a starter. The starting safety, Dakari Lester, was a senior and Division I college prospect. The secondary coach, Otis Collier, was frank with me. He told me not to expect much playing time my junior year. But if I used the opportunity to learn from Dakari and hit the weight room to build muscle and strength, I might start my senior year.

I had a good spring training camp. I made some interceptions, and the hard tackles our coaches wanted to see us make. I earned the respect of the other players. When we broke for the summer, I couldn't wait to get back on the field my junior year.

Yet it was not to be. At practice five days before our first game, I broke my finger during an interception drill. I spent a lot of time the first week after my injury with our trainer and the students who volunteered to assist her. One of her assistants was nicer and more attentive to me than the others. By the middle of September, we were going out. What that meant in practical terms is we would hold hands in the hallway between classes, eat lunch together in the cafeteria and hang out together with the same group of friends after football games. It was the kind of innocent first romance kids seem to skip these days or start much earlier than they should.

I had a new girlfriend and plenty of friends at school, and I played varsity football. I had finally settled into life in Miami, and was happy we had moved back. But in October, our family's fortunes took a sudden turn for the worse. I came home from school one day and knew from the look on my mother's face that something terrible had happened. It was a look you expect to see when someone has been told they or someone they love is dying. And that's exactly how I felt when she told me that earlier that morning Orlando had been arrested on drug charges.

I was stunned by the news. Like my parents, I had never suspected Orlando was involved in a criminal enterprise. His arrest and subsequent trial and imprisonment distressed the entire family, but Barbara and my parents bore the brunt of the hardships it caused. Even decades later, my sister and mother would be forced to relive the shame of the ordeal.

My family's troubles didn't diminish my enthusiasm for the upcoming football season. I was as eager as ever for it to begin. I didn't get a lot of playing time my junior year except during blowout games. The team had a great season. In our last regular-season game Coach Collier put me in early in the fourth quarter. I noticed that the opponent's tight end ran only two routes when he lined up to our left: an out pattern and the seam route our offense ran in practice. On one of the last drives of the game, I saw the opposing quarterback drop back to throw and look to his right. I made a beeline for the spot where I expected him to throw the ball to the tight end. I drove my face mask into the tight end's chest just as he grabbed the pass, knocking him flat. I heard the crowd roar its approval. I then realized I had popped the ball into the air and our cornerback had intercepted it. My teammates mobbed me when I came off the field. Coach Collier was giddy over my performance as if it was all he needed to convince our head coach, Sam Miller, to give me a shot as a starter. We won our first play-off game the following Friday; then we lost the sectional title game the following week. It was a close game with several lead changes and a last-minute miracle play by our opponent. I didn't play a single down, but to this day I still dream about the game.

I enrolled in summer school that year to improve my math skills and my prospects for admission to college. South Miami didn't offer summer school, so I took an algebra class at Coral Gables High. I began serious weight training that summer, working out daily at South Miami's gym as soon as my algebra class finished for the day. In less than two months, I added ten pounds of muscle—a noticeable transformation that would impress my coaches. It impressed the girls at Coral Gables High, too.

For the first time in my life, more than one girl showed an interest in me. I began to have doubts about staying in a committed relationship, and imagined what it would be like to spend my last year of high school dating several different girls. I felt guilty, though. My feelings alternated throughout the summer between appreciation for the great girlfriend I had and not wanting to hurt her feelings to wishing I were free to date other girls.

I began senior year with the wind at my back. I was the starting free safety on the varsity football team. I had gone from being a social recluse to being pretty popular, especially with girls. My relationship with my girlfriend didn't survive the first week of school.

The Cobras started off hot that season, winning our first four games and becoming one of the top-ranked teams in Florida. But it fell apart after that. In our first game, I tried to tackle the tight end, and just bounced off him while he ran for another thirty yards. That was the end of my career as a starter. We lost a bunch of games and were knocked out of play-off contention. We missed the guys who had graduated. And we had issues in the locker room that affected our play.

African Americans were about 25 percent of the student body at South Miami High; the rest were mostly Hispanic kids. I had been the only non–African American starter on the Cobra's defense, and one of only three white starters on the team. I've always considered sports to be a nearly perfect meritocracy, and I believed our coaches made personnel decisions based strictly on which players would give us the best chance to win. But some of my Hispanic teammates felt differently. They thought Coach Miller, who was African American, unfairly favored the black players. A few Hispanic players and students tried to stoke the racial-preference grievance as the reason I had been benched. That was nonsense.

I had been replaced by a bigger, stronger and faster kid who made more plays than I did. That's all there was to it. Our defense required the free safety to do some pretty difficult things. The system was designed for Division I prospects like Dakari Lester. I was better suited to playing a traditional free safety, who roamed the deep middle of the field, read the QB and made a play on the ball. I wasn't benched because I was Hispanic. I was benched because I wasn't strong enough to do consistently all the things our defensive system asked of me.

There was some racial tension at South Miami. A few years earlier, the football program and the school were rocked by a racial split after a losing game that turned violent and made it into the newspapers.

When I rejected claims that my status on the team had something to do with racism and remained friends with my black teammates, I became an object of scorn to some of my fellow Cuban students.

Despite my encounter with racial turmoil and my disappointing football season, my senior year proved to be the time of my life. I dated several girls. I spent my free time, which I had plenty of in the absence of football and a serious commitment to academic achievement, with friends at the beach, wandering around Coconut Grove and at house parties. In addition to the friends I had already, I became friends with many kids in Veronica's social circle.

I put my popularity to the test when I competed in our school's annual male talent contest, King Cobra. I had a decent singing voice. Many of the contestants lip-synched their songs. I actually sang mine, Lionel Richie's "Still." For laughs, I adopted an obnoxious braggadocio personality. I strutted around the stage, smirked, threw my microphone and stalked offstage after I finished the song. My friends got the joke. The judges did not—they voted me second to last. They thought I had behaved like a jerk. I had. Were I to judge a contest like that today, and some kid behaved as I had behaved, I'd vote him last.

I was a frequent disruptive force in the classroom. One teacher wanted me out of his class so badly, he promised to give me a C-minus if I didn't come to class, and threatened to give me an F if I showed up again. I finished my senior year with a 2.1 grade point average. I hadn't applied myself, but I hadn't failed, either. I was allowed to participate in the commencement ceremony with my class, but I had to complete a social studies class in summer school before I officially graduated.

Despite the fun I had and my occasional obnoxious behavior, I still kept an eye on the future. I wanted to go to college, get out of Miami and play football. I did just enough not to ruin my chances. My grandfather and parents had convinced me that I had to go to college if I were to succeed in life. I knew if I stayed in Miami, I wouldn't play college football and I probably wouldn't take my studies seriously, either.

Two schools offered me a chance to play football: Wagner College in Staten Island, New York, and Tarkio College in northwest Missouri. I chose Tarkio for two reasons: they offered the most aid, enough to cover my entire tuition and room and board, and they would let me try out for wide receiver. I was tired of being an undersized defensive back, and I thought my skills were better suited for the offense.

Orlando was convicted and sentenced during the spring of my senior year in high school. My most powerful memories of that time are my recollections of my sister and parents in the difficult years after his conviction. One night, Barbara called me and invited me to her house to eat pizza and watch movies. I declined. I was enjoying my socially hectic senior year, and pizza parties and movies weren't fun for me anymore. Barbara was lonely, and I avoided her. She had to move in with us a few weeks later. I came home late one night from a party, and saw my pregnant sister and my nephew, Landy, asleep on our living room sofa. My parents would eventually ask their tenants to vacate the garage apartment so Barbara and her boys could move into it after the baby was born. The image of her the night I discovered her asleep in our living room has remained with me all my life: the older sister I had long looked up to, reduced to moving in with her parents and sleeping with her son on a foldout sofa.

I look back on that time with admiration for Barbara and my parents. I admired how tenaciously she fought when her world turned upside down, how hard she worked and how devoted she was to her children. I admired how faithfully she stuck with her marriage.

At a time in their lives when they should have been anticipating retirement and finally having time for their own enjoyment as the last of their children neared adulthood, my parents assumed responsibility for the welfare of their older daughter and her children. They helped Barbara raise her sons from infancy to adulthood. I think Danny, Barbara's younger son, grew closer to my dad than I had been to Papá. While Barbara was at work, our parents fed them, changed their diapers, rushed them to the doctor when they got sick, picked them up after school and took them to baseball practice. They were in their late sixties and early seventies when they began raising two more children, and they never complained.

It was in these heartrending circumstances that the time arrived for me to leave home. I had to report for football practice in early August. I would live a great distance from the security and comfort of my family, in the unfamiliar Midwest, a place that would seem even stranger to me than Las Vegas had first seemed. I didn't expect to return until Christmas break. I had no money, so I would have to limit my contact with home to one brief phone call a week on Sundays after seven o'clock, when the rates were cheaper.

I was more anxious than excited the day of my departure. My parents, Veronica and a few friends accompanied me to the gate, where we said our good-byes. Loneliness hit me as soon as the plane took off. For the first time I was separated from my parents and their protection, on my own and friendless.

CHAPTER 9

College Daze

A S I LEFT THE KANSAS CITY AIRPORT, MY FIRST THOUGHT was the reports about Tarkio's remoteness had been exaggerated. An hour later, however, all I could see were the stars in the night sky. I had never seen so many. There wasn't a trace of civilization anywhere.

I arrived at Tarkio College in the middle of the night after a two-and-a-half-hour drive from Kansas City. I was shown to my dorm room and instructed to be at my first practice no later than eight thirty the next morning. I picked the top bunk, climbed in, closed my eyes and fell asleep wondering what my friends in Miami were doing that night.

Practices at Tarkio were easy compared to South Miami practices. At South Miami, Coach Collier loved to run what he called the "hamburger drill." Two players would lie on their backs; one of them had the football, while the other was the defender. Coach would blow his whistle and both players scrambled to their feet and ran toward each other at full speed. As a 140-pound high school junior, I had given away as many as thirty pounds to my opponent. I gave the hamburger drill my best effort, but I couldn't overcome the laws of physics. Bigger, faster opponents ran over me.

We didn't run hamburger drills at Tarkio. Nor did we run twelve-minute sprints in the ninety-plus-degree heat and stifling humidity of a Miami summer. The players were quite a bit bigger at Tarkio, especially the linemen, but they were also slower than the players at South Miami.

Tarkio had a junior varsity as well as a varsity football team. Varsity played on Saturdays, junior varsity on Sundays. Early in the season I dressed for the varsity games, and then started at wide receiver for junior varsity the next day. Midway through the season, three starting defensive backs suffered injuries in the same game. Coach asked me to switch to defensive back until the starters healed, and I agreed, playing cornerback in practices that week.

I started at cornerback in the next JV game, and played one of my best games ever. I started getting more practice with varsity at cornerback, and when the starting varsity cornerback left our next game with a concussion, I replaced him.

My assignment was to cover the opponent's star wide receiver, an all-conference speedster who had been burning us the entire game. A good offensive coordinator will always target a backup, especially if he's a freshman. I knew they would come at me right away. I ignored my responsibility and dropped back into deep coverage, anticipating a long pass to their star receiver. And that's the play they called.

He still managed to catch it for a touchdown. But my coaches were impressed. When we reviewed the film the next day, they were surprised that I had been in the perfect position, running stride for stride with one of the fastest receivers in the conference. The team did not finish the season with a winning record, but I was feeling good about myself. I was coming to grips with the fact that I did not have NFL talent. But for the first time in my life, I was a significant contributor on a football team.

The academics at Tarkio were an unpleasant surprise, however. No one took class attendance as they did in high school. We took notes while a professor lectured, and our grades were entirely determined by our mid-term and final exams. I was terribly unprepared. I didn't know how to take notes, and I had no idea how to study for a college exam. In high school, I had merely tried to memorize facts in my textbooks to prepare for multiple-choice exams. At Tarkio, the exams were essay form. I didn't spend a lot of time trying to improve these deficiencies, either, and as a result my first-semester grades were abysmal. Had I wanted to play a second-semester sport such as basketball or baseball, I would have been declared academically ineligible.

I couldn't blame my poor grades on my active social life. With fewer than five hundred students, there really wasn't much of a social scene. We played video game tournaments in our dorm rooms, and on weekends we went to keg parties at an apartment complex off campus, where a lot of upperclassmen lived. If we wanted to go to a movie or even eat at a McDonald's, we had to drive to St. Joseph, Missouri, or Davenport, Iowa.

Tarkio's residents were the nicest people I have ever met. It took me a while to get used to it. In Miami, people only exchanged greetings if they knew one another. But in northwest Missouri, even strangers said hello to you.

I liked the people and the football, but just about everything else at Tarkio made me miserable. I missed my friends in Miami, and my social life there. I struggled to adjust to life in a small town that didn't have a movie theater or a restaurant other than a single Pizza Hut. I wanted to go home and decided I would surprise my parents by returning to Miami for Thanksgiving. I surprised my friends, too, when I showed up for a pep rally before a South Miami football game. Everyone greeted me warmly. Coach Miller seemed glad to see me, and Coach Collier congratulated me for getting in good condition and making the varsity team. He acted as if my success confirmed the potential he had seen in me that others hadn't. His evident pride in me meant a great deal to me then and still does.

I also got to meet the newest member of our family while I was back, my nephew Danny. My mother recounted for me how lonely and difficult Barbara's life had been since Orlando had left. Three years earlier, when Landy was born, Barbara's hospital room had been crowded with flowers, balloons and friends. When she gave birth to Danny, the only flowers in her room were brought by my parents, her only visitors.

I returned for my second semester at Tarkio to ominous warning signs that the school was in dire financial straits. A series of newspaper reports examined the state of Tarkio's finances, which incited rampant rumors that the school was bankrupt and would have to close. I was alarmed. If Tarkio closed, some of my college credits wouldn't transfer to a school in Florida. If the school could keep its doors open for only another two years and I stayed enrolled there, up to a quarter of my credits could be nontransferable. Even more worrying was the prospect that Tarkio would have to cut its athletic budget. Since football was by far its most expensive sport, it was more than likely the school would terminate its football program first. In addition to my concern about Tarkio's precarious future, I had also begun to worry about the value of a degree from a small and unknown school.

I began to explore transferring to another school. I wanted to keep playing football, so I reached out to the coach at Wagner College who had recruited me. Wagner didn't work out, either. The difference between the aid they could offer me and my tuition was more than I could afford. For a while, I tried to convince myself that my best option was to remain at Tarkio and take my chances that the school and its football program would survive another few years. At Tarkio, I played in front of crowds that were smaller than the crowds at my high school games. But where else could I be a starter and possibly an all-conference standout? And a degree was still a degree even if it came from an obscure school. I was leaning toward staying when I encountered a new dilemma that would change my immediate situation and the future I envisioned for myself.

My neck had bothered me throughout my freshman football season. After games, I often woke up with excruciating pain that caused numbness in my right arm and hand. After the season ended, so did the pain, but the numbness persisted. I was having problems in the weight room because my right arm had become much weaker than my left. Eventually, my conditioning coach told me I wouldn't be allowed back in the weight room until the team doctor had examined me and cleared me to return.

After a quick examination, the doctor informed me he needed to run a series of diagnostic tests to determine the problem. My description of the pain suggested I might be suffering nerve damage, and I wouldn't be allowed to play or practice unless they determined that wasn't the case. When I pressed him, he told me that if I did have nerve damage in my neck, one more hit could leave me permanently impaired.

That was all I needed to hear. As a boy, I had dreamed I would one day play in the NFL. But I never really had the size or speed. That dream was over. I accepted who I was and who I wouldn't be. I made a practical, adult decision. I had to transfer to a school that would prepare me to do something important with my life, something other than play football. But I didn't want to move back to Miami—I would be too distracted there. And given how poorly I had done in my first semester at Tarkio, I couldn't afford any distractions. I wanted to go to the University of Florida, but I didn't have the grades to be admitted there. I heard a couple of kids in the class below me at South Miami High were going to attend Santa Fe Community College in Gainesville, and it sounded like a good fit for me. I decided to attend Santa Fe for a year, improve my GPA and apply for admission to Florida the following year.

I spent the summer in Miami working as a messenger for a courier service that did a lot of work for Miami law firms. I drove a blue 1983 Pontiac Firebird, which my father had bought for me from his sister, to courier packages between the law firms on Brickell Avenue and downtown Miami. I saved money for college, and squandered a little of it on the weekends. In late August, I packed up the Firebird and left for Gainesville.

I moved into a one-bedroom apartment in Gainesville only two miles from the University of Florida with a high school friend, Alex Sarmiento. His girlfriend was a student at UF and also happened to be one of Veronica's best friends. As soon as we unpacked and got our bearings, we began scouting the Gainesville party scene. The best parties in town were held at the university's fraternities and sororities. They dominated student social life at Florida. Since neither Alex nor I was a Florida student, we obviously couldn't join a fraternity. Nor could I have afforded to join one—I could barely pay my tuition, books and living expenses with my grants, loans, summer savings and the occasional twenty dollars from my parents.

Gainesville is a fun town, especially on football weekends, and I enjoyed myself there. But I had made a serious resolution to apply myself academically. I spent most weekends studying in my apartment. The University of Florida had become more selective in its admissions policy, and my grades would have to be very good to compensate for my poor performance at Tarkio. I dedicated myself to the task, and received the best grades in my life my first semester at Santa Fe.

When I returned from Christmas break for the start of the new semester, financial difficulties almost caused me to quit school. I had exhausted my savings, and the loans and grants I received weren't enough to cover all my living expenses. My parents couldn't help me, and I prepared to return to Miami to find work and save enough money to return to school in the fall.

I called my parents and explained my predicament and my plan. Then I prayed. I asked God for the strength to accept His will and whatever disappointment awaited me. After I finished my prayer, I went to collect my mail. I found an envelope addressed to me in our mailbox. Inside was a check sufficient to cover the shortfall in my finances. It was a small grant I had applied for and forgotten about. I called my mother again, and told her what had happened. She praised God, as did I.

My second-semester grades were even better than the previous semester's. I wasn't a social recluse, and life in Gainesville wasn't a ceaseless academic grind. But I spent most of my time studying and learning how to become a serious student. Early that summer, I got my acceptance letter to the University of Florida for admission in the fall of 1991.

My political science classes, and Iraq's invasion of Kuwait in the summer of 1990 and the U.S. response, Operation Desert Storm, rekindled my interest in politics. I had always paid attention to politics, but after my grandfather died my interest became episodic. That summer, I phoned the office of our local congresswoman, Ileana Ros-Lehtinen, and inquired about internship opportunities there. I was invited to the office for an interview and offered a summer internship.

The internship involved the kind of grunt work—answering phones, copying documents, sorting and responding to constituent mail—that some people find unrewarding. But it was a networking and résumé-building opportunity that paid dividends for me down the road. I met several people in the office who one day would help open doors for me to other political opportunities. I learned the nuts and bolts of constituent service and why it's a critically important function of a congressional office. I use the constituent service methods I learned in Ileana's office as the model for constituent services in my Senate office.

I took a math class at Miami-Dade Community College that summer as well. But my schedule still left plenty of time for socializing, and I made the most of it. I spent a lot of time with a friend from high school, Javier, and his girlfriend, Jenny. One evening at Jenny's house, I met her best friend, Jeanette Dousdebes, a beautiful seventeen-year-old brunette.

I had seen her before at one or two social gatherings, but we had never spoken. Javier spent a long time talking with Jenny and her parents in another room, leaving Jeanette and me alone in the living room. I don't really recall what we talked about; I just remember we talked for a long time. I knew that night I was very interested in her, but I had no idea if she felt the same way.

Javier told me a few days later that Jeanette had made a few favorable comments about me to Jenny. She hadn't said she liked me or even expressed an interest in meeting me again. But I was encouraged enough by Javier's report to start scheming for another opportunity to see her. I coaxed Javier into organizing a group of friends to go to the movies. I told him to make sure Jenny invited Jeanette. It had to be a small group so I wouldn't have much competition for Jeanette's attention, but not so small that she would feel she had been tricked into a date with me.

We went to see *Robin Hood* with Kevin Costner in the title role. I managed to sit next to her. I don't remember what I said, but Jeanette claims I talked so much she couldn't watch the movie. The movie's theme song was by Bryan Adams. To this day, whenever I hear the song, I remember the night I started to fall in love with Jeanette Dousdebes.

Despite my talkativeness, Jenny's report the next day was encouraging: Jeanette was interested in me. I worked up the nerve to ask her out, and she accepted. We spent our first date at a Mexican restaurant, El Torito, and we continued dating for the rest of the summer. As the middle of August approached, I prepared to go back to Gainesville. Our summer romance had been fun, but we didn't know if it would survive our separation. We would spend time socializing on the weekends with couples while a distance of 350 miles separated us. We would both be tempted to see other people. Nevertheless, we decided to give it a try and see what happened. Maybe absence would make the heart grow fonder; maybe it wouldn't.

I was out of sorts almost from the moment I arrived at the University of Florida. I had no interest in going out with friends or meeting new people. I didn't enjoy parties or any social activity. I missed Jeanette constantly. I tried to put her out of my mind, but I only thought about her more.

Running low on money, I didn't have the luxury of making frequent, expensive long-distance phone calls. So I wrote Jeanette numerous long letters, sharing with her the most insignificant details of my day in the hope that the comprehensive chronicle of my existence would somehow secure her affection for me. By the middle of October, I couldn't take it any longer. I jumped in my car one Thursday afternoon after classes and drove five hours straight to Jeanette's house. She was having dinner with her family when I arrived, but seemed neither surprised nor displeased by my sudden appearance. We spent all the time we could together that weekend. I went home to see her several more times that semester, including a trip at Halloween just a couple of weeks after my first surprise visit.

My disinterest in a social life in Gainesville gave me ample time to concentrate on my studies. I stayed in on weekends and worked. It was all I could think of to pass the time until I saw Jeanette again. I had worried I wouldn't be able to meet Florida's higher academic standards. But by the time I went home for the winter break, I was certain I would. My grades were excellent. My second-semester grades were even better.

With newfound academic confidence, I began to consider my future. I decided I wanted to go to law school, and looked for a major that would help toward that end. I got a great piece of advice from a professor who told me the smartest thing I could do is not worry about majoring in a subject that was considered good preparation for the law, but choose a major in the subject that most interested me. I would make better grades in classes I liked than in classes I felt obliged to take. Since Florida didn't offer a major in football, I decided on a political science major. I enjoyed the classes and excelled in them. I let nothing interfere with my studies except Jeanette. My weekend visits to Miami became more frequent. And I looked forward to summer, when I could spend part of every day with her.

I took a math class at Florida International University that summer to help make up for the Tarkio credits that Florida hadn't accepted. I worked on my first political campaign as well. I called the campaign office of state senator Lincoln Diaz-Balart, who was running for Congress, and asked to volunteer. I was told to come to the office in Hialeah and begin working that day. I spent the entire summer learning Miami politics from the ground up. I met people who would be of invaluable assistance to me someday, and I learned how to run a grassroots campaign in Miami's Cuban exile community, which would serve me very well over the next decade. The rest of my time I spent with Jeanette.

Our relationship became very serious. I had now dated Jeanette longer than I had ever dated anyone. As the summer ended and I began my senior year of college, we were both more confident about the strength of our commitment and more relaxed about our necessary separation. I still hated being apart, but the end was near. I would be home by May, and for good, I assumed.

Our separation foreshadowed our future life together. I would always be away from home for extended periods in pursuit of my ambitions. Jeanette would always stay behind to manage our most important responsibilities. My mind would always be focused on future challenges and opportunities. She would always have to attend to the demands of the present. Had she known then that our separation when I was a student at Florida would set the pattern for our future, I doubt she would have stayed in the relationship. Her parents had divorced when she was six; her mother had remarried and divorced again. Jeanette longed for a more stable married life, for a husband who would be a constant presence in her life and an equal partner in the responsibilities of marriage and parenthood. She wouldn't get that kind of life. But she would get a husband who loves her deeply and can't imagine life without her.

Just before I returned to Gainesville, local news stations began reporting the approach of a brewing hurricane. Having lived in the Miami area for seven years, I was accustomed to hurricane warnings, and to how predictions of their devastation were often exposed as unduly alarmist as the storms suddenly veered in another direction. People in Miami took hurricane warnings in stride if they paid them any heed at all. It became popular in Miami to hold hurricane parties to celebrate the newest natural disaster to threaten us, which would surely prove less fearsome than advertised. So, as usual, I didn't pay much attention to the new warning.

But then the reports became graver and more urgent. We had forty-eight hours to prepare. The storm was coming. It would be massive and devastating. And nothing would change its course. Aunt Lola and Uncle Armando happened to be visiting us that summer, and the storm trapped them in Miami. They helped us prepare the house for the hurricane, although our preparations were woefully inadequate for the magnitude of destruction that might be visited on us. Then we all hunkered down and waited.

Hurricane Andrew made landfall later that night. I had never seen anything like it. I looked outside as the storm ripped trees from the ground and tore tiles off roofs. We lost power almost immediately after the storm hit. Andrew's winds howled through our attic, and we were certain the storm would blow the roof off the house.

But it didn't. The winds slowly subsided and the clouds eventually cleared. By early morning the storm had passed, and our house had been spared. In contrast to the historic devastation the storm left behind in the southern part of the county, most of our neighborhood escaped serious damage.

I was worried about Jeanette and tried to drive to her house to make certain she was okay. But the roads were impassible. Immense trees that had stood for decades were uprooted, their massive bulk blocking all traffic. Downed power lines, some of which were still live, were strewn across the streets as well. I got out of the car and walked, and picked my way carefully around the obstacles until I reached her house. She was fine, although her neighborhood seemed a little worse off than mine.

Power wasn't restored at my house or Jeanette's for three weeks after the storm. But I escaped the inconvenience when I returned to Gainesville for my last year of college. I was back in Miami a few weeks later to help the Diaz-Balart campaign on Election Day. Lincoln won, and would serve in Congress for eighteen years until December of 2010.

I followed the presidential election closely and with great interest. I had tried to volunteer for the campus effort to help reelect President Bush, but I hadn't received a callback. Early one cold autumn morning, as I rode my bike to campus, eight men ran up to me at an intersection, where we all waited for the light to change. After a few seconds I realized it was governor and soon-to-be president Bill Clinton and his Secret Service detail out for his morning jog. I attended his rally on campus later that morning, curious to see what kind of a campaigner he was and what a Democratic rally looked like. I don't remember it making much of an impression on me.

As I considered what law schools to apply to, I briefly flirted with the idea of applying to schools far from Florida, like Georgetown and New York University. But the costs were prohibitive. I would graduate in the top 10 percent of my class at Florida, but that wouldn't be good enough to win a scholarship that would pay all my tuition. I would stay in Miami, and live near Jeanette. I couldn't ask her to put up with another three years of a long-distance relationship, and I was worried I would lose her if I didn't come home.

I applied to two schools in Miami. The first, St. Thomas University, quickly accepted me and offered a scholarship that would cover half my tuition. My preference, however, was to attend the University of Miami School of Law, which had a more prestigious reputation than St. Thomas. But I had reason to be concerned that Miami wouldn't accept me. The school prided itself on its national reach. It recruited students from all over the country, which made it more difficult for a Floridian, especially a Miamian, to be admitted, even with good grades. It was also very expensive. If I was accepted there, I would graduate with sizable student loan debt. But I knew if I was accepted, I would borrow the money and go. I worked hard on my application. In my essay, I expressed my intention to use my law degree one day to help construct a new legal and political system for a free Cuba. Lincoln and Ileana wrote recommendations for me. I was accepted.

That summer was a quiet time of transition. The only important event that year was the news Veronica had won a place on the Miami Dolphins cheerleading squad. I had passionately followed the Dolphins my entire life. I had played football in high school and college. I had dreamed of playing in the NFL. And the only person in our family who would ever set foot on an NFL football field was my sister. I wasn't envious, though. Each cheerleader received two season tickets for Dolphins home games. Veronica gave hers to me.

CHAPTER 10

Law School

THE FIRST YEAR OF LAW SCHOOL IS THE INTELLECTUAL equivalent of boot camp. It's not designed to impart new information to students as much as it is to teach them a new way to think. Before law school, if someone showed you a chair, you would acknowledge it's a chair. After your first year in law school, you should be able to present a plausible, if not persuasive, argument for why it's a stepladder with a backboard to prevent you from falling forward.

I had been an active reader my whole life, but I had never read as much as I had to read that year. It was the first time in my life I felt physically tired from mental exertion. I had little time for anything else. I lived with my parents a few blocks from school. I didn't have to make my own dinner, shop for groceries or do my laundry. I saw Jeanette every day. And I read.

I set an ambitious goal for myself. I wanted to make the law review, an honor reserved for those who earned the best grades their first year. Law school grades are determined solely by your final exam results. The exams are essay form, and unlike undergraduate exams, your conclusions are less important than your reasoning. I didn't grasp this difference in my first semester of law school. I prepared for exams as I had in Gainesville, and while my scores were fine, they were nowhere near the top of my class.

After my first semester, I prepared for exams by reviewing the exams my professors had given in the past. Law school professors have a habit of asking the same questions year after year. I was better prepared for my exams in the spring, and my scores improved dramatically. It was too late to make the law review, but I set a new goal for myself: I wanted to graduate with honors.

I had been told if I survived the first year, the rest of law school would be comparatively easier. That year was the most intense academic experience of my life, and a great change from my checkered past as a student. I was glad it was behind me. My second and third years were considerably less intense, and allowed for elective courses and extracurricular activities.

I found a job the summer between first and second year as a law clerk for a personal injury attorney, a sole practitioner, who rented office space in a building owned by a small law firm. After a few weeks I started working for another sole practitioner, who had an office in the same building. I didn't learn much from the experience. Both lawyers spent most of their time filing personal injury claims against insurance companies. My work mostly involved writing claim letters. But I earned enough to get through the summer and save a little spending money.

I was consumed by my studies and it affected my relationship with Jeanette. In February of 1995, she told me she wanted us to spend time apart for a while. We had had a few fights during our three years of dating. We had even broken up a few times, but quickly made up. Something was different this time. She was no longer certain our relationship was more than a comfortable habit we had both fallen into, and she wanted to find out whether our commitment to each other was genuine.

I know now that I had caused our estrangement. For three years our relationship had been ordered around my life. My school, my schedule, my plans for the future were the center of gravity of every decision we made. Naturally, she had begun to resent it, and this resentment had now reached the boiling point.

At first, I assumed the separation would be another of our brief break-ups, but after a few weeks I realized it was more serious than that. She seemed genuinely interested in exploring life without me. She didn't appear angry. She didn't treat me rudely. She just had an air about her of someone who was ready to move on with her life.

After weeks of unsuccessfully trying to repair the breach, I had a brilliant idea. I would show her how much better off I was without her. For the next three months, I abandoned the regular pattern of my days—classes in the morning and studying in the evening—and threw myself headlong into Miami nightlife. I went clubbing, and I liked it.

It was an exciting time in South Florida nightlife, especially the South Beach social scene, where in the company of friends from high school I became a regular. We got to know all the doormen at all the clubs and never had to wait in line. The peak of the South Beach social season runs from early January to the end of April. I don't think I missed many nights during the season in 1995. I was often exhausted by the time the weekend started.

I was having a grand old time, but I still knew this particular passage in my life was a temporary aberration. The curtain would soon fall and the rest of my life, my real life, would begin. I might have acted the life of the party, but I partied like someone who had something to lose.

In May, Jeanette started calling me again. She wanted to get back together. Now I demurred. Several times she warned me that if we didn't get back together now, we never would. The breach would be permanent. I told her the breakup had been her idea, and she would have to live with the consequences. I was spiteful, prideful and filled with false bravado. And I was a fool.

One night, near the end of the South Beach season, my friends and I made plans to attend one of our favorite South Beach haunts for a "foam party," where oceans of white foam are dropped from the ceiling and you find yourself dancing in it up to your waist. Jeanette told me if I went out that night, there would be no turning back. We would be over forever. I went out anyway. She had brought this on herself, I told myself. If we got back together, it would be on my terms, not hers.

That night, near midnight, I looked up and watched the foam descend from the ceiling. It was a sight to behold. Then my beeper buzzed. It was Jeanette's number. I knew she was calling to see if I had gone out. If I called her back and told her where I was, our relationship would end. If I didn't return her call, I would have to let her know the next day. I waded out of the foam to find a quieter place to consider my options. As I contemplated my predicament, I looked down at my shoes. They were perfectly white. They had been black when I arrived. The foam had somehow bleached the color out of my cheap and obviously fake leather shoes.

Maybe because I took it as a sign the life I was leading was phony and unsustainable or just that I had suddenly found myself wearing white shoes, a South Beach fashion faux pas, I left the club and found the nearest pay phone. I called Jeanette and told her what I had done. She gave me another chance. Go home now or never see her again. Something told me I was facing an important decision in my life, maybe the most important decision. I hailed a cab and went home. It was the best decision I ever made.

Despite my nightlife adventures, I still managed to make good grades. I was on track to graduate with honors. That summer I worked as a legal intern in the local prosecutor's office. I went to the courthouse every Monday morning and looked for a courtroom where a long line of people waited to be vetted for jury duty. Then I introduced myself to the lead prosecutor and offered to assist in the case. I worked on several felony prosecutions that summer, including a second-degree murder trial where the prosecutor allowed me to question one of the investigating detectives. During breaks in the trials, I would observe capital cases that were tried in one of the main courtrooms upstairs.

Every aspect of a trial intrigued me: selecting the jury, introducing your case, supporting with evidence and testimony every claim made in opening arguments, summarizing the case persuasively in closing arguments. Years later, I would employ in political campaigns and debates the organization and techniques of arguing a case before a jury. I introduce my hypothesis to my audience, and then use facts and figures to support it. I close by summarizing my argument in a style I hope is memorable and emotionally provocative. By the time my internship ended, I was certain I wanted to be a prosecutor. I loved the action of the courtroom, the drama of criminal cases and witnessing justice being served. The work seemed to suit me.

Florida Republicans were gearing up that fall for the 1996 presidential election. In November, the Florida GOP would host "Presidency 3," or P3, a three-day state party convention culminating in a presidential preference straw poll. All the major Republican candidates were spending significant time and resources preparing for the event, signing up local volunteers as delegates. David Rivera, a young political operative I had met on the Diaz-Balart campaign, recruited me to the Bob Dole campaign. Despite his youth, David had already had an eventful career in Miami-Dade politics. He had been prominently involved in a factional fight over control of the local Republican executive committee. The same warring factions would use the straw poll as a proxy battle. David had used his Washington connections to help him get an appointment to organize Dole's P3 effort. His rivals joined the Lamar Alexander and Phil Gramm campaigns. Dole won the straw poll and solidified his standing as the Republican front-runner, and we continued working for his campaign.

I spent as much time working on the Dole campaign that fall as I did on my law school classes. In early January, the campaign chartered a plane and flew some of us to Concord, New Hampshire, where we walked door-to-door, handing out Florida oranges to voters and asking them to support Senator Dole. I'm not sure how many voters we persuaded, but the trip went well enough and we had a lot of fun. A few of the younger volunteers stopped at a local liquor store and bought bottles of vodka. On the flight home, about ten of us celebrated our successful foray into New Hampshire politics by holding a vodka shot competition. I was one of the few still standing when the contest ended.

Halfway through the flight, I started to feel sick. I knew I had to get to one of the plane's bathrooms before something unfortunate happened. I made my way to the front of the aircraft clutching a motion sickness bag when I realized I wasn't going to make it. I was going to throw up in full view of some of the most prominent Republicans in Florida. Congresswoman Ileana Ros-Lehtinen sat to my right. To my left sat a well-known political operative who had volunteered on the campaign. I could either vomit on a congresswoman or on a fellow volunteer. I chose the latter. I tried to get as much of it into the bag as I could, but most of it ended up on his jacket. I ran to the bathroom, cleaned myself up as best I could and locked myself in there for the rest of the flight.

I was beyond embarrassed. I was convinced my brief career in Republican politics had just come to an abrupt and humiliating end thanks to my own immaturity. When a flight attendant knocked on the bathroom door and informed me the plane wouldn't land until I took my seat, I refused. She persisted, and eventually I summoned all the courage I could muster and walked back to my seat covered in shame, literally and figuratively. John Thrasher, a future speaker of the Florida House, was on the plane and witnessed my humiliation, which he would playfully remind me of years later when he swore me in as a new member of the legislature.

The year 1996 would bring great changes to my life. I would graduate in the spring, and after I passed the bar exam I would practice law, preferably as a prosecutor in the state attorney's office. I interviewed for a prosecutor's job that spring. If all went according to plan, I intended to propose to Jeanette that Christmas. After Senator Dole wrapped up the nomination, David offered me the job of South Florida coordinator for the Dole campaign. I was interested, but I had also landed the prosecutor's job. I explained my predicament to the state attorney's office, and they agreed I could start after the November election.

I had skipped my commencement at Florida, but I had no intention of missing my graduation from law school. On Mother's Day that year, my parents watched with pride as I accepted my diploma. All my life, they had exhausted themselves to give me every opportunity. Through all those years of ceaseless toil and sacrifice, they had made almost every decision with an eye to my future success. Now I had a juris doctor degree. It was the furthest anyone in my family, in the entire history of our family, had ever gone.

I visited Papá's grave the next day. I remembered holding his hand as he slipped away. I remembered him squeezing mine as I swore to him I would work hard and make something of myself. Twelve years after his death, I had finally made good on my promise. It was the first time I experienced a feeling I would experience again in the years to come: my parents and grandfather living vicariously through me. They had given me their dreams—dreams they had once had for themselves. And with my every accomplishment, I was giving their lives purpose and meaning. I proved they had lived and loved and made sacrifices that were not in vain. Their lives had mattered. I felt my grandfather's presence as I walked from his grave, and I feel it still.

CHAPTER 11

The Start of the Rest of My Life

I SPENT THE SUMMER AFTER GRADUATION SETTING UP THE Dole campaign's South Florida operations and studying for the bar exam. My job in the state attorney's office was contingent on passing it the first time. I signed up for a review course and spent every free moment studying. I sat for the exam in August, and felt confident I had done well. Over 80 percent of people who take the exam pass it on their first attempt. Still, as I waited for the results, I had occasional bouts of panic that I was deluding myself and had failed.

Later that month, Jeanette and I flew to San Diego for the Republican National Convention. The campaign had asked me to work as a floor manager. In the old days of brokered conventions, the job of a floor manager had real authority. But in the modern era, when nominating conventions are coronations rather than contests, the job mainly entails making sure people cheer at the right time and hold up the right signs. Still, for someone new to the business, the convention was exciting and, for a brief moment, the center of the political universe.

When I came home the following week, I opened the Miami campaign office in Little Havana, renting space in a building that a few months earlier had been the studios of Radio Mambí, the leading anti-Castro Cuban exile station in Miami. Running a high-profile campaign in Miami had been a graveyard for the careers of more than a few aspiring Miami politicians.

Balancing the various political factions and pleasing the sensitive egos in local Republican politics was complicated work that had proven beyond the competence of many young operatives before me. My detractors, having failed to deny me the job, now relished the prospect that the rivalries and antagonisms in Miami politics would bring an abrupt end to my fledgling career. But, again, my naïveté spared me from recognizing their ill wishes and the possibility I might not be up to the job.

Senator Dole was a heavy underdog. During the primary season many of us supported him because he was the candidate most likely to win the nomination. But by the fall it had become increasingly difficult to build any excitement for the campaign. It was frustrating as well as difficult work, but on the whole a valuable experience. I became one of a tight circle of young, first-time operatives who remained loyal to Senator Dole's campaign and worked doggedly for his election. We would remain closely associated for the next fifteen years.

David Rivera would serve as the rules committee chairman in the Florida House when I was speaker and now serves in Washington as a member of the Florida delegation in the U.S. House of Representatives. Alina Garcia would be my first legislative aide in the Florida legislature, before working for David in the same capacity in the legislature and later in Congress. She is also the godmother of my youngest child, Dominick, and her brother, Wilfredo, is a priest who baptized two of our four kids. Monica Rodríguez was another of my earliest legislative aides; her husband, Len Collins, served as my parliamentarian when I was speaker, and as legal counsel in my Senate office. Carlos Lopez-Cantera served with me in the Florida House, where he became an important committee chairman and later majority leader. Nelson Diaz was my legislative assistant in Tallahassee before going on to law school and a successful lobbying career. Jose Mallea worked for President Bush's chief of staff Andy Card, and then as chief of staff to the mayor of Miami before managing my Senate campaign.

By late September, everyone knew Senator Dole would lose, and other than our small but dedicated group and a few loyal volunteers, it was hard to get anyone else to care about, much less work for, a losing campaign. In the end, I was never really in any danger of alienating prominent figures in Miami Republican politics. None of them wanted to be involved in the campaign.

I put in long hours, though, arriving at the office early every morning and often staying until midnight or later. Most days involved mundane but important tasks: setting up phone banks, organizing sign wavings, addressing whatever small problems walked in the door on a given day. Sometimes, I represented the campaign at public events. One of those occasions I will remember the rest of my life.

A representative of a local Spanish-language radio station called the office and asked for a Dole surrogate to debate a Democrat on air. I called every Spanish-speaking Republican legislator I could find. They were all unavailable or unwilling to do it. So I had to do it myself. It didn't go well.

I was not well prepared. My opponent was an experienced Democratic operative who had done this kind of thing many times. He knew all of Senator Dole's vulnerabilities and easily countered the few obvious talking points I used to criticize President Clinton. He made short work of me. Several Republicans called the campaign office and the state party office to complain about my performance and demand I never be allowed to represent the campaign again in a public forum. It was a valuable, if painful, lesson. I vowed I would never again show up for an interview, speech or debate before I had done all I could to make certain I was the best-prepared person in the room.

The radio debate debacle notwithstanding, I received generally positive reviews for my work on the campaign. Local Republicans respected my dedication to a losing cause. People began commenting for the first time on my tenacity and concentration, which would be valuable attributes in a political career, were I to pursue one.

Jeanette, however, didn't consider it a virtue that I had the ability to focus on a political campaign to the exclusion of all else. She complained, rightly so, that I had been completely consumed by the work. Even when I wasn't working, when I spent a few hours with her on the weekend, the campaign was all I could think and talk about. "It feels like you're cheating on me," she told me. And I was. Except the object of my obsession wasn't another girl. It was politics, and it wouldn't be the last time I would make her feel politics took precedence over our relationship. I was chasing my ambitions, and I left her chasing after me.

Senator Dole lost the election, and although the outcome had been expected, it stung nonetheless. But the experience was invaluable. I had never before led anything bigger than a weekend pickup game of football.

Now I had run a local grassroots campaign and learned the tactics and skills required to do it successfully in the future. I had impressed prominent Republicans in Miami-Dade politics, including Al Cardenas.

Al, a partner in Miami law firm Tew Cardenas, had been involved in Miami-Dade politics for a long time. He had run unsuccessfully for Congress in the late seventies against the legendary Claude Pepper, and served as vice chairman of the state party. After the election, he offered me a job as his associate at Tew Cardenas.

The job at Al's firm offered a starting annual salary of $57,000. The job in the state attorney's office paid less than $30,000 a year. I wanted to be a prosecutor. I wanted to gain courtroom experience. I relished the excitement of trying cases and had little interest in the land use and zoning law that Al practiced. But I had student loans to repay. I wanted to get married. And I wanted to help support my family so my father could at last retire.

For years I had ended my nightly prayers with the same request. I prayed that my parents would live long enough to see me succeed, and that my success would allow them to enjoy a comfortable old age. I was haunted by the fear that one or both of them would fall ill and die without ever receiving a reward on earth for all the sacrifices they had made for us. My father was seventy years old. He was still working late evenings and weekends as a banquet bartender, as he had done twenty years earlier. On nights when he came home late from another wedding or bar mitzvah at the Mayfair House, and I was in bed but awake, I would hear him limp tiredly up the steps to our house, fumbling with his keys while he searched for the right one. The memory has stayed with me all my life.

A salary of $57,000 seemed like a great deal of money to me at the time. It was more than my father had ever made, and more than enough, I thought, to cover my student loan payments and help pay our household bills. I could afford to get married soon, too. I accepted Al's offer, and in late November 1996 I began working as an associate attorney at the law offices of Tew Cardenas.

My decision allowed my father to retire from bartending, and I am profoundly grateful for that. My dad didn't have any hobbies—he didn't golf or fish or enjoy any recreation that other men of his age enjoyed in their retirement. We knew he wouldn't be happy in retirement unless he had something useful to do. So we found him a job as a school crossing guard with the

Miami-Dade Police Department. He loved it, and in less than a year he was temporarily promoted to supervisor. The promotion didn't last, however. My father's lack of a formal education made his daily reports appear as if a child had done them. Many times I saw him sitting at the kitchen table staring blankly at his paperwork, confused, not knowing where to begin. From time to time he would ask me to review his work the way a child asks a parent. He did the best he could, but it was apparent from what he wrote that he lacked basic reading and writing skills, especially in English.

I worked primarily for Al at the firm. Most of our work was on zoning cases, but I helped as well with some of his other government relations work. I spent most of my first year learning how to persuade local zoning authorities to accept our clients' applications while preserving the option to appeal to the courts should the application be denied. In addition to my zoning work for Al, I helped with a few cases for the Miami-Dade School Board, for whom the firm handled construction litigation.

I had wanted to be a litigator in law school, which I assumed would keep me in the courtroom a lot, arguing before judge and jury. In reality, the life of a litigator, especially a commercial litigator, is considerably more mundane. It involves countless hours of research and writing, and precious few courtroom appearances. The time that is spent in the courtroom is seldom entrusted to a young associate. I didn't particularly enjoy the work, but I did like the other advantages of working at Tew Cardenas. I developed a camaraderie with the other associates there. And working for Al meant I could stay active in Miami politics. He always had a hand in important local races, and often enlisted my assistance.

I had other things to occupy my attention as well. I was almost twenty-six years old. Jeanette and I had dated for six years, and our relationship had continued on the assumption we would marry after I had finished law school. Jeanette never pressured me to get married. On the contrary, I talked about it more than she did. The prospect of marriage seemed to frighten her a little. The only marriages she had observed closely—her parents' and then her mother's second marriage—had ended in divorce. I had no reservations about the institution of marriage in general or marriage to Jeanette in particular. I think I had known I would marry her almost from the moment we started dating.

I am not by nature the most thoughtful romantic. But I wanted our proposal to be a moment neither of us would forget. I wanted Jeanette to know, despite my many defects, that I could rise to the occasion and let her know how much I loved her. New York was Jeanette's favorite city in the world. She had dreamed of living there one day. I had never been to New York. When I pictured the city, the only landmark that came to mind was the Empire State Building, which I decided would be the ideal location for proposing marriage to Jeanette Dousdebes, on Valentine's Day 1997.

I told her I wanted to take her on a surprise one-day trip to a cold-weather city. She didn't discover our destination until we arrived at the departure gate. After we landed at LaGuardia Airport, I asked the cab-driver to take us to the Empire State Building. It was a cold and windy morning, and Jeanette balked at the idea of sightseeing on the observation deck, where we would be at the mercy of the elements. I pleaded with her that *King Kong* had been my favorite movie as a boy, and I couldn't leave New York without visiting the location of the film's most famous scene.

She was right about the weather. It was freezing, and I knew I would have just a couple of minutes to propose before she insisted we go back inside. So I reached into my coat pocket, retrieved the ring and asked her to marry me.

I think she had suspected New York was our secret destination, but from the shocked look on her face, I knew I had managed to surprise her anyway. She hadn't expected the proposal, but she accepted without hesitating. We went inside to phone her mother. We spent the rest of the day enjoying the sights and pleasures of the city. I caught her glancing at her ring frequently. Her fear of marriage would reemerge a few more times in the coming months, but not that day. That day we were all smiles.

Jeanette's sister Adriana had been a Miami Dolphins cheerleader for several years. In the spring of 1997, soon after our engagement, Jeanette decided she wanted to try out for the squad. I supported the idea. I wanted her to be able to do anything that made her happy, and to have something in her life that was hers and not mine as well. I'm sure the possibility of free tickets to home games was a consideration as well.

Making the cheerleading team had become more competitive in recent years. The year before, the Dolphins had brought in a veteran member of the Dallas Cowboys cheerleaders to revamp the Miami squad and make it more glamorous. But Jeanette survived every cut and made it to the final tryout. The night before, she stayed up all night practicing with Adriana. I nervously waited for her at her house, and was thrilled when she returned and told me she had made the team.

The job didn't pay much, just a small sum per game, and a more generous fee for public appearances. It also required a substantial commitment of time. She had to practice every weeknight and arrive at the stadium early on game days.

I made it to all the home games that year, and would pester her afterward about exchanges between the players she might have overheard during the game. One Sunday, she was designated the "cheerleader of the game," and her picture was featured prominently in the layout of the team program and on the Jumbotron screen during the game. I told everyone seated around me she was my fiancée. When we have kids, I thought to myself, I can tell them that one of their parents had made it onto an NFL field.

I was doing well at Tew Cardenas. But when I look back on my years there, it's clear that while my time might have belonged to the firm, my heart belonged to politics. Al was deeply involved in two local elections, in Miami and Hialeah, in 1997, and he pressed me into service as well. The culture at the firm expected lawyers to remain at their desks all day. As far as the senior partners were concerned, if you weren't in the office, you weren't working, and if you weren't working, you weren't billing hours. Doing campaign work didn't sit well with the other partners, and a few of them told me I would have to decide soon whether I wanted to be a lawyer or a politician. I told them what they wanted to hear. I wanted to be a good lawyer. If I decided to enter politics seriously someday, it would be years from now. But that wasn't true. I liked the law. I loved politics. And I was already looking for a way to do what I loved.

I was approached that summer to serve on the city of West Miami Code Enforcement Board. I told Al about it, and he discouraged me. He had struggled for years with the competing demands of politics and a law practice, and knew how difficult a balance it was to maintain, especially for an attorney in his first years of practice. The board didn't require much of a time commitment, and wouldn't take time or attention from my work for the firm. I saw the position as merely something to add to my résumé as I established myself as a lawyer. But Al saw it as a first step down a slippery slope to a career in politics and not the law. He didn't encourage me, but he didn't prohibit me, either, and I accepted the position.

He was right in one respect. My seat on the board would whet my appetite for a career in politics. Since I had sat at my grandfather's feet and listened to him talk about politics and politicians, the profession had fascinated me. I never viewed politics and government service in the way it is often popularly viewed, as a self-interested and corrupt business. I always believed it was an honorable way to distinguish yourself, and an opportunity to advance the causes you believe in and oppose the ones you don't.

By November of that year, after serving on the code enforcement board for a few months, I started planning the beginning of my own political career. I decided the best place to start was in my own city of West Miami by seeking election to the city commission. West Miami is a small city, and I felt confident the campaign and my service on the commission wouldn't interfere with my work at Tew Cardenas. I thought it was a manageable commitment that would let me practice law until I was financially stable, while I kept a low profile in local politics in the event I might run for another office in the future.

I knew I couldn't win without the blessing of West Miami's popular mayor, Rebeca Sosa. I had been introduced to her a few months earlier by Republican committeewoman Liliana Ros, who told her I wanted to get involved in West Miami politics. The introduction had led to my appointment to the code enforcement board. I went to see Rebeca at her home in early December, where I found her putting up Christmas lights. I told her I wanted to discuss the upcoming city elections, and she invited me inside for some Cuban coffee.

I didn't know what to expect. I assumed she had close relationships with the city commissioners and worried she would think my intentions were presumptuous. But to my surprise and relief, she told me she was unhappy with one of the two incumbent commissioners seeking reelection, and offered me her full support.

I would have to get permission from two people before I could officially commit to the race: Al Cardenas and Jeanette. I hadn't mentioned my intentions to either of them yet, and I wasn't looking forward to it now. The conversation with Jeanette turned out to be easier than I'd expected. She had always assumed politics would eventually play a big part in our lives. This was a little sooner than she had expected, she said, but if that was what I wanted to do, it was fine with her.

Al would be a harder sell. I expected that rather than tell me he didn't want me to do it, he would tell me the other partners would object. I decided to preempt the argument and go straight to the firm's senior partner, Tom Tew. I explained that the commission met only four hours a month and wouldn't interfere with my cases. Nor did I anticipate any conflict of interest between city commission work and the interests of our clients. It would be no bigger a commitment than serving on a condominium board, I assured him. He wasn't enthusiastic about the idea, but he didn't object. He had been involved in litigation concerning the 1997 Miami mayoral elections, and, I suspected, had been a little bitten by the political bug himself.

I met with Al next, and as I expected, he expressed concern that the other partners would be displeased. I told him I had already received Tom's permission. There wasn't anything he could say to discourage me after that. I know he was worried that in a few months, when he became the state party chairman, his partners would complain he was spending too much time on politics at the firm's expense. Now he would worry I couldn't be relied on to pick up the slack in his absence. But he let me do it anyway, and I was grateful.

I would run for my first political office in 1998 and, with a little luck, win it. I would also get married to the woman I loved, who would eventually have cause to wonder if the major events of my political career and our life together would always coincide.

CHAPTER 12

First Campaign

THE CAMPAIGN BEGAN WITH THE START OF THE NEW year. With the election scheduled for early April, I had just three months to introduce myself to voters and persuade them to support me. West Miami has only five thousand residents, and even in a high-turnout election, only a little more than eight hundred people vote. You reach them by walking the streets of their neighborhoods and knocking on their doors.

I knew the mechanics of that kind of campaign well from my time volunteering for Lincoln Diaz-Balart in 1992 and for Senator Dole in 1996. I needed good walk lists, lists of registered voters organized the way courier routes are laid out for mail delivery.

I needed a message, something to say to voters when they opened their door that would make a good first impression. And I needed literature to hand them that included my name, picture and the office I was running for to remind them on Election Day that they had met me and I had seemed like a nice enough fellow.

I started knocking on doors the first week of January. I calculated it would take twelve weeks to visit every voting household and speak personally to a voter. I rarely walked alone. Rebeca Sosa introduced me to a local activist, Gerardo Ramos, who usually walked with me. Rebeca often accompanied me, too, and personally introduced me to voters. She was immensely popular in West Miami, and her support gave me instant credibility.

I had another frequent companion on my walks: my father. He was a natural at it. Personable and helpful, he impressed voters, especially elderly voters. West Miami has a large elderly population. Many voters were reluctant to open their door to a stranger, especially a young male stranger. But an appeal from a friendly seventy-one-year-old Cuban American who wanted to visit with them about his son, the aspiring politician, was a disarming and welcome request. After decades of friendly interaction with people across a bar in the hope his affability would encourage a generous tip, my father knew how to charm people.

He was never happier than when he was helping his children. He enjoyed campaigning and working for a purpose that was dear to him: his children's success. And I enjoyed the gratifying sense that I had made him proud of me, as my brother had done on the football field three decades earlier.

He was particularly adept at helping supporters who didn't drive or who, for other reasons, couldn't vote on Election Day. We gave their names to my dad, and he would pay them another visit and help them fill out a request for an absentee ballot. His visits often took a long time. Many of the voters he helped lived alone. Their children were gone and starting families of their own. Those who didn't drive spent most of their days inside their homes, and ventured into the world only for an occasional visit to the doctor. They were lonely.

They offered him coffee, and began to talk about personal matters. They discussed their children and grandchildren. They shared recollections of their lives in Cuba, and the years of striving in America to make a better life for their families. He always left his telephone number with them. When they received their ballots in the mail, many of them called and asked him back to help them fill out the ballots.

The home visits I made during the campaign had a profound effect on me. I had grown up in a Cuban American home, but I don't think I had understood the community and my place in it until this experience. I don't think I really knew where I was from and who I was until I spent hundreds of hours in the company of the people who claimed me as one of their own.

To maximize the number of voters we contacted, we knocked on the doors of younger voters between six and eight at night. They greeted you at the door, listened to your pitch and then sent you on your way. They were tired after a long day of work, and had to make dinner and help their kids with homework. Sometimes I encountered them in their driveways as they were arriving home from work or returning from an errand. They would give me only a few minutes to make an impression. Older voters were different.

I met as many widows as married couples. Grandchildren often roamed their homes after day care and school had finished for the day and before their parents came home from work. They were usually reluctant to open their door to me. I might have been some young hood or con artist who preyed on the elderly, trying to trap them in an elaborate hoax or get them to open their door to an intruder posing as a politician. The first few minutes of conversation were through a screen door and sometimes a closed one. More often than not, though, I was eventually invited into their homes to discuss my candidacy over the inevitable cup of Cuban coffee.

The coffee is prepared in a metal Italian-made coffeepot. The first few percolated drops are poured into a measuring cup partially filled with sugar to make a syrupy substance called *espumita*. After the rest of the coffee is percolated, it is poured into the *espumita* to sweeten it and give it a light foam. While the coffee brewed, they aired their grievances and asked my views about them. Did I think the cost of living was too high? Why had their auto insurance premiums increased when they had never had an accident, and their property insurance premiums, too, when they had never filed a claim? Why had gas prices doubled? Did I think crime in West Miami was becoming a big problem?

When the coffee was served, my hosts would steer the conversation away from the campaign and begin to talk of more personal things. I always noticed the pictures first: the decade-old high school graduation photos of their now grown and absent children, the pictures of their grandchildren's christenings and graduations and inductions into the military.

They told me the stories of their lives. They were, most of the time, stories of loss. It often seemed as if they were recalling it for their own as much as my benefit, as if seeking their own affirmation—not another's—that their lives had virtue and meaning and importance.

They reminded me that they had lived in Cuba when they were my age, and had once had plans to become a doctor or lawyer or business owner. And then they had to leave. They came to Miami or New York, expecting to return to Cuba in a few months or a few years. Cuba had fallen into the hands of dictators before, but it never lasted more than a few years at most. They could wait it out. They took whatever work they could find: at a factory, a janitor's job at a hotel or apartment building, loading trucks. Then they started looking for ways to make a little more money. They were going to be here for only a little while, but why not make the most of it. So they opened a side business. They sold car parts from the trunk of their car. They rented a small storefront and opened a business. They bought some brushes and painted houses. Or they were promoted at work. They became a supervisor at the factory or head custodian at a Miami Beach hotel. Nothing had changed yet in Cuba, but still they believed the regime would end.

But it never did end, and the years passed so quickly. So they saved their money and bought a house. The kids were growing up now, speaking more English than Spanish. And then the children were gone, and grandchildren arrived. Now here they still were, some of them alone, readying to leave the world and knowing they would die having never seen their homeland again.

They had made their lives here in the houses where I visited them, different lives than they had expected to lead. Here they had realized they would never do the things they had dreamed of when they were young. Here was where they had relinquished those dreams and dedicated their lives to their children's happiness. Here they lived vicariously through their children's achievements. Here, on every wall and shelf, were diplomas and certificates and other tokens of achievement and success they revered, often well out of proportion to their real-world significance. All parents are proud of their children; this was more than pride. This was affirmation. Their lives had purpose. They had lived for a reason. They had made their mark.

I found heartache, too: anguish over adult offsprings' unwillingness to make something of their lives; pain over a son or daughter's recent divorce; the loneliness of separation from loved ones who had died or moved away, and from busy children who paid them less attention than they deserved.

When it was time for me to go and they walked me to the door, many would remark they were pleased to see a new face in politics. They were glad there were young people interested in running for elective office. The desire for change is common in American politics. We're an often dissatisfied people, and we often have cause to be. But I sensed they meant more than that. Many told me I reminded them of their son Carlos, or their grandson Ernesto, or any number of other children and grandchildren. My ambitions, too, they wanted me to know, affirmed their sacrifice.

They had lost everything: their youth, their culture, their country. They had to settle for something other than their dreams. They had built a new life, often a good life, but different than the life they had once wanted. Now, in their final years, they wanted to be sure of the purpose of it all. Who were they? What did they do? What would they leave behind? What difference had they made?

Who was I really to them? Someone who bore a physical resemblance to a son or grandson? No. I represented their children and grandchildren's generation. My success, and the success of any Cuban American of my generation, was their answer. Our lives, accomplishments and contributions were a lasting tribute to theirs. Even as a boy, I had grasped that my family's emotional investment in my happiness and success was as great as their investment of time, work and self-denial. Now I recognized that an entire generation of Cuban exiles had the same emotional investment in my success.

On the streets of the small city of West Miami, in the early months of 1998, I discovered who I was. I was an heir to two generations of unfulfilled dreams. I was the end of their story.

I raised about $10,000 for the campaign—enough to pay for a couple of mailings, some campaign signs and handouts for Election Day. We didn't do any polling, and I didn't know if I would win or lose. I badly wanted not to lose my first race but tried to prepare myself emotionally in the event that I did. As it turned out, the election wasn't close. I, and another candidate Rebeca had supported, finished well ahead of the other two candidates running for the two open seats. The results were announced by the city clerk just outside city hall. I celebrated my victory in the courtyard of a nearby community center with my family, friends from the Dole campaign and supporters. At one point in the party, I noticed my mother sitting in a chair with her head down, weeping. My mother is an emotional person. It isn't hard to make her cry. But my first political victory moved my parents more deeply than anything I had accomplished before. They had never pushed me toward one profession or another. They had never encouraged me to be an attorney or a politician. They wanted me to dream my own dreams, and live them, as they had never been allowed to do.

My political career began that night. But something more important had happened. That night I realized that whatever I did with the opportunity I had just been given would reflect on my parents as well. They wanted me to succeed—they *needed* me to succeed. For in my success, they could find their rest, assured they had lived for something. My dreams were theirs, and my success as well.

CHAPTER 13

A Married Man

I MADE A POINT OF ARRIVING EARLY FOR WORK THE MORN-
ing after my election. I wanted the partners to see I was committed to the
firm and wouldn't let my new civic responsibilities distract me. When I got
there, I was called into the managing partner's office. Three senior partners, including Al, were waiting for me, and quickly got to the point. As far
as they were concerned, my election didn't change anything. I was a junior
associate and was expected to put in the same hours the other junior associates worked. I said all the right things in response and thanked them
for supporting me. But I left the meeting a little taken aback. I thought the
reminder was an overreaction, and the timing, the morning after my election, seemed odd. I never felt the same about the firm after that.

My swearing in took place a week later in the small commission cham-
bers on the second floor of city hall, followed by a small reception with
family and friends. I settled easily into my responsibilities on the commission, which met only twice a month to consider mostly uncontroversial
matters. The only contentious issue we faced all year was a proposal to
change the local code to permit the construction of two-story houses.

I was approached that summer by a law firm that specialized in land
use and zoning law, Ruden McClosky, to gauge my interest in joining their
practice. The firm's main office was located in a neighboring county, but it

had recently opened a Miami office and hired a politically active Cuban American attorney, Armando Lacasa, to run it.

It wasn't a difficult decision. I didn't think my prospects for making partner at Tew Cardenas were very good. The firm's culture didn't value its government relations practice, and it didn't really consider land use and zoning matters legal work at all. I still had a bad taste in my mouth from my meeting with the partners, and Ruden McClosky had offered me a $13,000 raise. I gave Tew Cardenas two weeks' notice, transferred my cases to another attorney at the firm and went to work for Ruden McClosky.

I wasn't nearly as busy there as I had been at Tew Cardenas. They had brought me in as part of a plan to expand the Miami office, but they didn't have enough work yet to keep me fully occupied. I worked as Armando's associate, and most of his work involved facilitating business deals in Latin America. So I dabbled a little in bank loan document work, and spent a lot of time trying to bring in new clients and representing the firm at public events. On most days I was home before seven.

I decided to use the time before my wedding in October to tie up any loose ends in my life. Jeanette and I searched West Miami for a house to buy. We found a nice two-bedroom house only two blocks from my parents. Jeanette's mother generously offered to buy the house for us with the understanding we would buy it from her when we had saved enough money.

Jeanette and I had dated for seven years. I wasn't frightened or nervous about getting married. Marrying her seemed the most natural and sensible decision in my life. The night before our wedding, I went to bed for the last time under the same roof as my parents. I had gone away to college, but I had lived with them most of my life. Veronica had married two years earlier. Now the last of their children was leaving home. I felt nostalgic and a little sad. It was the natural order of things, but I couldn't help feeling I was abandoning them, even though I would live only two blocks away. Before I went to sleep I said a familiar prayer, a prayer I had offered thousands of times before, but had special meaning to me that night.

> God, I ask You that if it is at all possible within Your will, that You will let me live long and healthy enough so that I can make them proud. I pray that You let them live long enough so they can know that all their hard work and all their sacrifices were not in vain.

On the evening of October 17, 1998, two hundred of our family and friends gathered to watch Jeanette and I exchange our vows at the Church of the Little Flower in Coral Gables. I waited at the altar and looked down the aisle as the church doors opened and my impossibly beautiful bride, angelic in her white dress and veil, entered. Most brides make a striking appearance. And most grooms believe their brides to be the loveliest of all. But they didn't see Jeanette that night.

I don't remember being impressed at the time with the homily Father O'Brien, the priest we had asked to officiate, gave at our wedding. But years later, when I listened to it again on videotape, I was struck by how prophetic he had been. He said love isn't a feeling, it's an action. Marriage isn't supposed to be the Hollywood version of romance, but rather a real-world union in which two people agree before God to share all of their lives and all of themselves with each other, the good and the bad. In the years that ensued and to this day, Jeanette and I have faced the bad as well as the good.

We have been blessed. We have four healthy, happy children. We are not wealthy, but we have more than our parents ever had. We have shared the highs and lows of my career, and we have had the opportunity to see and do things neither of us would have imagined possible on our wedding night.

We have struggled, too, and she has borne the brunt of it. Our life is far different than the one she hoped we would have when we married. Naturally, there are regrets. Regrets for the trips we haven't taken as a family, the nights she has cared for our children alone, the school plays and concerts I've missed, all the demands on my time that keep me away from my family and distract me when I'm home. She has accepted a life she never wanted, only because she believes the influence I can have on important issues is worth the sacrifices she makes.

I joined the band and sang two Sinatra songs to her at our reception: "My Way," which seems all too fitting now, and "New York, New York," as an ode to our engagement. We honeymooned in France, spending five days in Paris and five more in the Normandy countryside. Paris was Paris, as enchanting as advertised, and impossible not to enjoy. But we enjoyed Normandy just as much. We rented a car and drove to the landing beaches, toured the German fortifications and visited Pointe du Hoc, where Americans, barely older than boys, had scaled the steep cliff under fire. We stared wordlessly at the endless rows of crosses and Stars of David in the American cemetery.

We moved into our new house as soon as we returned from our honeymoon. We had modest plans for our immediate future. I would concentrate on my work at the firm, and Jeanette would continue working as a bank teller part-time and enrolling full-time in design school. We would save money and establish a foundation for our future financial security before we considered having a family. And for the time being, I would restrict my political aspirations to serving on the West Miami City Commission, where my duties didn't demand much of my time. But life often surprises with unexpected opportunities and blessings that make a hash of your plans.

From my days as a volunteer on Lincoln Diaz-Balart's campaign, and even earlier, when I was a young boy following the 1980 Democratic convention, I had been fascinated by campaigns and the process of politics. But it was my service on West Miami's city commission that instilled in me an appreciation for the privilege of public service. Neither then nor now do I believe government is the solution to all our problems. On the contrary, when government assumes too great a role in our economy and private affairs it crowds out the individual initiative and risk-taking entrepreneurism that are the engine of our prosperity and the essence of Americans' problem-solving genius. Government at its best can make a positive difference in our lives when it listens to the people, and responds to their concerns effectively without exceeding its mandate and assuming responsibilities that we are able and prefer to manage ourselves.

When I walked door-to-door in my first campaign for office, I listened to my future constituents raise concerns about their neighborhoods and the responsibilities of city leaders to help address them. I promised them that if I were elected I would do all I could to make certain the commission responded to their concerns. I tried to be true to my word after the election, and by the end of my time on the commission, I understood, much better than I had before, how government within its limited scope of activities can help improve the lives of ordinary people.

One experience from that time has remained with me ever since as a reminder of that lesson. During the campaign, several people in one neighborhood complained to me that the city had planted trees along the right-of-way of every neighborhood but theirs. When the commission initiated the next city beautification project after the election, I made sure it included the purchase of trees for the neighborhood that had none. It was a small thing, to be sure. But as I stood there and watched landscapers plant the trees, I realized it was happening because of me. Through my seat on the city commission I had made possible this little improvement in the quality of my neighbors' lives. I had listened to the people I served, and used my office to help them. Campaigns can be fascinating and exciting, but they are not, by themselves, fulfilling. Public service is or can be. It can give our lives greater meaning not because of the titles and privileges it confers but because of the impact it can have on the lives of others. I enjoy politics. But on the city commission of the small city of West Miami, I found my purpose.

I became close friends with the Lacasa family during my time at Ruden McClosky, especially Armando's oldest son, Carlos. He was a member of the state legislature, in line to become the next budget committee chairman, a position of considerable influence. Florida voters had approved eight-year term limits for legislators in 1992, which meant that half the state's districts would have open seats in the 2000 election. One of them was in the district adjacent to mine, and in 1999 Carlos encouraged me to consider running for it.

The Florida House seemed like the logical next step in my political career, but this opportunity came too soon. I had planned to spend ten years practicing law full-time, and in the less intensely scrutinized world of West Miami politics before I considered running for another office. But Carlos argued convincingly that the 2000 elections might be a once-in-a-lifetime opportunity for me. Not only were there an historic number of vacancies in the house, but, were I elected, I could gain influence in state politics quickly because there would be relatively few veteran legislators left to contend with.

I had reservations. I didn't think Jeanette would approve of a sudden change in the plans we had just made. She was busy with her design school studies and didn't need the distraction of a political campaign. I didn't think the firm, despite Carlos's support, would approve of it, either. The Florida House meets in session for nine consecutive weeks every spring. That is an awful lot of time for a junior associate to spend away from the firm's business. To my surprise, though, neither Jeanette nor the firm's partners objected to the idea. At Carlos's suggestion, I decided to open an account for campaign donations as a way to gauge support for my candidacy and to reserve my option to run. I wouldn't have to make a decision until early in the new year. Then life interrupted my plans, again.

Late one night in August, Jeanette mentioned she had been feeling ill. When she described her symptoms, I remarked they sounded like the symptoms of pregnancy. She dismissed my diagnosis curtly. I got in the car and drove to the nearest pharmacy, where I bought the most expensive and, therefore, to my mind, most reliable pregnancy test kit I could find on the shelves. I convinced Jeanette to take it, which she did grudgingly, handing me the stick when she emerged from the bathroom and returned to her studies.

I stared at the stick as a single line appeared, and then, a few moments later, a second one. I was holding a positive pregnancy test in my hand. I showed it to Jeanette. She was skeptical about the result, so I returned to the store and bought three different brands of pregnancy tests. All of them were positive.

I was ecstatic. I was going to be a father. Sure, it was a little earlier than we'd planned, but a blessing all the same. "It's God's will," I kept telling her. Jeanette's reaction was less enthusiastic. After the initial shock wore off, she started to cry and called her mother. We had been married less than a year, and she wasn't ready to have a child yet. She wanted to finish school, and her studies often kept her up well into the night. She wouldn't have the energy for a healthy pregnancy. We weren't financially secure. I was thinking of running for the legislature.

She was upset, and my joyful reaction to the news wasn't making her feel any better. I wasn't going to suffer morning sickness. My body wouldn't be transformed. I wouldn't endure labor. She would. Her reaction was understandable and temporary. By the morning, she was as excited by the news as I was.

The first three months were rough on Jeanette. She suffered severe morning sickness and had little energy for school; it subsided by the second trimester. Her belly started to show, and her spirits were good. And we had a new plan—a good one, I thought. Early the next year, we would decide whether or not I would run for the legislature. The baby was due in April, and, if I did run, I wouldn't have to start campaigning full-time until early June. Everything was coming along nicely in our lives—a little ahead of schedule, but manageable.

I was sitting at my desk at the firm when I heard the news from a local campaign consultant. One of the most powerful state senators in Florida had just cut a deal with prosecutors who had indicted him for Medicare fraud. He would resign from office that day. At first, the bulletin meant nothing more to me than being a piece of interesting political news that had no bearing on my future. But the consultant who broke the news to me explained that Carlos Valdes, the term-limited state representative whose vacant seat I was considering running for, wanted to remain in the legislature. The most obvious course for him would be to run for the just vacated senate seat in a special election. That meant Valdes's house seat would be contested in a special election as well. Anyone running for it would have to start their campaign immediately.

I had only hours to decide what to do. Valdes announced for the senate special election, and the election for his house seat was scheduled for the same time. The winner of the special election would be an incumbent running for reelection the following November, which would give him or her a leg up over any opposition. It's notoriously difficult to beat incumbents in the Florida Legislature. Moreover, the winner of the special election would have a seniority edge in a huge freshman class of legislators. And if I didn't run in the special election, another opportunity might not be available for years. I had to run now or wait for a very long while.

I discussed it with Jeanette and the firm's partners. With their blessing, I decided to run. The timing wasn't ideal, but how often is anything perfectly timed in life? It wasn't our plan. It was life.

CHAPTER 14

Running for the Legislature

AT FIRST IT APPEARED THE CAMPAIGN WOULD BE EASIER than I had imagined. None of my rumored opponents were well known or well positioned to run. That changed the morning Angel Zayon, a popular television news reporter and contributor for a highly rated drive-time radio show, announced his candidacy.

I wasn't too concerned initially. Angel had never run for office before. He hadn't raised any money and he didn't have an organization. But David Rivera was worried from the start. He appreciated what I had not. Angel was well known—better known than I was. In a short campaign, greater name recognition would be a huge advantage. I held out hope Angel would change his mind. But when he filed his candidacy and qualified for the ballot, I knew I faced a stiff challenge from a formidable opponent.

It felt odd to campaign during the holiday season, and challenging. People are a little busy at Christmas, and not likely to be preoccupied with politics. I walked door-to-door as I had done the year before in West Miami. More than once, I approached a house as the owners were putting up their Christmas lights.

My fund-raising head start gave me an advantage. None of the other candidates for the Republican nomination were able to raise as much money as I had. We were better organized, too, and I felt confident on primary day I would win with more than 50 percent of the vote. If I fell short of 50 percent, a runoff election between the two top vote getters would be held four weeks later.

The early returns suggested I had been overconfident. Angel was doing much better than I had expected. He was winning precincts I had been certain I would win. He was beating me in important precincts in Hialeah and clobbering me in absentee ballots. But he didn't get 50 percent, and I finished in second place with thirty-nine fewer votes.

We would have a runoff. I thought the night had been a disaster, and I felt pretty certain it would be repeated in the runoff election. With Carlos Lacasa's help, I had received campaign contributions from the state's major Republican donors, who had been convinced I would win. Now that Angel had finished first, they would want to hedge their bets and donate to him. He had come out of nowhere to beat me without money or organization. Now he would have both.

I suffered a psychological blow as well. Many supporters and local activists who had helped me jumped ship immediately after the first vote and joined Angel's campaign. It's fair to say, a sense of doom gripped my campaign. I had a choice to make. I could feel sorry for myself and give up or I could buckle down, figure out what I had done wrong and fix it.

My first task was to address my underperformance with absentee voters. Angel had aggressively pursued them. He had shown up personally at the homes of voters who had requested absentee ballots, carrying a roll of stamps. He urged them to fill out their ballots for him and mail them that day. I had to match his effort for the runoff, and pressed my family into service. My parents went out together every day to visit absentee voters. Using the daily county election lists, we anticipated when voters would receive their ballots and timed my folks' visits for the same day. I dispatched my sisters to do the same, and even Jeanette, who was five months' pregnant at the time, knocked on doors for me.

Next, I had to fix my problem in Hialeah. Although it was only a small part of the district, Hialeah is a politics-obsessed town. Its residents vote in higher numbers than any other place in Miami-Dade. Hialeah's longtime and powerful mayor, Raul Martinez, supported Angel because he believed I was allied with his rivals. I couldn't persuade Raul to switch allegiances, so I had to make a virtue out of his opposition. Raul was powerful, but he had many enemies, and I appealed to them for help. All I had to do was tell them that Raul was supporting Angel, and they were instantly motivated to help me.

None of Raul's enemies was more helpful to me than Modesto Pérez, known locally as the guy from Mr. Cool Appliances. Modesto was a self-made man who spent his days at the warehouse where he sold water coolers, using his political contacts to help his neighbors. When he agreed to help a candidate, he had a simple expectation in return. If you were elected, and he asked for your help on behalf of people who had come to him for help, you would give it. They were always legitimate requests: a small store owner who wanted to get a lottery ticket terminal, a grandmother who needed a letter of recommendation for her granddaughter's college application—that kind of thing. It was retail politics at its purest, and Modesto was a master of it.

I had never worked harder than I did during those four weeks. I walked every day from very early in the morning until it was so dark people wouldn't open their doors. After I finished, my father and I would put up signs until two or three in the morning. I felt certain I had done all I could by primary day, but far from certain it would prove enough to win.

On Election Day we confronted one disappointing development after another. Popular Miami city commissioner Tomas Regalado, who for weeks had assured me of his support, turned up at the polling site at St. Dominic Catholic Church and handed out literature for Angel. From another precinct, where we had lost badly in the first round, one of my most trusted supporters called to say we were likely to lose again. Throughout the day, we received reports that volunteer drivers for Raul Martinez's political machine were dropping off hundreds of voters at the polls, and I knew they weren't voting for me.

I had been working a polling station in the largest precinct in Hialeah when I felt the need to retreat to my car, rest for a few minutes and feel sorry for myself. As I sat there, I saw in the fading light my wife—who was then six months' pregnant, had never liked politics and would have been perfectly happy if I had never run for office—working harder than I was. I watched her approach voters and try to convince them to vote for her husband, who was off somewhere sulking. I thought of Father O'Brien's homily at our wedding. Love isn't a feeling, it's an action. I saw Jeanette's love in action, and I knew if I lost that night, I would be fine.

After the polls closed, we headed straight to our campaign headquarters at the Fraternal Order of Police hall in Little Havana. By the time we arrived, the results had already started to trickle in. We didn't have a television or Internet, so a volunteer stationed at the county elections department conveyed them over the phone. I trailed all night long, and was still behind with only one precinct's returns yet to be counted, St. Dominic's. But St. Dominic's was my strongest precinct, and I knew it would put me over the top. A few minutes later I received word over the phone that I had won the precinct easily and the election by a whopping sixty-four votes.

We rushed into the hall and made the announcement to a jubilant crowd of family, friends and supporters. Jeanette sat in a corner apart from the crowd, quietly tearing up with joy. My nephew Danny took a picture of her that I still have. She was happy and proud, and probably unaware how much our lives would be changed by my election.

The general election was still two weeks off, but it was a solidly Republican district, and I won it comfortably. I was twenty-eight years old, and headed to Tallahassee. The legislative session would begin in less than eight weeks, and Jeanette would give birth to our first child four weeks after that.

The firm had been very supportive of my candidacy, and generous with the time they gave me to campaign. But after I won, the partners informed me they were going to reduce my salary by the same amount I would earn as a state legislator. The news stung. I had counted on the extra money to help with the expense of the new baby. This, too, had not been in our plans. But, as I was beginning to learn, you make plans, and then life unmakes them.

CHAPTER 15

Welcome to Tallahassee

W E AWOKE ON A FEBRUARY MORNING IN 2000 TO FIND A thick fog covering Tallahassee. Jeanette and I, my parents and my sisters and their children had made the eight-hour drive to the state capital the night before in a three-van caravan. After breakfast we loaded everyone into the vans and made a right turn from our hotel onto the Apalachee Parkway, the broad street that leads uphill to the capitol building. The fog had begun to lift and I could see the dome of the Old Capitol and the twenty-two-floor capitol building behind it, where I would be sworn in that morning.

I was sworn in with another new house member from Miami, Renier Diaz de la Portilla, whose brother had vacated his house seat to run in the special senate election. I was allowed to say a few words at the ceremony. I thanked my family and supporters, and closed with a line borrowed from President Kennedy's inaugural address: "knowing that here on earth God's work must truly be our own."

The sixty-day legislative session wouldn't begin for another three weeks, but lawmakers had returned to the capital for a week of committee work. Half of the members of the house were termed out and would leave the legislature at the end of the session. Some had served there almost as long as I had been alive, and it was clear many of them didn't want to go. My committee assignments reflected my low status as a new member, and the reluctance of veteran legislators to share any of their authority before they were required to relinquish it.

Races for speaker of the Florida House usually begin years before the winner assumes the office. As soon as I arrived in Tallahassee I found myself thrust into the middle of the 2004 speaker's race. Three new representatives from Miami-Dade had been elected in the class of 1998. One of them, Gaston Cantens, a former prosecutor, aspired to be the first Cuban American to serve as speaker of the house beginning in 2004. I was immediately pressured by two members of Gaston's class to sign a card pledging my support for him. But one of Gaston's rivals for speaker, Randy Johnson, had been immensely helpful to my campaign. He had helped me raise money and had been at my campaign headquarters during the tense hours when the outcome was in doubt. Gaston had stayed on the sidelines during my campaign, reluctant to risk endorsing the wrong candidate and making an enemy of the winner.

I was greatly indebted to Randy, and the last thing I wanted to do was appear ungrateful by immediately turning my back on him. But Gaston's election to speaker was a matter of pride to the Cuban American community, and I knew I would have to support him eventually. I held back from making any commitment, and some of Gaston's supporters misinterpreted my reluctance as a signal that I wanted to be Florida's first Cuban American speaker. And although that was the furthest thing from my mind at the time, suspicions about my ambitions would persist for quite some time among some of my fellow legislators.

My first year in the legislature was like a redshirt year in college sports. Because I had been elected in a special election, the session didn't count against my eight-year term limit. I would have nine months' seniority and valuable experience by the time the rest of my freshman class arrived in November. I used the time to learn how the place worked, how decisions were made and how successful legislators accomplished things. I cultivated a relationship with Mike Fasano, who would serve as house majority leader in the new term under incoming speaker Tom Feeney, and I observed power beginning to shift from the current speaker John Thrasher to Tom in the closing weeks of the session. The nine months of seniority I accumulated would give the house leadership a rationale to promote me over other ambitious members of my class.

I had other things on my mind, however, in those early days in Talla-hassee. Jeanette was nine months' pregnant. I worried she would go into labor while we were in session and I would miss the birth of my first child. Luckily, I was at home for the weekend when her contractions started on April 3, 2000. We drove to the hospital and waited a couple of hours only to learn they were a false alarm. But since Jeanette was past her due date and we were at the hospital, her doctor decided to induce labor.

As every parent discovers, the birth of your child, especially your first child, is an experience unlike any other. Nothing really prepares you for the flood of emotions it summons, or the abrupt change in your priorities. It is the moment your heart admits a love that surpasses all others, and ego submits to a stronger attachment. You suddenly form a new consciousness, as if your life is turned inside out. It transformed me.

The very moment I first saw Amanda, I felt such a surge of devotion and protectiveness it overwhelmed me. She slept most of her first night of life, and I couldn't stop staring at her, my mind gripped not only with un-familiar sensations but with imagining the whole of her life. I pictured her first day at school and the day I would drop her off at college and the day I would walk her down the aisle at her wedding.

When we brought her home, I felt possessed by a responsibility greater than any that had ever been expected of me. Amanda was a colicky baby. She cried uncontrollably after being fed, her face red and her little body stiff in distress as we tried to comfort her. We suffered many anxious, sleepless nights our first months with Amanda, and even though honesty obliges me to confess I looked forward to getting some sleep when I returned to Tal-lahassee, it was still hard to leave her. But I did—the first of many separa-tions I have regretted over the years.

Not long after Amanda was born, another child's welfare captured my attention, and the attention of the entire country. In November 1999, a six-year-old boy and his mother boarded a small, crowded aluminum boat with a faulty motor in the hope of escaping oppression in Cuba for a better life in America. The mother and ten others perished on the journey when the motor quit and their boat swamped. The boy, Elián González, survived and was found floating on an inner tube by two fishermen who rescued him.

The Immigration and Naturalization Service placed him in the cus-tody of relatives in Miami. Elián's father, with the support of the Castro regime, demanded his return to Cuba. Elián's Miami relatives refused, and the stage was set for an intense confrontation that would divide the Cuban American community from many of their fellow Americans.

The vast majority of the Cuban exile community, including me, wanted Elián to remain in the United States, and his father to join him here. The notion that he be forcibly returned to a regime his mother had given her life to rescue him from was unfathomable to us. In the 1960s, hundreds of Cuban parents had sent their children to live with foster families or orphanages in the United States to save them from life under communism. For those who had lived through the experience, returning a child to Cuba against his dead mother's wishes was too much to bear. To most other Americans, however, reuniting a motherless child with his father was obviously the right decision.

Attorney General Janet Reno set a deadline of April 13, 2000, for Elián's relatives to turn him over to federal authorities while his custody case was adjudicated. They refused to surrender him, and a crowd of hundreds of supporters and media kept a constant vigil at their modest home in Little Havana.

The Elián González saga became more than a custody battle. It became a cause that polarized Miami and much of the nation. In some quarters, support for his father's custody rights took on a distinctly antiexile undertone. Many longtime friendships between Cuban Americans and non-Cubans ended in bitter arguments over Elián's fate. Many non-Cubans thought it outrageous that Elián's relatives thumbed their noses at the authorities and dared them to take Elián forcibly from them. Many Cubans felt their antagonism was intended as a deliberate insult to their community.

The deadline came and went, and for a while it seemed the standoff would continue indefinitely. Jeanette and I were talking about the case on the evening of April 21. It was Good Friday, and I was home for the Easter break. I remember predicting to Jeanette that if the authorities were going to seize Elián that weekend they would do it the next morning, and not on Easter Sunday.

I awoke to Amanda's cries at four o'clock that morning. After I fed her and she had fallen back asleep, I decided to go by the house in Little Havana where Elián was staying. I expected something could happen that morning, and I wanted to be there to see it. The streets were empty as I made the short drive until I reached the neighborhood where Elián's relatives lived, and found a police car with its lights flashing blocking an intersection. Seconds later several vans sped past me toward the house. I waited in my car at the intersection, and a few minutes later the same vans sped by me again traveling in the opposite direction. I parked my car and sprinted the three blocks to the house. Hundreds of people were wandering around in disbelief, many of them coughing and looking for a hose to wash pepper spray off their faces. Media trucks and camera crews were everywhere. Reporters interrupted early-morning broadcasts with breaking news that Elián González had been seized in a predawn raid by a Border Patrol SWAT team.

I, too, was in disbelief, but less so over the raid itself—I knew the government would eventually enforce its authority—than over the raid's immediate aftermath. The Cuban exile community had always been a bastion of pro-American sentiment. Exiles loved America and Americans. My grandfather and parents had been deeply patriotic, and regarded their new country with reverence and gratitude. Most Cuban Americans were pillars of their communities, deeply invested in our nation and always on the side of law and order. Now, perhaps for the first time in their lives here, they felt they were on the outside looking in: raided by federal agents, vilified in the national media as lawless and disrespectful.

Some Miamians harbored deep-seated resentments for Cuban Americans. The controversy exposed many of those resentments and forced Cuban Americans to confront them. Many were shocked to hear from non-Hispanic friends how much it bothered them when they couldn't place an order at Burger King in English or when Cuban associates at work spoke Spanish to each other in front of them. I think the discovery encouraged many Cubans to reexamine the way they lived and be more attentive to the sensitivities of non-Cubans.

The Elián González incident was a watershed moment in Miami politics and in the history of the Cuban exile community. Its most immediate impact was felt in the 2000 elections. Arguably, it cost Al Gore the election. Gore lost Florida and the presidency to George Bush by a little more than five hundred votes. Cuban American anger over the Clinton administration's seizure of Elián and dissatisfaction with Gore's ambiguous position on the controversy motivated most of them to vote to punish the administration. As for Elián, he returned to his father and Cuba, where he became an active member of the Communist Party and loyal supporter of El Co-mandante, the ridiculous title given to Fidel Castro.

When the sad ordeal concluded, I returned to the pressing concerns of my fledgling political career. My primary opponent, Angel Zayon, whom I had very narrowly defeated, was making noises about challenging me again in August. He was convinced that low voter turnout in the special election had been the primary reason for his defeat and felt his chances would be much better in a regular primary, where the turnout would be higher and his name recognition advantage would be greater. I started knocking on doors in the district, raising money and sending every signal I could that I was prepared for battle.

In the end, it wasn't necessary. Angel had been upset with me over a misunderstanding. I was being interviewed on a talk radio program, when a caller made a disparaging remark about Angel's daughter. I had misun-derstood his comment and hadn't rebuked him. I met with Angel to discuss it, and subsequently apologized on the same radio program for uninten-tionally failing to reprimand the caller. In response to my apology, Angel announced he wouldn't run.

Without an opponent, I spent the summer campaigning for Republi-can candidates who would be elected to my incoming freshman class. Sup-porters of Gaston Cantens's bid for speaker misinterpreted it as further evidence I had ambitions for the office. I had signed Gaston's pledge card at the end of the regular session, and I saw no harm in traveling the state and supporting my future colleagues. And if I helped myself in the process by making allies for a possible leadership bid in the future, I didn't think there was anything wrong with that, either.

In hindsight, I understand I should have handled myself better. Gaston had worked very hard to be elected speaker, and believed correctly that the house wouldn't elect two consecutive speakers from the same region. If some of the freshmen I campaigned for that summer believed I was likely to run for speaker in the next election, they might be inclined to withhold their support from Gaston. I can understand why Gaston's allies viewed my campaigning as a threat, and why they would continue to regard me suspi-ciously in the coming months and years.

I watched the returns on election night with friends from the Dole campaign in the living room of my former aide and Dole campaign alumna

Alina Garcia, who had resigned from my staff to run for a house seat. She lost, but by that point we were resigned to her defeat. We didn't expect the unfolding drama of the presidential race, however. We monitored the returns on David Rivera's computer, and David relayed them by phone to Al Cardenas, who was our party chairman. Al relayed them in turn to Governor Jeb Bush, who was sitting in the Texas governor's mansion with his brother, the candidate. As the returns from different counties came in, I could hear Al swearing on the other end of the call.

Then the bottom fell out. NBC News called Florida for Vice President Gore. It seemed premature—some of the strongest Republican counties hadn't reported their returns yet. Al and David argued that the result couldn't possibly be known yet. But the rest of us thought they were crazy. The networks never call a race unless they're certain they've got it right.

Soon thereafter, the counties David and Al had mentioned started to report their results, and the numbers started to move. Within the hour, NBC retracted its prediction, and put Florida back in the "too close to call" category. After pronouncing Senator Gore the Florida winner and retracting it, the networks then gave the election to Governor Bush. Gore called Bush to concede and then called him back to retract it. I finally gave up and went to bed around three o'clock in the morning, certain that when I woke up we would have our new president. But we didn't. And I would begin my second year in the Florida House as the body was stuck in the middle of the most controversial presidential election in modern American history.

CHAPTER 16

Majority Whip

T HE FLORIDA LEGISLATURE CONVENES AN ORGANIZA-
tional session after an election to swear in members, elect a speaker
and pass rules for the new legislative session—it's an occasion marked by a
good deal of pomp and ceremony. As I drove to the capitol to begin my first
full term as a member of the Florida House, it was quite apparent the session that began two weeks after the 2000 election would be special for reasons that had nothing to do with us.

All roads leading to the capitol were clogged with satellite trucks.
Available hotel rooms were scarce, most of them occupied by the vast media
horde that had descended on Tallahassee. Another new member jokingly
asked me, "Does the first day always get this much attention?"

As it turned out, the resolution of the election crisis would prove anti-
climactic in the house. The U.S. Supreme Court effectively declared the
winner on December 12, before the legislature had to take definitive action.
Nevertheless, it was a very unusual start to a new legislative session.

The session was memorable for other reasons as well. The incoming
majority leader, Mike Fasano, appointed me to his former job, majority
whip. After only nine months in the house, I had vaulted into the leadership. It was a major coup, and I was thrilled. The news wasn't received en-
thusiastically by Gaston Cantens's allies, however, whose suspicions about
my ambitions only deepened.

After the election crisis concluded, the rest of the legislative year seemed largely uneventful by comparison. As majority whip, I was given a few opportunities I might not otherwise have had to speak on the floor about several important bills. I hoped to impress colleagues with my leadership skills and public speaking, which I knew could give me an advantage over the competition were I to decide to run for speaker. When the 2001 session concluded in May, I was generally satisfied with the direction of my political career, and worried sick about my finances and my legal career.

My leadership role took more time from my work at Ruden McClosky and strained my relations with the firm's partners. The weeks I spent in Tallahassee consumed nearly half the year. And when I was back at the firm, I was usually distracted. None of the firm's work was as interesting to me as my work in the legislature, and it showed. The partners had good reason to be displeased with me.

My annual review at the firm was rapidly approaching, and I knew nothing good would come of it. The partners would either reduce my salary further or ask me to leave the firm. My salary was $72,000, more than my parents had ever made combined. But it barely covered our basic expenses. My student loan payments at the time were close to $900 a month. Rent was $1,500. Our car payments were another several hundred. I agonized over our monthly budget, and searched for expenses we could live without. We considered having Jeanette go back to work even though we had wanted her to remain at home until Amanda was old enough for school. But when we factored in the cost of child care, her net income would be negligible. So we decided to sell my car and move in with Jeanette's mother for the time being. Even with these economies, we couldn't afford any further reductions in my salary. I reached out to a professional headhunter with a difficult request. Find a firm that needed a land use and zoning attorney, and wouldn't mind if I was absent half the year.

We were living in my mother-in-law's house. I had given up my car. Still we were struggling to make ends meet, and I was facing either a catastrophic reduction in my salary or unemployment. My understanding wife, who had already sacrificed so much for my political career, now had to worry that I couldn't provide for our family. I had never been so despondent. The only solution, I concluded, was to resign from the legislature and practice law full-time again.

I got in the car and started driving to clear my head. Eventually, I drove to the Church of the Little Flower, where we had been married and where I had often attended daily Mass. I entered the church, walked to the front pew, opened the kneeler and prayed. Why had God allowed me to come so far only to let me fail? Why had doors opened to me and then suddenly closed again? What did He want me to do? I prayed His will be done, and for the strength to accept it.

When I think of that moment now, I wonder if my despair was as great as my father's and grandfather's had been when they had suffered far worse misfortune. How anguished must my grandfather have been when he lost his railroad job, his home and the social and economic status that had meant so much to him, when he wandered for miles leaning on his cane in search of menial jobs to support his seven daughters, when he was refused work because of his disability? What did my father feel when he considered moving back to Cuba, when his small businesses failed, when he lost his job and our apartment at Toledo Plaza, when he searched in vain for work in Las Vegas and had to accept a job as a bar boy?

My grandfather and father had once been my age, and had ambitions no less dear to them than mine were to me. They both had known success for a brief time, and both had seen it taken away, never to be recovered. They endured and made the best of their circumstances, and gave their children a better start in life than they had ever had. But they had to settle for less of a life than they had wanted, hoping their children would never face the same disappointment.

Now I imagined telling my children someday that I had once been the majority whip of the Florida House but had lost my job and had to leave politics to make a living. I had a family to provide for and their future to plan for. Maybe, like my family before me, I would lose my dreams, too, and hope my children would live theirs.

I left the church still worried, but resigned to accept whatever happened. On my way back to my mother-in-law's house, my cell phone rang. After weeks had passed without hearing from her, the headhunter was calling to let me know a law firm in Broward County, Becker and Poliakoff, had expressed an interest in my services.

I had just been on my knees in prayer asking God's help. Now a door suddenly appeared to open and offer me a way out of my predicament. Was it a miracle? I don't know. I do know that whatever fortune or misfortune we encounter in our lives, God expects it to lead us closer to Him.

The headhunter put me in touch with the firm's senior partner, Alan Becker, who had once served in the legislature, too. I met with him a few days later at his office in Hollywood, Florida. Becker and Poliakoff had a very successful land use and zoning practice in Broward. Alan told me they wanted to expand the practice to Miami-Dade. We spent most of the interview discussing the challenges of practicing law while serving in the legislature. We seemed to hit it off on a personal level, but he couldn't make me an offer until he had discussed it with his partners and gotten their approval.

The next Monday, Alan called me and offered me the job, with a salary of $93,000—the precise amount I had budgeted before Ruden McClosky cut my pay. I didn't hesitate a moment. Two weeks later, I drove to the firm's Hollywood office for my first day in my new job.

I woke up early to beat the traffic. As I reached for my wallet before walking out the door, I saw the yellow sticky note attached to it:

Good Luck Tomorrow!
Don't be nervous,
Make sure you're on time,
Break a leg and
Remember I Love You!!!
(P.S. I got you the bars as a snack when you get hungry)
Love, Jeanette

The additional money gave us a little breathing room and would allow us to move back into our house in West Miami soon. I vowed not to make the same mistakes I had made at Ruden McClosky. I intended to arrive at the office before seven every morning. It wasn't an election year and I would be able to spend more time in my law office that summer. Either I would make this opportunity work or I would have to give up my political career. I was determined to make it work.

I flew to Tallahassee for the start of committee work on a Tuesday morning in September. I was in my house office in a meeting when my aide Nelson Diaz passed me a note informing me that a bomb had exploded at the World Trade Center. I had visited the towers just four weeks earlier when I had traveled to New York for a conference. Speaker Feeney had hosted a fund-raiser for our Florida House candidates at Windows on the World on the 107th floor of the North Tower. I had brought Jeanette and Amanda with me, and I remembered having a hard time getting Amanda's stroller onto one of the tower's escalators.

Nelson soon corrected his early bulletin. It wasn't a bomb explosion— an airplane had crashed into the North Tower. Like most people, I initially assumed it had been an accident; the pilot of a small aircraft had probably flown too close to the New York skyline and had somehow lost control of the plane. We watched on television as the second plane struck the South Tower, and we realized the United States was under attack.

Within minutes the Florida capitol was swarming with heavily armed police. I appreciated the quick response but thought it was an overreaction. I didn't believe that terrorists who had just struck New York and Washington would be interested in attacking the sleepy capital of Florida. Nelson reminded me that the governor, whose office was four floors beneath mine, happened to be the president's brother. I decided that getting out of the capitol might not be a bad idea after all.

I wanted to go home as soon as possible, but all flights were grounded after the attacks. I drove to Miami the next morning with three of my colleagues. We lived just a few miles from the airport, and I had become accustomed to the sound of aircraft overhead. Now there was just an eerie silence above, and the empty sky seemed surreal.

The shock and uncertainty that gripped Americans in those first days and weeks after 9/11 began to subside slowly as people resumed their lives and things returned to what would become the new normal. I managed my time better and my work at the firm was going well. Our financial situation was much improved. We were growing more accustomed to the changes in our lives necessitated by my political career. We were as content as we had been in some time. And when Jeanette announced in October that she was pregnant again, we were both happy and excited about it. We hadn't planned it, but we were thrilled Amanda would have a brother or sister close to her age.

The legislature would soon begin the politically charged, highly technical, once-in-a-decade process of redistricting. I had no official leadership role in redistricting, but I managed to become a key player in the design of the house districts, and a principal defender of the final plan. In the process, I gained favor with my Republican colleagues and with Johnnie Byrd, the next speaker of the house.

I didn't know what my next role would be in the new legislature. After two years as majority whip, the logical next step was to run for majority leader. But with so many members ahead of me in seniority, I appeared to be a long shot.

Jeanette was scheduled to have an induced labor on June 18 that summer. The night before, I had an uneasy feeling about it. Researching all the potential complications of childbirth had made me a nervous wreck the day Amanda was born, and I attributed my anxiety that day to the memory of that experience.

Her labor went much more quickly than it had the last time. It seemed mere minutes had passed before I was introduced to my newest daughter, Daniella. We hadn't known the sex of the baby in advance, and I was happy Amanda would have a baby sister and Jeanette would have two little girls to keep her company when I was away from home.

Jeanette delivered her in a birthing suite, a large and comfortable room intended to make the experience more like giving birth at home. Although the room was spacious, there were so many people present during the delivery that it didn't feel large. The doctor, nurse, myself, Jeanette, her mother, my mother, Veronica and Jeanette's three sisters were all present when Daniella entered the world. As soon as she was born everyone was instantly mesmerized by her without realizing that something was seriously wrong with her mother.

Jeanette was suffering from an obstetric complication called placenta accreta in which the placenta becomes so deeply attached to the uterine wall that the obstetrician has to remove it surgically. Women in this condition often hemorrhage, and the result can be a hysterectomy or even death depending on the severity of it. I could tell by the look on the doctor's face that he was having trouble. He is a very calm and composed man who has delivered many of the children in our family. So when he suddenly ordered everyone except me to leave the room, we all knew something was wrong. He ordered three units of blood and told the nurses to have the operating room prepared. I heard one of the nurses page the anesthesiologist to report to the operating room as soon as possible. As they wheeled Jeanette out of the birthing suite to surgery, I overheard the doctor tell the nurses what was going on.

The next thirty minutes were the longest half hour of my life. I paced right outside the surgery, praying for my wife's recovery. I watched nurses race out of the operating room to retrieve more units of blood. I could hear our family in the waiting room, joking and laughing, unaware of the severity of her condition. I fought to keep from contemplating the worst.

We were fortunate our doctor succeeded in stopping the bleeding with a relatively minor surgical procedure that averted the necessity of a hysterectomy. I waited until Jeanette was back in her room and settled before alerting the family to the situation. The next twenty-four hours were critical. She had lost so much blood that even a little more bleeding would require urgent attention. I spent almost the entire night staring at her while she slept, watching for any sign of distress.

Later that night, the doctor came to her room and explained what had happened. There had been some difficulty stopping Jeanette's bleeding when Amanda was born, and we had survived an all-out crisis with Daniella. He strongly advised us not to have any more children because he believed Jeanette suffered a predisposition to the condition. I was so relieved she and Daniella were okay, the last thing I was concerned with was having another child. Jeanette felt differently. She believed we would have more children, and considered his recommendation to be a casual caution. We went home a few days later with the admonition Jeanette needed to take it very easy for the next six weeks.

Primaries to nominate house candidates were held that summer. I decided to stay out of them for the most part. I wanted to spend time with Jeanette and the girls, and I didn't want to further antagonize Gaston's allies. Gaston was frantically traveling the state campaigning for candidates who would support him for speaker in the 2004 leadership election. If enough of them won, he would have the votes to defeat his rival, Allan Bense, and become the first Cuban American speaker of the Florida House. Had I campaigned, some of the candidates I would have helped were not Gaston's supporters. So I limited my activity to supporting two Dole campaign alumni, David Rivera and Carlos Lopez-Cantera.

The primaries were held in late August. David won and Carlos lost. But the biggest news of the night was that not enough of Gaston's candidates had won. He dropped out of the speaker's race that night and declared his support for Bense. That race was over, and I knew my colleagues would soon start concentrating on the next race for speaker of the house, in 2006, who would be chosen from my class.

I didn't have a burning desire to be the first Cuban American speaker. But after Gaston's bid failed, there wasn't any reason I should dismiss the idea. Two speakers would serve before my class chose one. Whatever assignment I received from the next speaker, Johnnie Byrd, would determine whether or not I had a decent shot at becoming speaker in 2006.

I wanted to be majority leader. It would give me a platform to become involved in all the major issues addressed by the house, while a committee chairmanship would restrict my involvement to issues within my committee's jurisdiction. But every supporter I talked to discouraged me from going after the job. They said I could kiss good-bye any ambition for speaker if I were majority leader. I would be in the vote-counting business, and would have to twist arms on difficult votes, making as many enemies as friends in the process.

I saw the job differently. First, there was no guarantee I would be elected speaker, but I had a good chance right now of joining the senior leadership of the house. I had confidence in my communications skills, too, and believed the majority leader's job would give me ample opportunity to communicate the Republican message on important issues.

Mike Corcoran was a consultant to incoming speaker Johnnie Byrd who also did some work for me. I asked him to help persuade Johnnie to restructure the majority leader's job, proposing that the majority leader's responsibilities be limited to communication, and all vote-counting responsibilities given to a more powerful whip's office. After several weeks of pitching, Speaker Byrd offered me the newly restructured majority leader's job.

I had been whip in my first two years, and I was about to be majority leader. Soon, I would have to make another, much more difficult decision, a decision that would affect not just my political future, but the happiness of my family.

CHAPTER 17

Running for Speaker

IN ONE RESPECT, A CAMPAIGN FOR SPEAKER IS SIMILAR TO a primary campaign. You don't need bumper stickers or signs or television ads, but you do travel the state and meet with the voters. They are a very select group of voters, to be sure. But as with any group of voters, their interests are various. Some colleagues want assurances their support would be rewarded with a committee chairmanship. Others simply support the candidate they like the best. Most, however, want to be with the winner, and wait to pledge their support to a candidate until they have a good idea who's going to win.

I knew if I ran for speaker I would have to overcome several obstacles. I represented a district in Miami-Dade, the most populous region in Florida, and the least popular with house members from the rest of the state, who believed South Florida received a disproportionate share of the state's budget. There had not been a speaker elected from Miami-Dade since 1971, the year I was born.

To have any chance at all, I had to have the united support of the Miami-Dade delegation, which has a long history of fractiousness. At least one of Gaston's supporters in the delegation believed I had undermined his speaker's bid by not ruling out a run of my own. A newly elected member of the delegation was upset with me because I had supported his primary opponent. I was far from assured of unified support within my own delegation.

A few weeks after he withdrew from the speaker's race, Gaston asked to have lunch with me, and urged me to run. To his credit and my good fortune, he hadn't believed I had tried to undermine him. He didn't hold me responsible for the defeat of his aspiration to be Florida's first Cuban American speaker of the house. On the contrary, he told me he had gotten the ball to the five-yard line, and was now relying on me to get it into the end zone. He was proud of how close he had come, and prouder still he had made it more likely that a Cuban American would eventually be elected speaker.

I decided to run, and from the start I made a series of terrible blunders. The first and most egregious was my failure to consult with Jeanette. She should have had a veto over my decision. I took for granted she would support the idea. My presumption was a mistake, and a selfish one, since Jeanette would have to assume even more of the responsibilities for raising our children and running our household than she already disproportionately shared. The travel and time the campaign required would come at the expense of my family. Jeanette would be publicly supportive of my bid. But privately, she resented the way I made my decision, and had every right to.

My second mistake was to let the *Miami Herald* know I would run before I informed most of the members in the Miami-Dade delegation of my intentions. I had conferred with a few of them about my decision, but most of them learned about it when they read it in the newspaper. They all eventually supported me, but many of them would show little enthusiasm for my campaign.

I opened a political committee to cover the expenses of my campaign for speaker. But I decided Jeanette and I would manage the fund-raising and reporting for the committee ourselves. That decision proved to be a disaster. I had estimated I would need to raise between $30,000 and $40,000 to pay for my travel, dinners and other events I would host, and to dispense campaign donations to Republican candidates. I seriously underestimated the costs, and raised and spent considerably more than I had anticipated. I was in over my head trying to do everything myself. I often used my or Jeanette's personal credit cards to pay for many of the campaign's expenditures. When I received my statement, I would spend hours trying to figure out which were political, and which were personal.

I asked Jeanette to serve as the committee's treasurer, putting her in an impossibly difficult situation. She didn't accompany me on most of my trips or attend many of the events I attended in South Florida. She had to jog my memory to determine which credit card purchases were campaign expenditures, sometimes weeks after I had made them. It was an imperfect accounting system, to say the least.

Years later, my lack of bookkeeping skills would come back to haunt me. The press and Governor Crist raised the matter during my U.S. Senate campaign, implying I had pocketed money from my finance committee and used it to pay for personal items. It wasn't true, but I had helped create the misunderstanding my opponents exploited.

The legislature's 2003 session was a miserable experience for all involved. The legislature failed to deliver a state budget on time despite having a surplus of revenue. And the political capital Speaker Byrd possessed when he entered the office was exhausted before he gaveled the session to order.

I spent much of my spare time during the session cultivating personal relationships with members and with people who might influence them. I used Gaston to keep our delegation united in support of me, while I met with members from the rest of the state. In that effort, I had two key allies, Stan Mayfield of Vero Beach and Ralph Arza from Miami. Both had entertained the idea of running for speaker, but Ralph had decided to support me and persuaded Stan to do the same. As the first member from outside South Florida to back me, Stan was a hugely important recruit.

The morning Allan Bense was designated the next speaker, we began securing pledges. I was off to an early start with fifteen pledges—thirteen from the South Florida delegation, Stan Mayfield's pledge and another from John Carassas, a colleague at Becker and Poliakoff.

My closest competitor was Dennis Ross. Dennis looked and comported himself like a speaker. He was a mature, intelligent and well-respected member of my class. He had ten pledges. Several of the other candidates had three or four. The race looked like it would be close and protracted, not unlike the Bense/Cantens race that preceded it.

I had a pretty good idea where most members stood. That summer, David Rivera had traveled the state and met with most members in his class. He took detailed notes of his conversations, and knew what each of his classmates thought about me. Some thought I was too close to Johnnie Byrd. Others didn't like Stan or Ralph, and expected they would receive the best leadership positions if I were elected. Others liked me, but weren't ready to make a commitment yet.

Stan and Ralph devised a plan to collect second-choice commitments from members, so I would have the lead in pledged members and the lead in members who pledged to support me if their candidate dropped out of the race. It proved to be a smart move.

I was at home on a Tuesday night when David Rivera called to tell me he had just heard from someone in Lakeland, Florida, where Dennis Ross lived. Dennis had told friends he was dropping out of the race. I started speed-dialing members who had pledged to him but had committed to me as their second choice. The next morning, I drove up I-75 with my aide Sebastian Aleksander to districts in the western part of the state and appealed in person to members who had supported Dennis. By the end of the day, I had twenty-nine pledge cards.

On Thursday morning, I started reaching out to my rivals to convince them to drop out and support me. By Thursday afternoon the last of my competitors had quit the race. Not all of them committed to me, but I was the only candidate left. I had thirty-nine votes, and I rushed to get the rest.

On Friday, we chartered a plane and flew from Ft. Lauderdale to Tampa, where about twenty house freshmen were meeting at State Representative Kevin Ambler's house to deliver their pledge cards to me. I invited Gaston to come with me. He had done so much for me, and I wanted him to be there to share in our historic success. But I invited so many people to fly with me there wasn't a seat for David Rivera, my friend and most loyal supporter. He had done more for my candidacy than anyone else, and I left him to drive to Tampa on his own. Just as I had once taken Jeanette's support for granted, so, too, had I taken David's for granted.

Earlier in the week, all indications were it would be a long and hard-fought battle for speaker. By the end of the week, in a flurry of activity, I had secured all the votes I needed. Just four years earlier, I had been a city commissioner in little West Miami, and an unknown candidate in a special election for the house. Now I was on the verge of becoming speaker of the Florida House, the first from Miami in over a quarter century, and the first Cuban American ever.

CHAPTER 18

Come Home to Rome

I WOULD NOT BE OFFICIALLY DESIGNATED SPEAKER UNTIL November 2006, three years after I had secured the necessary pledges, and in that long interim anything could happen. Rumors that an attempt might yet be made to challenge me began circulating almost immediately after the last of my opponents had quit the race. My first concern was to keep my voters on board, no matter what enticements might be offered them to reconsider their commitment.

Early in 2004, I hired Richard Corcoran to run my political organization. An attorney from Crystal River, Florida, Richard was smart and highly regarded. His first task was to reorganize my political committee, which was an accounting mess, and after a quick review he decided to close it. Once I appeared to have the votes to be elected speaker, money had begun pouring into the committee. It had to be carefully accounted for and wisely spent. We opened a new committee, which Richard would run, and hired a professional accounting firm to keep the books.

During my campaign for speaker, members repeatedly expressed to me their frustration with their lack of influence over how the house was managed and the policies the leadership decided to pursue. They resented the top-down management style of previous speakers, and insisted on a more collaborative process. I agreed with them, and assured them that as speaker I would leave it to members to create and pursue policy priorities, while I oversaw the management of their agenda.

Richard and I spent many hours devising a leadership structure that would give more power to the members. Critical to the success of any leadership team is choosing the right people for it, and Richard and I gave a lot of thought to finding the right ten to fifteen people to serve as my inner circle. I was influenced by Jim Collins's book *Good to Great* and his advice that a leader's most important function was to get the right people on the bus and assign them seats where they would make the best use of their talents. Once I had the right people, the team would decide the bus's destination.

I also wanted the house to become a vibrant laboratory of ideas, a place that conceived and pursued big, bold policy ideas. In that endeavor, I was most influenced by the creativity and daring of Governor Jeb Bush, who was a one-man idea factory and had used his intelligence, innovation and the authority and bully pulpit of the governor's office not just to improve the status quo on the margins, but to overcome it and change it. His last term would end eight weeks after I became speaker. For eight years, his office had set the policy agenda in Tallahassee, and his retirement would leave a huge policy vacuum in state government. I wanted the house to fill it.

To that end, Richard came up with the idea of writing a book that could serve as a guide for a policy agenda similar to the Contract with America that had helped Republicans win a majority in the U.S. House of Representatives in 1994. Governor Bush pointed out to me that some of his best policy ideas had come from e-mails he'd received from regular Floridians. I decided to follow his example. I traveled the state over the next two years, joining other members at events with voters we called "idearaisers." We picked the best ideas they offered and turned them into a contract with Florida, which we later published and titled "100 Innovative Ideas for Florida's Future."

As I traveled the state in 2003 to prepare for my speakership, Jeanette usually stayed at home. Veronica invited her to services at a local church she attended, the First Baptist Church of Perrine. I had become so immersed in my political career that I had lapsed considerably in my spiritual responsibilities to my family. First Baptist, which would later change its name to Christ Fellowship, sparked a spiritual awakening in Jeanette's life, and eventually in mine, too.

The church's pastor, Rick Blackwood, is a gifted preacher very adept at connecting real-life experiences to biblical teaching. Christ Fellowship's congregation grew immensely under his stewardship. One of the reasons for its popularity and its appeal to Jeanette and me was the excellent children's program it offered on Sundays. I have often heard parents complain about how hard it is to get their children to want to go to church on Sunday. Since Jeanette started attending Christ Fellowship, Amanda and Daniella practically begged us to take them to Sunday services. I saw my children's enthusiasm, and I saw how my wife's faith was deepening and enriching her life, and concluded I shouldn't let denominational divisions disrupt the awakening in their faith. More than anything else, I wanted my children to grow up with a strong faith influence in their lives. I also wanted my family to be part of a wholesome, family-oriented church, and Christ Fellowship provided that. It was a case of history repeating itself.

My parents began attending services at Christ Fellowship as well. My father, who had never been a regular churchgoer, often began insisting to my mother that they attend Sunday services. On Sundays, my entire family—my parents, my sisters and their families, my wife and daughters and I—went to church together, and then had lunch together. Christ Fellowship brought my family closer together and closer to Christ. By the end of 2003, Christ Fellowship was the church where we regularly attended services, and the church we tithed to as well. It was our church.

Yet, theologically, I hadn't left the Catholic Church. Despite our growing relationship with Christ Fellowship, all of our children were baptized Catholics. And on many occasions, especially during the Lenten season, something in me still yearned for my Catholic roots.

One of the reasons so many Roman Catholics like me wander away from the Church in search of something more is because so many of us don't appreciate or understand the fullness of the Catholic faith. The scriptural basis of the Catholic catechism, the theology behind the Church's liturgy, its symbols and sacred traditions—these aren't fully understood by many Catholics, even Catholics who attend Mass regularly and receive the sacraments. And when the Church's teachings or practices are challenged, too many Catholics don't know how to answer them.

Americans increasingly receive their news and information in creative and entertaining ways. And some want to receive their faith that way as well. The gospel, preached by a gifted pastor who ties its message to the routines, problems, aspirations and temptations of our everyday lives, is sometimes more accessible and comprehensible to twenty-first-century Americans in search of a closer relationship with Christ.

Sometimes it seems as if the American Catholic Church struggles to connect its ancient rituals and centuries-old practices steeped in the Old World traditions to the lives of the faithful. I've heard some Catholics say they often leave Mass feeling unfulfilled and detached, as if they just participated in an elaborate ceremony that didn't reveal its purpose or draw them closer to God.

Many Catholics don't understand the richness of our ancient faith, or the powerful purpose behind every moment of the Mass. Every gesture, every word has a purpose and a meaning. Some are taught the practices but not the origins of our traditions, and don't realize the connections of every part of our liturgy to biblical and historical truths.

That was me, unaware of the fullness of the liturgy and the intimate relationship with God the Church's sacraments establish. And so I lapsed and joined another church, a place that provided my family a spiritual life that was more personal and comprehensible.

I admire Rick and the other pastors at Christ Fellowship. I respect how hard they work to meet the spiritual needs of their flock. Every Sunday, I watched desperate, hurting people make the walk to the front of the church and accept Christ into their lives. It is a deeply moving experience to witness.

Every Sunday, I witnessed a powerful message of the gospel that applied to the challenges I was facing, to the fears and doubts I had. It was a message of salvation. But it was also a practical guide to how our faith can influence and guide every aspect of our lives.

I loved Christ Fellowship—I still do. And yet, despite the power of its message, I could never shake the feeling that for me something was missing. Maybe that is why we were never baptized there, or why we never enrolled in the church's introductory class that was a prerequisite to becoming full-fledged members of Christ Fellowship.

The church's services offered a powerful teaching of Christian faith. But I felt I wanted something more. After some reflection, I finally figured out what it was. I craved, literally, the Most Blessed Sacrament, Holy Communion, the sacramental point of contact between the Catholic and the liturgy of heaven. I wondered why there couldn't be a church that offered both a powerful, contemporary gospel message and the actual body and blood of Jesus.

There is an old saying, "Once a Catholic, always a Catholic." I am not sure that is true for everyone, but for me the observation refers to more than nostalgia for the religious institutions and practices of my youth. Something greater than just old habits drew me back to the Catholic faith. It wasn't my memories but my heart that compelled me, a deep sense that the Church holds the fullness of the faith that Jesus Christ founded. That it is built on the full truth, and I felt a calling for this truth.

In late 2004 and early 2005, Ralph Arza, my friend and early supporter of my campaign for speaker, helped lead me back to my Church. Influenced by the strength of his wife's faith, Ralph had become a very active Catholic. He shared with me the books of Scott Hahn, a former Protestant minister who had become a lay evangelist in the Catholic Church. I even read the entire catechism of the Catholic Church.

A deep, almost mysterious, emotional attachment pulled me back to my church. The challenges to the Church's teachings and sacred traditions inspired me to not just practice Catholic liturgy, but comprehend it.

I learned that the Church has answers, not only to the criticism it receives from other churches, but to the incompleteness and yearning that causes people to seek a fuller relationship with God. Every sacrament, every symbol and tradition of the Catholic faith is intended to convey, above everything else, the revelation that God yearns, too, for a relationship with you.

There are plenty of resources at our disposal that communicate that truth. In early 2005, I found a wonderful monthly Catholic publication, *Magnificat*, which I began reading faithfully. When I was in Tallahassee, I attended Mass with Ralph every morning. But I knew I faced a dilemma.

I was becoming a more devout Catholic, while my wife and daughters were growing in another faith tradition. In the pursuit of my temporal ambitions, I had neglected my spiritual responsibilities at home, and my wife and daughters had found their own spiritual home. I had no standing to insist my family return with me to the Church I had fallen back in love with.

I met with a priest to discuss my predicament. He wisely told me I should be grateful that my wife and children were growing stronger in their faith in Jesus Christ. I needed to take charge of my own spiritual growth, he advised, and trust God to take care of the rest. And that is what I did. I attended Mass during the week in Tallahassee, and often alone on Sunday mornings, before accompanying Jeanette and the girls to services at Christ Fellowship.

Our faith journey continues today. On most Saturday nights, we still attend services at Christ Fellowship, especially if Pastor Rick is preaching the sermon. His sermons still inspire me to grow in my Christian faith. On Sunday, we all attend Mass at St. Louis Catholic Church. My children are enrolled in CCD classes there. The girls received their first Holy Communion last May.

Some of my Catholic friends occasionally express concern over my continued association with Christ Fellowship. But I don't think you can go to church too often or spend too much time in fellowship with other Christians, whatever denomination they confess. I fully accept the teachings of the Roman Catholic Church. But God used Christ Fellowship to bring me closer to Him and ultimately to the Catholic Church. As it is often said, He works in mysterious ways.

Some of the biblical teachings I listened to at Christ Fellowship helped make the Catholic Mass come alive for me, and I now see clearly the biblical basis for every word written in the Catholic liturgy. The Church's liturgical calendar is no longer a meaningless routine to me. The days before Christmas are now Advent, the season of hope in anticipation of the greatest gift humanity has ever received. Christmas isn't one day, but a twelve-day celebration of the birth of our Savior. And the bread of the Eucharist isn't just a symbol of Christ's sacrifice for us, but the living Christ, available to us every day of our lives.

To paraphrase a title of one of Scott Hahn's books, I have come home to Rome, but with a real appreciation for the work being done by my brothers and sisters in Christ, who live their faith in other traditions.

As I have dealt with my faith journey in the context of my public life, I have learned to accept the powerful lesson contained therein. Our temporal ambitions are infinitely less important than our spiritual progress, but they are the stuff of life, too, and often beguiling, and they tempt us constantly to misplace our priorities. It's a lifelong temptation, one which I have often succumbed to, and which tempts me still. We all crave to make our mark in this life, and sometimes forget that our place in the next one matters more. I have been ambitious for worldly success. I hope I have been for the right reasons. But I know my own failings well enough to admit that I am prey to the desire to achieve distinction for my own sake, in the mistaken belief that there is happiness in it. It's a struggle to remember that when you've invested so much time and trouble in your success you're likely to value it too dearly.

As for politics, the 2004 legislative session was just as difficult as the previous year. Speaker Byrd was running for the U.S. Senate and almost every decision he made was viewed by the press and many house members as politically motivated. But on an individual level, when the house adjourned in the summer of 2004, I was pleased with my personal progress. My political committee was well organized and well run. I had identified the members I would ask to join my leadership team. Many of them hadn't initially supported me, but they were talented legislators and the right people for the jobs I had in mind for them. I believed we had identified worthy goals for my speakership and devised a good plan to achieve them. I didn't think things could get any better. But they did.

CHAPTER 19

Speaker in Waiting

T HE SPEAKER IN WAITING DOES NOT HAVE FORMAL POW-
ers in the legislature, but the distinction does come with political responsibilities. Beginning in early 2005, I was expected to lead the Florida
Republican Party's support for our house candidates in the 2006 election
cycle. It wasn't an official office, but by long-standing tradition, the next
speaker is responsible for raising millions of dollars to fund the house campaign's operation, and makes the hiring and spending decisions there as
well. I would also be expected to fill in for incoming speaker Allan Bense
when he was unable to attend a fund-raising event for the party or one of
our candidates.

I was still mostly unknown to Floridians outside my district, but my
leadership of the campaign committee and my impending speakership
were the beginning of my ascent to statewide political prominence. I was
eager for the responsibilities and enhanced public profile my new leadership role would give me. I was not, however, prepared for the greater scrutiny accorded to prominent political figures. In the months following my
election as speaker, I would make political and personal decisions that
would cause me considerable political difficulty and embarrassment in the
future when I tried to explain them to a skeptical press.

I spent much of the summer of 2004 cultivating relationships with the
party's leading donors, many of whom didn't know me. I authorized my

political committee to pay a retainer to my fund-raiser, Bridget Nocco, who organized the meetings and would later serve as the finance director for house campaigns. I paid my consultant Richard Corcoran a retainer so he could afford to take time away from his law practice and help my political operation. And in the fall of 2004, I also authorized my committee to hire my nephew Landy, as well as Jeanette's brother Carlos and her cousin Mauricio, and I sent them to help several house campaigns around the state. They were too young to rent a car, so we rented my mother-in-law's old van to use as transportation.

I didn't consider these decisions to be anything less than practical and appropriate. Bridget and Richard were instrumental in organizing my political activities. And I needed young, inexpensive campaign aides to help me, and Landy, Carlos and Mauricio were capable and available. But years later, as a U.S. Senate candidate, some of the press would see things differently. The retainers paid to Richard and Bridget would be deemed lavish. And I would be accused of funneling money to my relatives. I didn't have enough experience to know it then, but I would learn in the years ahead that every decision I made, even the smallest personnel and spending decisions, could be potentially exploited by my political adversaries.

I had my own reelection race in 2004. A young Democratic activist challenged me, and while my district was safely Republican, I didn't want to take any chances. As the future speaker of the Florida House, I couldn't afford to win reelection by a smaller margin than expected, which might encourage a late challenge to my speakership. I raised a considerable sum for my campaign and used it to run television and radio advertisements. I would win reelection by a wide margin, but the full-scale campaign I ran had an additional benefit as well. Most state legislators are unknown outside their districts—some aren't even very well known in their own districts. My 2004 reelection campaign raised my profile considerably, not just in my district but throughout South Florida.

My personal circumstances greatly improved in 2004 as well. That summer, Mike Corcoran introduced me to attorneys at Broad and Cassel, a large firm with offices in several Florida cities. The firm's Miami office, its founding headquarters, had become stagnant, and they were looking to revitalize it. They offered me a $300,000 annual salary to be of counsel to the firm—nearly three times what I earned at Becker and Poliakoff. I was torn. I had been in difficult financial straits when Alan Becker had offered me a job, and I was indebted to him. But I couldn't afford to refuse the financial security the Broad and Cassel offer would provide. I was thirty-three years old and the sole income earner in a young family. I had a mortgage, student loans and other debts, and we lived paycheck to paycheck. We had outgrown our two-bedroom home in West Miami, and my salary at Broad and Cassel would make it possible for us to buy a bigger house and settle some of our debts. I asked Alan if he could match the Broad and Cassel offer. He couldn't. I felt terrible about leaving Becker and Poliakoff, but knew it was in our family's best interests that I accept the offer.

In October, we learned Jeanette was pregnant with our third child. After the scare at Daniella's birth, our joy was tempered with worries for her health. We hadn't planned her first two pregnancies and the third wasn't an exception. It was a blessing, and we accepted it as such. So we took every precaution to ensure she wasn't predisposed to postpartum hemorrhaging. She had five ultrasounds during her pregnancy and, to our relief, every one indicated a normal pregnancy and uncomplicated delivery.

We found a place two blocks from our current home in December 2004. The two-story, four-bedroom house with a pool hadn't been built yet and the address was still an empty lot when we put down a deposit to buy it for $550,000. Like all preconstruction homes during the overheated real estate boom, the house would appreciate in value once it was built. We added several upgrades to it as well, which we paid for in cash. When we closed on the finished house a year later, it was appraised at over $700,000, which made it possible to apply for a home equity loan. We used the line of credit to add more upgrades and buy furniture.

I had much to be thankful for as 2004 came to a close. We were expecting a baby in the summer of 2005. We were financially secure for the first time in our married lives. We would move into our new house by Christmas the following year, and we had paid off some of our debts. I would be speaker of the Florida House in two years' time. And my future, after I retired from the legislature and returned full-time to my legal career, looked bright.

I wanted to use the two years before I became speaker to concentrate on building the leadership team and governing structure I would need to succeed. So I spent much of 2005 and 2006 working on issues important to my district, strengthening my relationships with my colleagues and running house campaigns.

Running a statewide political operation is expensive. In addition to the traditional responsibilities of the incoming speaker to conduct meetings and fund-raisers with candidates and donors in every part of Florida, I also participated in the "idearaisers" we had conceived as the basis for the policy agenda I would pursue as speaker. All these activities incurred expenses. There were expenses associated with travel—airline tickets, hotel rooms, car rentals, meals. Equipment costs were substantial as well. We couldn't use state property for political purposes. The equipment used for every phone call I made or e-mail I sent or speech I wrote for house campaigns had to be paid for with political funds. And there were a variety of incidental expenses, like flowers for a donor who had suffered a death in the family.

In the past, previous incoming legislative leaders had these costs defrayed by asking lobbyists to pay them. It was not unusual for some members to ask a lobbyist to call his credit card number into a restaurant to pick up the tab for a meal the committee hosted or to ask a lobbyist to lend the committee his private plane. Richard Corcoran strongly advised, and I agreed, that I should discontinue the practice. Lobbyists could still make financial donations to house campaigns, but we wouldn't rely on them to pay our bills.

I could have paid for my travel and other expenses and then sought reimbursement from the state party. But rather than see my name appear dozens of times in the party's financial reports, I used a party-issued American Express business credit card from February 2005 through November 2008 to pay for party-related expenses. There was nothing unusual about it—the party typically provided charge cards to legislative leaders to pay for party-related expenses. The monthly statements made it easy to identify and itemize specific political expenditures for the financial report the party filed quarterly. Unlike most credit cards, you can't roll over American Express charges from month to month. The balance has to be paid every month. The card was secured under my name and Social Security number and with my personal credit. I would be responsible for paying any charges that were not incurred in my work for the party.

From January of 2005 until October of 2008 I charged about $160,000 in party-authorized expenses on my party-issued American Express card.

Eighty-nine percent of it was for travel, lodging, car rentals, fuel and meals. In fact, during my two years as speaker, we saved Florida taxpayers $32,000 by having the party, and not the state, pay for my travel costs to and from Tallahassee.

But from time to time a few personal expenses were charged to the card as well. For example, I pulled the wrong card from my wallet to pay for pavers. My travel agent mistakenly used the card to pay for a family reunion in Georgia—a single expenditure that represented 65 percent of personal charges on the card. Each time, I identified the charges and paid the costs myself, directly to American Express. The Republican Party of Florida didn't pay a single one of them.

Nevertheless, in hindsight, I wish that none of them had ever been charged. When the statements were later leaked during my Senate campaign, they invited press skepticism, confused some of the public and allowed an opponent to suggest the party had paid for personal expenses. As often as it is remarked, it always bears repeating: in politics appearances are as important as reality.

In my final legislative session before becoming speaker, Speaker Allan Bense appointed me the chairman of a select committee he had created in the wake of the U.S. Supreme Court's decision *Kelo vs. City of New London*. The gist of the ruling held that a government could seize private property by eminent domain and transfer it to another private party if it deemed it to be in the public interest. The decision sent shock waves across America, angering Americans who believed their property rights were sacred. States scrambled to figure out ways to get around the ruling. It wasn't a partisan issue. Democrats and Republicans opposed it. My job as chairman of the select committee was to deliver a bipartisan legislative fix that could serve as a model for the nation.

But for a brief stint as chairman of the House Claims Committee, I hadn't much experience running a committee. I had always been in leadership, and hadn't needed a committee chairmanship to acquire influence in the house. This would be a big test of my leadership abilities, and I could sense people were watching for clues to how I would conduct myself as speaker. We spent several months taking testimony from members, the public and outside experts. We carefully crafted both a bill and a constitutional amendment in an open and collaborative process. I let a freshman member, Dean Cannon, offer the legislation and manage the debate. Years later, Dean would become speaker, and I think that early opportunity to demonstrate his leadership helped him win the office. When we finished, I was commended by all involved, including the most prominent Democrats on the committee, which gave my colleagues confidence I could lead the house fairly and productively as speaker.

I attended the Super Bowl in Jacksonville in January of 2005. My fondest memory of the experience had nothing to do with the game. I saw a father and his little boy both dressed in Philadelphia Eagles jerseys and caps, both of them excited to share a cherished experience they knew they would always remember, just as my father and I had at many Dolphins games in the past and were doing that day. For the first time in my life I felt a strong yearning for a son. I had two beautiful daughters, whom I loved so completely I had never felt a moment's regret that I didn't have a son. But when, a little more than four months later, Anthony Luis Rubio was born, I was ecstatic.

I was terribly anxious when Jeanette went into labor because of her experience after Daniella's birth. The doctor who delivered him was as prepared as he could be in the event she hemorrhaged again. He had three of his best nurses in the maternity ward assisting him, and an operating room and anesthesiologist on standby. As it turned out, Jeanette's labor was the briefest and least complicated of her four pregnancies, and there were no complications after Anthony's birth.

That morning I held my infant son in my arms and, as I did with all our children, I imagined our lives together. Of course, it included football.

I would be officially designated speaker that September, and sworn in as speaker in the next legislature. Even that experience, the realization of an ambition I had worked hard to achieve, could never compare to the experience of holding your son for the first time, and the pure, almost otherworldly love you experience when your children are born. I try to remember that as I make my way in this world, so I don't forget where my heart truly belongs.

I spent the summer after Anthony was born working on the speech I would give when I was designated speaker, devising a writing regimen around his feeding schedule. Jeanette would go to bed around eleven; I would feed him at midnight, get him to sleep and write until dawn. Then I would go to bed until nine.

I rewrote the speech many times. I wanted it to accomplish several things. I wanted to honor my parents and the sacrifices they had made for me. I wanted to acknowledge the Cuban exile community that had helped raise me and then elected me to office. Finally, I wanted to show the house the purpose I had for my speakership. For years, the driving force behind all significant policies in the state government had been the vision of the man I most admired in Florida politics: Governor Jeb Bush. I didn't believe any of the candidates running to succeed him as governor would follow his example of bold leadership, but the house could fill the vacuum he would leave.

On the day of my designation, the chamber was packed with virtually every prominent Republican in the state, who had all come to hear me deliver the most important speech of my political career to date.

I used the speech to announce my plans to travel the state and join legislators as they asked their constituents to give us their recommendations for our policy agenda. I wanted to make the announcement in a dramatic way. I had book jackets printed for "100 Innovative Ideas for Florida's Future," and a copy of the book placed in each of their desks. I asked them to look in their desks and open the book they found there. When they did, they saw the pages were blank. I let a few moments pass before I told them the pages would be filled by the time we met in session in November 2006, after we had enlisted the help of our constituents and selected their best ideas. The people of Florida would set our agenda; their priorities would be ours.

I closed the speech by telling the hypothetical story of a young woman.

Today, somewhere in Florida, a young single mother will give birth to her first child. Maybe she comes from a broken home, or maybe, even worse, she has grown up bouncing from one foster home to the next. In either case, she's probably grown up in poverty, trapped in failing schools. She reads at a fifth-grade level. She never graduated high school. Lost and alone, she has spent the better part of her young life in search of someone to love her. And, in that quest, she has been in and out of a series of relationships with irresponsible and abusive men, including the now absent father of her new child. While she receives a significant amount of public assistance, it has done little to improve her life. She is trapped in poverty. Up to this point in her life, little has gone right for her. But, today, her life has changed forever. Today, she held her firstborn child in her arms for the first time. And, at that moment, she was no different than parents all over the world, rich and poor, privileged and disadvantaged alike. Today, when she looked into the eyes of her child for the first time, she saw what your mother saw in your eyes and what my mother saw in mine. She saw all the hopes and dreams she once had for herself. And in her heart burns the hope that everything that has gone wrong in her life will go right for that child, that all the opportunities she never had, her child will.

When I finished, I noticed several people in the audience apparently tearing up, including our lieutenant governor, Toni Jennings. It had been the most powerful part of my remarks and I had almost been convinced not to include it in the speech. All of my advisers had opposed using it, worried it made me sound like a Democrat. Only one person had felt strongly I should keep it in the speech: Jeanette. Not for the first nor the last time, I was glad I had listened to her.

I wanted to use the story to achieve two objectives. The first was to remind the members we had an obligation to use our time in public office to make a positive difference in the lives of the people we served. The second was to emphasize the importance of empowerment and upward mobility, and make that the purpose of our work.

We hung up pictures in my office of Florida's "Unsung Heroes," ordinary people throughout our state who were making positive differences in others' lives. They were a reminder to us, and to anyone who entered our office, that our obligation was to the people of Florida—not to politics, not to power, but to people.

I knew from my own life's experience that the purpose of my parents' lives was to help their children achieve the dreams they had been unable to achieve for themselves. In my campaigns, I learned that was not just my family's story but the common aspiration of people everywhere. The opportunity to give your children the chance to do what you could not do is what makes America special. I wanted Republicans to be defined by how well we helped every mother and father in Florida give their children a decent chance to live the best of their dreams.

The day was and always will be a special memory for me. It was obviously a milestone in my public career. My parents were there. They saw their son enjoy the success and distinction they had dreamed for me and sacrificed everything for so I would have the opportunity to attain it. My children were there, as I hope to be with them someday to witness their successes.

My speech was broadcast to Cuba on Radio Martí. I don't know how many people in the country of my ancestors actually heard it, but if only one person had, I would have been very pleased. For I am the child of immigrants, an American with a history that began somewhere else and with a special place in his heart for the land of lost dreams his parents had left so their children wouldn't lose theirs.

CHAPTER 20

Speaker of the House

B Y THE TIME I WAS SWORN IN AS SPEAKER OF THE FLOR-
ida House of Representatives on November 20, 2006, I was certain I
had done everything right. I had planned my transition carefully. I had
designed a new leadership structure for the house that would give greater
authority to and demand greater accountability from its members. I had
initiated and led an outreach to Florida voters to solicit ideas for an ambitious policy agenda. I had hired some of the most talented political profes-
sionals in the state as my staff. I wanted my speakership to be innovative,
bold and accomplished, and I didn't want to waste a minute of my term on
anything that didn't advance that ambition.

Politics, however, doesn't operate with that degree of efficiency, no
matter how prepared and determined you are. It's a great business for
teaching humility, even if you don't believe you require a lesson in the
virtue.

I chose twelve members to serve as my leadership team. We met regularly in different parts of the state in the months preceding my swearing in,
occasionally holding focus groups with voters. The focus groups helped us
communicate the policies we would pursue in the coming year. More important, they gave us the opportunity to listen to voters' concerns. At the
time, Florida's economy and the national economy were still strong. Yet
there was a real sense of unease among the voters in our focus groups, as if

they anticipated an imminent downturn. They sensed that rising property insurance rates and rising property taxes were the edge of an oncoming economic storm that would soon engulf them. The intensity of their worries influenced the selection of our policy priorities as much as it influenced the language we used to advocate for them.

I had been very deliberate in choosing the members of my leadership. I knew I would depend on each of them for the support and counsel I needed to be the kind of speaker I wanted to be. But I would lose two of them before I had even taken the oath of office.

Jeff Kottkamp was the first to go. He had been one of my rivals in my race for speaker, but I admired his ability and trusted him. That summer, Charlie Crist chose him to be his running mate. I was happy for him, but sorry to lose him, and I had to scramble to find a replacement.

Before they decided on Jeff, the Crist team had approached me to see if I would agree to be vetted for the lieutenant governor's nomination. I don't think they seriously considered me—I suppose it was an attempt to flatter the incoming speaker of the house. I turned them down. Had I been interested, and had word got out I was under consideration, it would have created chaos among house Republicans as members scrambled to join the race to replace me as speaker.

My decision would prove fortunate for another reason. Had I agreed to be vetted, I would have given the Crist campaign an enormous head start in their opposition research when I decided to oppose him for the U.S. Senate nomination three years later.

Losing Jeff was a blow. But it was the loss of another member of my leadership team that would be one of the most painful experiences of my entire political career. Ralph Arza and I hadn't always gotten along. We had once had the same ambitions and viewed each other as rivals. But we eventually became close friends and allies. Ralph had been one of my most loyal and active supporters. Ours was a genuine friendship and not, as political friendships can be, an acquaintanceship of mutual convenience. My nephew Landy dates Ralph's oldest daughter.

Ralph had gotten into a political tug-of-war with the Miami superintendent of schools. The dispute turned ugly when several people claimed Ralph had used a racial slur when referring to the superintendent, who was African American. One of his accusers was a fellow Republican member of our Miami delegation. And when in October of 2006 Ralph left a voice mail for a fellow legislator in which he used the same slur he was accused of using before, he was forced to withdraw his bid for reelection.

I wanted the house to operate differently than it had in the past, when the speaker had so much authority that members could always assign the blame for any failure to the "fourth floor"—code for the speaker's office. The speaker had always decided which committees would have jurisdiction over legislation, and his decision could mean life or death for a bill. If he assigned it to one or two committees, a bill had a decent chance of passing. If he assigned it to five or six committees, the sixty-day legislative session would expire before all the committees had disposed of the bill.

I decided to relinquish the most important power a speaker possessed, and give it to the members of my leadership team who would chair the house committees. Committee chairmen would decide which subcommittee would consider a bill or if the full committee would assume that responsibility. I combined the budget and policy authorities in each committee as well. Committees would now receive a budget allocation and they would decide how to fund their policies within the limits of their allocation.

Under my speakership, committee chairmen would have more power than ever before, but a greater share of responsibility as well, and greater accountability. I trusted the leaders I had chosen. I had spent a lot of time with them during the months before I was sworn in, and I had a good sense of their abilities and interests, which informed my decisions about which responsibilities to assign them.

A series of devastating storms in Florida over the last few years had nearly wiped out the private property insurance market in the state, and the few companies that were still offering property insurance were charging exorbitant rates. It was the biggest political issue in Florida. Just weeks after I was sworn in as speaker, the new governor, Charlie Crist, called the legislature into special session to pass his proposal to resolve the crisis. It was a purely political remedy. He wanted to go to war with the insurance companies. He wanted to give the state-run insurance carrier the authority to compete in the private insurance market. He didn't worry about the long-term consequences of his approach. He knew in the short term the move would be met with widespread approval from Floridians who had become very angry with insurance companies. The longer-term consequences of his solution, however, could make them even angrier. If the public carrier, which was, of course, subsidized by the state, was unable to pay claims after another devastating storm or series of storms, taxpayers would have to cover the shortfall.

The politics of opposing the governor's plan were daunting. A newly elected Republican governor with the support of Republicans and Democrats in the Florida Senate would accuse any member of the house who opposed his proposal of being in the pocket of the hated insurance industry.

We tried to modify the bill with some small successes. We limited the public carrier's ability to expand, and got everyone to agree that the measure would be temporary. When the private market recovered and rates came down, the public carrier would begin to exit the private market. But other than these small changes, the legislation gave the governor most of what he wanted. The house leadership team decided to take the small concessions we had gotten, pass the bill and live to fight another day.

Nothing seemed to go smoothly in my first months as speaker. I learned that the press covers the speaker of the house differently than they cover the speaker in waiting. The fun started just a few days after I was sworn in.

During the transition, outgoing speaker Allan Bense had asked us for our input on making improvements to the house office complex. We made several suggestions, one of which was to turn an unused, nondescript space on the third floor into a members-only dining room. The space already had a kitchen, and the only improvements required were to knock down a wall and furnish it with plastic tables and chairs. We had two purposes for making the suggestion. The first was simply to give members a place where they could buy breakfast or lunch without being surrounded by lobbyists.

The second reason was to help improve bipartisan comity in the legislature. Many members hardly knew each other personally. In the era of term limits, members simply weren't around long enough to form close relations with members of the other party. Most knew one another only from debates on the floor or in committee. The house had become less civil than it should be, and we thought a dining room open to all members might serve as a place where legislators from both parties could get to know one another better, which might improve the civility of the place. Anticipating some criticism in the press, we showed the new dining room to reporters before I was sworn in. None of them seemed particularly interested in it.

Changes we had made to the committee structure in the house also necessitated some changes to house offices. I had created a position of Democratic ranking member on the committees, and gave Minority Leader Dan Gelber the authority to choose his ranking members—an authority no speaker that I know of had ever given the leader of the opposition before. But now we needed office space for the new ranking members in the committee suites or near them. And because we had combined budget and policy authority in the committees, we had given the committees more staff, which also required additional office space. The only change I made to my own office was to remove a spiral staircase that connected the speaker's office to the majority leader's office.

I didn't expect any of these changes to be controversial. But multiple media outlets would soon report them as an extravagant waste of public funds, claiming we had spent hundreds of thousands of dollars to remodel my office and build a fancy dining room. It was inaccurate, sensationalized reporting, to say the least, and disappointing. Even more disappointing was the failure of Democratic members, the beneficiaries of many of the improvements, to defend my decisions.

The reports were followed by editorials implying I had gone on a wild spending spree in my first days as speaker. It was my first experience with intense media scrutiny, and I can't say I enjoyed it much. The fact that we had inexpensively furnished an existing space didn't stop some reporters from claiming I had built a fancy dining room. Neither did the fact that almost all the changes we had made to existing committee office space discourage them from reporting that I had spent thousands to spruce up my own office.

Many of Jeb Bush's aides were available when he left office. They were smart, talented policy experts who had helped build Jeb's reputation as an innovative, bold and effective executive. I admired them and valued their expertise and creativity. We hired dozens of them. They were already on the public payroll, so the hires were lateral, which meant they could keep the salaries they had made in the governor's office. Almost none of them worked for me directly; most of them were hired as staff directors for the committees. They, too, became targets for reporters.

Just weeks in the office, and I was taking quite a beating. I had hoped the press would first focus on the one hundred innovative policy ideas the house would pursue during my speakership. But that was naive of me. The experience taught me an unpleasant although useful lesson about how reporters, especially print reporters, are under constant pressure to uncover controversy and scandal even where none exists.

The year 2007 began with the challenge of Governor Crist's populist approach to the property insurance crisis, and the different style he brought to the office of governor. Jeb was bold in policy, a man of ideas and ideals. He was mature in judgment and unafraid to hold fast to an unpopular decision if he thought it was right. Charlie Crist was his opposite. He is a polite and pleasant man, but he didn't really have any fixed ideals or a particular interest in policy. And rather than attempt to persuade an angry public to be careful not to demand policies they might come to regret, he was the first to pick up a pitchfork and storm the castle. He had beaten us in a game of chicken over the property insurance bill, threatening to veto anything that didn't meet his demands. We won a few concessions and let it go. I had passed a bill I didn't like. I had been mired in a press firestorm about office construction and staff hires. I had lost Ralph Arza. In February, my chief of staff quit to run for an early opening in the state senate, as did two more of my twelve leaders, including my speaker pro tempore, Dennis Baxley. It had been a rocky start, to say the least.

CHAPTER 21

Drop Like a Rock

JEB BUSH WOULD HAVE BORROWED A TERM FROM JIM Collins and called it a B-HAG, a big, hairy, audacious goal. Eliminating property taxes on homes and replacing them with a consumption tax was the boldest reform in our 100 Ideas project. Soaring property taxes had become a crushing burden on many Florida families. A consumption tax would have taken less of their income. When you ran the numbers for them and showed them their tax burden would be smaller, you could convince them to support it. But it was an easy position to demagogue, and a very heavy political lift. Opponents would focus on the increase in the sales tax, ignoring the elimination of the property tax.

The leadership team debated whether to chance bold reform, settle for a more modest approach or adopt the purely cosmetic changes Governor Crist had proposed during his campaign. We voted to go big.

We unveiled the plan a few weeks before the start of the regular session, and it dominated the news throughout the state. I was pleasantly surprised at the initial reaction. Local governments expressed concern with the proposal, but most political figures offered support for it or reserved judgment. Then the gravity of politics set in, and we had a huge fight on our hands.

Democrats who had at first supported or shown interest in the idea received instructions from their party leadership to begin attacking it, and retreated to their default position of opposing it as a boon to wealthy home owners. The Florida Senate played the usual Tallahassee game of seizing a major house initiative as a hostage to use in negotiations over the senate's legislative priorities. Even Republican house members were nervous. Senate veteran legislators employed consultants and lobbyists to warn members they would expose themselves to attacks in the next election for supporting a sales tax increase.

The press, too, became skeptical. Only one editorial board gave the idea fair consideration. The others cast it as some sort of supply-side trick to help the rich get richer and bankrupt local governments. Some even implied I supported the plan because I would personally profit from it, calculating how much I would save on my property taxes if the legislation became law.

We had taken the plunge, though, and there was nothing to be done but fight our way through, win or lose. I was shorthanded in the fight. My chief of staff, who had been instrumental in organizing the leadership and our agenda, had left, as had four of the original members of my leadership team. Then one of my closest friends in the leadership, Stan Mayfield, was diagnosed with esophageal cancer, and would spend most of the session in Houston, where he was treated. We had spent over two years choosing and building our leadership, and creating an esprit de corps among us. Now almost half of them were gone, replaced by people who hadn't been involved in our planning. We also started too late. We should have begun advocating for the plan in the summer before the election so we could have claimed it as a mandate. Or, at the very least, we should have started when we released "100 Innovative Ideas for Florida's Future." But it took much longer than I'd expected to reach consensus in the leadership, and by the time we did there were only two weeks left before the session convened.

Our first task was to shore up support with rank-and-file members. I couldn't afford to lose more than a couple of Republicans when the issue came to a vote. But I knew winning the public opinion battle was more difficult and more important if we were to overcome Democratic opposition, and the reluctance of the governor and the senate. I traveled the state extensively, attending rallies in support of the plan. I did countless television and radio interviews explaining and defending the plan. Support for the measure didn't appreciably increase. It remained a fifty-fifty proposition. But we did succeed in making property taxes the biggest issue in the state.

The experience made me a better public servant. I learned how to fight a big political battle. I had to convince voters our plan was sound and in their best interests. I had to defend it from aggressive attacks. I had to answer tough questions about it from the media. I had to work closely with activists across the state. I didn't realize it at the time, of course, but the seeds for my election to the U.S. Senate in 2010 were planted in the spring of 2007.

We passed the plan in the house with almost unanimous support from Republican members. But the session would adjourn before the senate took up the legislation, and it was clear to us that Governor Crist was working with senate Republicans to undermine us. I had never had a very good relationship with Charlie Crist. He, and especially his staff, viewed me suspiciously from the outset. I had been close to Jeb Bush, and I had hired several staffers who had worked for Crist's opponent in the Republican primary. The property tax fight hardened their suspicions, and bred what can be fairly described as mutual antipathy. Crist was determined not to be outflanked on the issue by us. In a press conference, he boasted he would demand that a new law cause property taxes to "drop like a rock." The plan he had advocated as a candidate to double the homestead exemption (a property tax exemption on the first $25,000 of value you could claim on your primary residence) would have reduced property taxes only negligibly. But that hardly mattered to him. His real purpose was to make certain he got the credit for whichever plan passed.

The senate could wait out the session without taking action on the plan. But it couldn't avoid it forever—the issue had become too salient. We insisted that a special session be convened to resolve the issue, and the senate had to agree. The governor lobbied the senate to pass his plan. The idea polled well, which was why he had proposed it during his campaign. But I criticized it publicly, explaining to the press and anyone who would listen that doubling the homestead exemption most certainly would not make property taxes "drop like a rock."

We would do our best, but our plan to replace property taxes with a consumption tax would never be popular enough to prevail. Without the governor's support, we couldn't put enough heat on the senate to pass it. I made the pragmatic decision to give up the idea of scrapping the entire property tax system and push for serious reform of the existing system instead. Many house Republicans were upset with my decision. They had taken a tough vote in the house, and many of them felt they had put their reelection at risk only to see our plan abandoned. Some of the staff thought we were showing weakness by caving under pressure.

It's always easier in the legislative process to defeat an idea than to pass it. The side that wants something is always at a disadvantage to the side that wants to stop something. Property tax reform wasn't a priority for senators—they had been forced to do something about the issue because we had made it a priority for Florida voters. But we hadn't succeeded in making our plan the public's clear preference.

Time wasn't on our side, either. I would have a year left as speaker in the next session, and the closer I got to the end of my term, the less clout I would have. I worried, too, that when house Republicans returned home they would be raked over the coals by their local governments, and return to Tallahassee reluctant to take up the issue again. I was convinced the special session in the summer of 2007 would be our last and best chance to pass meaningful reform. Even though it was not our original plan, we had an obligation to get the best deal we could for our constituents.

That summer, the house and senate agreed to substantial reforms. They weren't as far-reaching as we had hoped, but the bill wasn't what I called a Tallahassee Special—reform in name only. The legislation made statutory reductions in the property tax code and contained an amendment to the Florida constitution that, if passed by the voters, would have reduced property taxes even further. Floridians would realize real savings on their property taxes.

We held a press conference to celebrate the achievement with the senate president and Governor Crist. The governor brought a rock to emphasize that, with the passage of the bill, taxes would drop like a rock. We hung a sign behind us that heralded the bill as the single largest tax cut in Florida's history.

If the story had ended there, it would have been an enormous legislative achievement. But before voters had a chance to have their say, the Florida courts declared the constitutional amendment "confusing and misleading" and struck it off the ballot. The pressure was back on to do something about property taxes, and another special session was convened in October.

The senate was out of patience. Senators had never wanted to address the issue but, thanks to us, had spent most of the year dealing with it. They felt they had acted in good faith and given it their best shot. We had passed a bill, and the courts had struck it down. Now they just wanted to be rid of the issue as quickly as it could be arranged. They lined up in support of Crist's original plan to double the homestead exemption, a plan I did consider a Tallahassee Special.

That October, in 2007, we put together another property tax reform plan in the house with nearly unanimous bipartisan support and sent it to the senate. In its eagerness to put the issue behind them, the senate ignored it. They took up and passed the Crist proposal, sent it to us and went home. Many of my colleagues were offended, and argued that after creating huge expectations for a bill that would dramatically reduce taxes, we would make a lot of people angry if we settled for the minor changes offered in the governor's plan. Better to reject it, they advised, go home and fight the issue again next year. They had a point.

But if we rejected it, there would be no property tax relief that year. And in order to get an item on the ballot for a special election in January 2008, the law required we had to pass something by the end of October 2007. I thought voters would be angrier if we passed nothing than if we passed Crist's proposal. Crist would blame us for the failure, and voters would think we had taken our ball and gone home rather than compromise. I suspected Crist was secretly rooting for us to block the bill, worried that if it passed voters would realize how little it accomplished. I figured he would rather have had a fall guy to shift the blame to than be held accountable for his own position.

I knew the bill wasn't good enough. I knew it would be hard to bring the issue back up if we passed it. But I also knew we had gone as far as we could. We had done our best, and fallen short. I accepted the hard reality of our situation, and let the bill pass.

The press hailed it as a big win for Charlie Crist, and a big loss for me and the house. I suppose it was, but it was a bigger loss for the people of Florida. A speaker's legacy is achieved in his first year, and his influence wanes in the second year. For better or worse, property tax reform would be my legacy, and it was incomplete, to put it charitably.

Our fourth child, Dominick, was born in late August 2007. As the year came to an end, I looked forward to my final year as speaker with a feeling that we had some unfinished business to address. We took another shot at meaningful property tax reform in the next session. We devised a new proposal. We held rallies to promote it. We collected signatures to get it on the ballot. We passed it in the house. But the senate, once again, disregarded it. The senate president wanted to concentrate his efforts on reforming the state's university system, and he refused to be drawn back into the property tax debate. Governor Crist didn't have much of a policy agenda in 2008.

I spent most of my final year in the Florida legislature managing the house rather than undertaking bold new initiatives. We did pass into law a number of policies from our 100 Ideas project that had been held up in the senate the previous year. We also confronted a few difficult issues we had not anticipated addressing. And I took a few more hits in the press that year as well.

I was accused by the *Miami Herald* of trying to rig the state bidding process for concessions on Florida's turnpike on behalf of a close, personal friend, Max Alvarez. Max had escaped Cuba as a young boy. He's a self-made man who owns dozens of gas stations in Miami. He talked to me several times about his concern that the Florida Department of Transportation had made it impossible for all but the biggest companies to bid successfully on contracts to own and operate gas stations on the turnpike by insisting that companies bid for both gas and food concessions together. The limited competition not only hurt smaller companies like Max's, but cost the state revenue. I'd seen this kind of fix before on the local level, when a bid's specifications are written in such a way that only one or two companies have a shot at a contract. I agreed to support legislation that required the concessions for food and gas to be bid separately.

Some folks at the Department of Transportation were displeased by my position, as were the handful of companies that could have bid on both concessions. They told the *Miami Herald* that I had intervened in the bidding process to give an advantage to a friend. Of course, the legislature couldn't award or deny a contract. Nor did any provision in the legislation give Max an advantage over his competitors. But the *Herald* apparently believed the story and insinuated that I had attempted to grease the skids for a friend and supporter.

I felt I was vindicated a few months later when a new contract was awarded to a large Spanish conglomerate, but not before a series of bid disputes were filed by the losing bidders, alleging that the bid had been rigged to give it to the largest company.

A few weeks later, the subject of my home equity loan became a matter of press scrutiny. I hadn't included it in my financial disclosure. That was my oversight, and I deserved to be taken to task for it. But the press also insinuated the loan itself was improper. Of course, it wasn't. And once we showed we paid a standard interest rate and that the home had been properly appraised, the issue went away. I was offended by the insinuation, and thrown off stride for a while. But I've come to accept that a thick hide is a prerequisite for the job.

I recovered my balance after the controversies subsided in time to finish our work on a few important issues before my career in the Florida legislature reached its end. The previous summer the governor had issued a series of executive orders instituting global warming cap-and-trade regulations, which would become law unless the legislature overrode them. We had the difficult task of coming up with a bill the governor would sign that would override his executive orders. We found a solution. We passed a bill that instructed Florida's Department of Environmental Protection to create an outline of a cap-and-trade plan for the state. However, the plan couldn't take effect unless the legislature approved it. The governor signed it because he could claim he got a signature initiative passed by the legislature. The legislature passed it because we knew we could stop it later, no matter what the governor did.

When we ran against each other a couple of years later, in an effort to convince Republican voters he was the more conservative candidate, Crist falsely claimed I had supported cap and trade. He cited an interview I gave in which I made the assumption that some form of cap and trade would eventually become national law. Both the Republican front-runner for president, John McCain, and the Democratic candidates, Senators Barack Obama and Hillary Clinton, supported a cap-and-trade system. I suggested that Florida should prepare for the inevitable by adopting a policy of its own. But I didn't support cap and trade. I wrote an opinion piece in the *Miami Herald* denouncing the governor's executive orders shortly after he announced them.

Several state immigration enforcement measures were proposed that year as well. I didn't want the state to assume a responsibility that properly belonged to the federal government, and I didn't want the house to waste time on legislation I knew the senate wouldn't pass. And many of our members didn't want to debate an issue that would divide the Republican conference along ethnic lines. I made my position clear in numerous public comments. But I did not instruct committee chairmen with jurisdiction over the issue to refuse to consider the legislation. They made the decision not to take it up. Nevertheless, some anti-illegal immigration groups charged I was responsible for preventing the house from addressing the issue, a charge they and Crist would repeat when I ran for the Senate in 2010.

For me personally, the most difficult issue we addressed that year concerned the treatment of children with autism. The advocacy group Autism Speaks had targeted Florida as part of a national campaign to mandate insurance coverage for autism. I knew very little about the disorder before 2008, but that changed when Jeanette and I began to meet families of autistic children. We met with parents who couldn't afford the expensive early intervention their kids needed—desperate, devoted moms and dads who loved their children dearly and wanted nothing more than to give their kids a chance to live productive lives. We were stunned by the number of our friends who had autistic children. I wanted to find a way to help families with autistic children or children with other disabilities, who deserved the assistance of a good and generous society.

I impaneled a special committee charged with improving the services the state provided to children with disabilities. I made sure to appoint both Democrats and Republicans who had expressed an interest in the issue. They produced sweeping legislation that could have helped thousands of families. It was late in the session, but I thought an issue that affected so many people, and moved so many others, would encourage the senate to act swiftly. But the old, tired politics of Tallahassee can thwart even the best of intentions.

A state senator who was in his last term had sponsored an autism bill

year after year and had never succeeded in getting it passed. It addressed
only services for autism, and not for children with other disabilities. It
wasn't as expansive as our legislation. As a tribute to him, the senate took
up and passed his bill, not ours, and sent it back to us, daring the house to
vote against it.

Once again, in my last days as speaker, I was trapped by the senate. I
had learned during the property insurance and property tax debates that
once the legislature addressed an issue, however ineffectually, it was extremely difficult to get it to revisit the subject the following year. If I agreed
to pass the senate's autism-only bill, I would disappoint thousands of families, including members of the house who had children with disabilities
and had worked so hard to put together and pass our bill. We had raised
their hopes, and settling for an autism-only bill would be a tremendous
blow to them. But if we didn't pass the senate bill, families with autistic
children would suffer, and we would be blamed. I had very little time to
make a decision, and I prayed for guidance.

Many of my colleagues were seething with anger. The senate always
does this to us, they complained. They do what they want, refuse to negoti-
ate and dare us to do nothing. We should teach them a lesson. Let the bill
die, and send our bill back to them in the next session. But I couldn't do it.
Helping some kids was better than not helping any. And after my colleagues got past their initial bitterness, they agreed to pass the senate
measure.

The autism-only bill was the last legislation we passed that session. It
had not been my purpose to outwit the senate. I had wanted to make a
difference in people's lives, people who had no one else to turn to. We had
had to settle for helping only some of them. It wasn't good enough, but it
was something.

My speakership was one of the most challenging and fulfilling experiences of my life. There were disappointments, of course. But I was proud of
the things we had accomplished. We balanced the budget both years, as
required by Florida's constitution, without raising taxes. We cut spending
and produced lower budgets than the governor requested and the senate
wanted, and forced government to make difficult, responsible choices Florida families have to make every day. And our 100 Ideas project was the
catalyst for a series of policy advances as well. I'm very proud that we

continued the accountability-based education reforms begun by Jeb Bush. We modernized Florida's education curriculum and raised the standards for math, science and language arts to better prepare students for college, for technical schools and for success in the global marketplace. We hadn't achieved the revolutionary property tax reform I believed would have revitalized Florida's economy, but we had made a difference in the lives of our constituents, and I was grateful for the privilege. It is customary on the last day of the session for the outgoing speaker to give a farewell address to the house, and I had given considerable thought to what I would say as I ended my nine-year career in the Florida legislature. My colleagues unveiled my official portrait and gave me a wonderful and much appreciated farewell gift: two years of season tickets to Miami Dolphins games.

I stood at the front of the chamber where I had given so many speeches before. I wanted to reflect on my entire life and not just my years in the house, so that I could pay tribute to my parents, who had sacrificed for my dreams, and to the country that had let me live them.

I had rarely discussed my faith in public. I hadn't hidden it, but I hadn't emphasized it, either. But time and again, throughout my thirty-six years, God had made His hand visible in my life. I had had opportunities to do things that the people who loved me had never had—not because I was better than they were but because I had been more blessed than them. I had been blessed with a strong and stable family. I had been blessed with good health and a good education. I had been blessed with parents who encouraged me to dream and a wife who helped me achieve my dreams. I had been blessed to be born an American.

"God is real," I told my colleagues. "He loves everyone who has ever lived."

I should have given the speech long before, but I had been conditioned by political correctness, by the prevailing notion that a discussion of one's faith didn't belong in the public realm. No matter how hard we try, though, we cannot keep God out of our lives, out of every moment, every aspiration, every failure and every success. Whether we acknowledge it or not, He inhabits our lives completely. It had taken me too long, but I was determined not to leave the house without paying public tribute to God, for the blessings He had bestowed on me and on our country. No one seemed offended. A few members appeared to have been genuinely moved by my remarks.

Then it was over. I left Tallahassee the first week of May with no plans other than to return full-time to my law practice. For twenty years I had set goals and achieved them. Now, for the first time in my adult life, I really had no idea what would come next.

CHAPTER 22

Calm Before the Storm

I TOLD ANYONE WHO WOULD LISTEN, INCLUDING MYSELF, that I couldn't wait to be liberated from public office—from its crowded, rigid schedule; from the news clips, phone calls and e-mails; from the too many nights spent away from my wife and kids. I was still technically speaker of the house until the November 2008 elections, but my legislative career was effectively finished when we adjourned in May. I went home to Miami.

I was hired by Florida International University that summer to work part-time at the school's urban policy think tank, the Metropolitan Center, and I discovered even a retiring politician can find himself unwittingly embroiled in controversy. FIU is the only public university in Miami-Dade. I would be involved with the public policy research and polling the center undertook for its clients. I would also teach a political science class each semester. I was qualified for the work—a nine-year veteran of the Florida legislature, where I had held three leadership offices. I was the first Hispanic speaker of the house, who would be teaching politics to mostly Hispanic students. There was no public money involved, either. I would be paid from private donations and client fees that I was expected to help generate.

However, cynics saw it as another case of a politician cashing in on his public service. As evidence, they noted the amount of public funds the university had received during my two years as speaker. The relevance of the school's funding was lost on me, since the legislature didn't determine which specific projects received funding—the independent state board that oversees Florida's public universities made those decisions. Some made the opposite argument, saying they found it disturbing that the school would hire me at a time when it was suffering funding reductions and layoffs. That wasn't a valid argument, either, since I wouldn't be paid with public money. In the end, it was worth the grief. Twice a week I had the chance to teach young students, most of them with a background just like mine. I hoped my story and my lectures would inspire some of them to enter public service one day.

When I wasn't teaching, I expected most of my time would be dedicated to expanding the land use and zoning practice at Broad and Cassel. In a healthy real estate market, developers frequently seek legal counsel about changes to the land use code and other existing regulations. But in the summer of 2008, Florida's real estate market was in full retreat, and a growing surplus of single-family homes and condominiums made new construction projects increasingly rare. Opportunities for a land use lawyer were scarce.

Broad and Cassel's partners discussed opening a new consulting business, which I would run with the full support of our statewide law firm. I agreed, and began looking for new clients who needed help building stronger relationships with local business and civic leaders.

The local Univision Spanish-language media group offered me a position as an on-air political commentator for the presidential election campaign that fall. I was expected to provide commentary on both their television and radio broadcasts and be available for interviews whenever their reporters needed insights from an experienced politician. I enjoyed the television work tremendously. I was usually paired with a Democrat, former Miami-Dade mayor Alex Penelas, to provide analysis after debates and the party conventions. The pay wasn't spectacular, but there were other advantages to the work. I learned the television business from the inside. I learned how news packages were put together, and what producers needed to produce an interesting segment. The knowledge would help me become a better interview subject. The on-air work also helped keep me in the public eye, especially with the Spanish-speaking voters in Miami-Dade who were my political base.

I also began an association with GOPAC, the national organization dedicated to electing Republicans to state legislatures. GOPAC paid for my travel that summer to speak to several Republican groups who were interested in our 100 Ideas project. I had other speaking engagements as well that summer, and I was pleasantly surprised that people were still interested in listening to me even though I was leaving public office.

I enjoyed my new assignments, and was especially excited about the challenge of building Broad and Cassel's new consulting business. I liked teaching and television work. I was grateful to have more time to spend with my family. But I still missed the excitement of politics and the fulfillment of public service.

Although it wasn't a substitute for the adrenaline rush you experience participating in a political campaign, the Miami Dolphins, as they often did, brought more excitement into my life. They went from being one of the worst teams in the NFL in 2007 to a play-off team in the 2008 season. I attended every home game that fall, thanks to the generous gift from my house colleagues, often in the company of my father.

When I was young, my dad had taken me to the games at the Orange Bowl in his old 1973 Chevy Impala. We would park a few blocks away, and stop on our way to the stadium at the same cafeteria for a Cuban coffee. When the Dolphins moved to a new stadium farther north, he would drive us to Florida International University, where we would catch a shuttle bus to the game. Now I picked him up and drove us to the games. I got the sense he didn't enjoy football as much as he once had, and that he accompanied me only to avoid disappointing me. The Dolphins' season ended with a play-off loss at home to the Baltimore Ravens. It was the last Dolphins game my father and I ever attended together.

Observing the presidential election of 2008 as a teacher and television analyst made me long for the thrill of campaigning—the battle of ideas, the clash of competing visions, the energy and ups and downs of campaigns. What made it harder to bear was the knowledge that the campaign was heading to the wrong conclusion: Senator Barack Obama's election to the presidency. It became increasingly obvious he was going to win. He was a compelling figure, with an extraordinary gift for public speaking. His soaring rhetoric, almost poetic at times, but always seeming so calm and reasonable, blurred the lines between right and left and spoke to a nation weary of angry partisanship. He seemed to offer a third way and hope to Americans exhausted by two long wars and terrified by an economic crisis that threatened their jobs and savings.

Hidden beneath his centrist message, however, was a decidedly left-of-center policy agenda—exactly what the country didn't need. His personality and language gave an impression of moderation, but his ideas and voting record revealed a dogmatic, big-government liberal. I found it frustrating that so many voters couldn't see the agenda behind the appealing personality, and I worried that at a time when our economy desperately needed the innovation, competition and creativity of the free-enterprise system, the country was going to choose a president who would rely almost exclusively on government for the solutions to our many problems.

But as I waited in Univision's studio on election night and watched the new president-elect give his victory speech, I was moved deeply by the historic significance of his election, and it overwhelmed my political concerns. As he reached the end of his speech and told the story of an elderly African American woman, born just two generations removed from slavery, braving a long line and cold weather to cast her vote that day for America's first black president, I saw the emotion and pride on the faces in the massive crowd that had gathered in Chicago's Grant Park to hear him. And I, too, became emotional with pride for my country.

In the sweep of history, it was just a moment ago when African Americans were denied their God-given rights and full citizenship in the country that had been founded to protect those rights. Two generations later, an African American had risen from modest beginnings to the highest office in the most powerful country in the world. I was so proud to be an American, and so moved by the powerful symbolism of the moment, I couldn't stop myself from tearing up.

I could see the shock on the faces of some of the people in the newsroom as they noticed my eyes begin to water. Some of them thought they were tears of regret for the election of a Democratic president. But they weren't. There would be plenty of time to oppose the new president's misguided policies. That night was a night to be proud of our country and grateful for the blessing of my citizenship, for the place I was privileged to call home, for the nation that had given my parents a second and third chance at a new life, and had given me an education, a standard of living and opportunities that were unimaginable for my family just a few decades before. America is a place where anyone from anywhere can accomplish anything.

The election marked the official end of my career in the Florida legislature, and in the weeks that followed I struggled with the idea that I might never hold public office again. There would be open seats in the state senate in 2010, but I wasn't really interested in running for one. I had occupied what many people considered the second most powerful office in the state, and I didn't believe I could have that kind of influence in the senate. I would only be running just to have an office, and in my heart I knew that wasn't a purpose worth the sacrifices it would impose on my family. Every state office was held by an incumbent who would be easily reelected. The only Democrat in the state cabinet, Alex Sink, was a former bank executive who, by all accounts, had done a competent job.

I had always been interested in foreign policy, but I had never been very interested in federal office. That all changed, though, with President Obama's election. While his election was inspiring, I knew he would use his presidency to lead the nation in the wrong direction, and we would need a strong conservative movement to restrain him. For the first time, I had a genuine desire to engage in federal policy debates, but no platform from which to do it. As a former state legislator without a national profile, my views wouldn't receive much attention. And there weren't open congressional seats in Florida. South Florida's three congressional districts were represented by strong, well-liked incumbents who weren't going anywhere. There would be an election for one of Florida's seats in the U.S. Senate, but the incumbent, Mel Martinez, a Republican and Cuban American, was assumed to be running for reelection.

I had risen swiftly in Florida politics—from city commissioner in West Miami to speaker of the Florida House in a little more than a decade. But there really wasn't anywhere for me to go now, and my political career seemed to have run its course. I had a hard time accepting that for a few weeks, but by December I was resigned to it.

This is what God wanted me to do, I told myself. I could take care of responsibilities I had neglected for a decade. I could make certain my family was financially secure. I could devote myself to being a good husband and father. I could succeed at something other than politics.

My grandfather had wanted to be a prominent business and civic leader in Cuba, and he had briefly experienced success. Then he spent the rest of his life struggling to make a living in Havana and Miami. My mother had wanted to be an actress. She dreamt of being a movie star, and had auditioned for a few acting roles. She would settle for menial labor and raising her children. My father had wanted to be a prosperous business owner, like the Spaniard who had given him his first job and then fired him. He had started several businesses in Miami only to see them all fail. He had settled for work as a bartender for thirty years.

I had reached my ambition. I had been elected to public office. When I faced personal financial challenges that had almost forced me to leave politics, I had found a new job that would let me continue. I had been a leader in the legislature for most of my time there, and been called the most effective member of the house of representatives. I'd been elected speaker at thirty-five, the first Cuban American to hold the office. My parents had seen me raise my hand and take the oath of my office. They had lived long enough to see me live my dreams. If it all ended now, I would have had a great ride.

I was only thirty-seven. I was married to a wonderful woman and I was the father of four wonderful kids. I was home for dinner every night, and I spent the weekends with my family. I had nothing to complain about. I enjoyed my work in television, and had recently had an offer from another local station that was interested in giving me a long-term deal to do political analysis and reporting. I loved teaching more than I ever thought I would. I was blessed and I knew it, and I should have been content to live a less public life.

But as I had discovered many times in the past, life doesn't always follow our plans. It often changes course when you least expect it. I didn't know it at the time, but those quiet, rewarding months right after I had left office were just the calm before the storm.

CHAPTER 23

An Opening

I N EARLY DECEMBER 2008, THE FLORIDA PRESS ERUPTED with the news that Mel Martinez, Florida's incumbent junior U.S. senator, would not run for reelection.

There had been rumors Mel might retire, but they had subsided, and everyone assumed he would be on the ballot in 2010. I had never run a statewide campaign. Out of office, I no longer had a fund-raising base. I wasn't very well known outside Miami. But, at least initially, if I made a run for his Senate seat the media would consider me a serious candidate—not the front-runner, of course, but credible.

I told Jeanette the news, and that I was interested in the race. I expected her to tell me I was out of my mind, that we had just decided to begin a new chapter in our life free of the demands of public life, and the toll they took on our family. Instead, she said we should think about it and pray for guidance. I was shocked. Jeanette didn't care for politics. She tolerated my political career because she knew it was important to me, and because I could be of service to people who needed help. But she, too, was worried about the direction of the country after the 2008 elections. For the next few days we discussed what a Senate race would entail for our family.

A few days after the Martinez announcement, rumors began to circulate that Jeb Bush was interested in running for the seat. Usually, when there had been speculation before that Jeb might come out of political retirement, he quickly shot it down with a firm denial. Not this time. Several people I trusted, including Mel himself, told me Jeb was seriously considering it. Jeb was still immensely popular in the state. If he were to run, no one would challenge him in the primary—certainly not me. The Democrats would probably offer only token opposition. Rather than spend several weeks preparing for a campaign that wouldn't happen, I decided to ask Jeb myself. I drove to his office in downtown Miami the day before Christmas Eve and met with him for an hour. I left the meeting convinced he would soon announce he was running for the United States Senate.

I asked friends to do a little preliminary organizational work in the event Jeb changed his mind, but otherwise, Jeanette and I let the matter drop. We had something more important on our minds. Doctors had noticed something unusual in my father's chest X-ray during his annual checkup: a lesion in one of his lungs. They ordered a biopsy, and in December we learned he had lung cancer. He was eighty-two and had smoked virtually his entire life. Previous checkups revealed he suffered from early-stage emphysema, but hadn't detected the cancer I had long feared he would contract.

A series of tests indicated my father had a small cancerous lesion that had not metastasized. Despite his age, he was a candidate for a surgical procedure, a lobectomy, which would remove the diseased portion of the lung. My father agreed to the surgery, which was scheduled for January. We spent the holidays at home worrying about my father, although his doctors seemed confident of a prognosis for a full recovery.

Just a few days after New Year's, I was in my office at Broad and Cassel going over financial projections for our new consulting venture when my cell phone rang. It was Jeb. I had been expecting him to call and tell me he was declaring his candidacy for the Senate. Instead he began the conversation by announcing, "I'm not going to do it." He asked if I was interested in running, and I told him I would give it a serious look. He was encouraging, but cautious, as if he were worried about whether my family and my finances were ready for the challenge. He sounded tired and hurried, and I suspected he had a number of similar calls to make that day. After we hung up, I called Jeanette and told her, "Jeb's not running. We need to talk."

I spent a lot of time in January trying to make up my mind. My father had his surgery early in the month and, as the doctors expected, was on his way to restored health. Not having to worry about my father's health was a relief that freed me to contemplate the possibility of a Senate run. The more I thought about the issues that were at stake in the next election, the more interested I was in running. The economy was in disastrous shape. I believed only the creativity and dynamism of an unleashed American free-enterprise system would rescue it, but over the last ten years Washington had increasingly relied on the federal government to stimulate economic growth. Now, with a Democratic president and Congress, I expected Washington would assume even greater control of the economy. I was concerned about the administration's approach to important foreign policy questions as well. President Obama and his allies had promised to reverse many of his predecessor's policies: closing Guantánamo, retreating from Iraq and trying terrorists in civilian courts. I thought their positions were not just naive, but dangerous.

I was frustrated, too, by the failure of Republicans to counter the leftward drift in Washington with distinctly conservative solutions to our national problems. There seemed to be a growing chorus of Republican voices who argued that to win national elections in the future, we needed to become more like Democrats. Some claimed it was simply a matter of demographics—the country was changing ethnically, culturally and politically, and to retain our appeal conservatives would have to be, well, less conservative. Right-wing purists had cost us the 2006 and 2008 elections, they argued. The future belonged to centrists, and the party needed to nominate candidates who sounded, acted and voted like centrists.

That didn't make sense to me. President Obama had won a decisive victory, but his election had not established that Americans believed any less in limited government and a free-market economy than they had in the past. He was the most effective political communicator since Ronald Reagan. He was the best-funded candidate in history, and had an enormous financial advantage over Senator McCain. He ran during the most serious economic crisis in a long time, when the incumbent Republican president was very unpopular. And, still, almost half the country had voted against him. The voters hadn't given him a liberal mandate, and he had been careful to campaign on a centrist, bipartisan message. His election hadn't been the consequence of a historic demographic and ideological shift. He was a very good candidate running at a very opportune moment for Democrats.

The argument that the Republican Party's future depended on fielding moderate candidates wasn't a new one. It had been building for a while, especially in Florida. Charlie Crist had won the Republican nomination for governor by veering as far to the right as he plausibly could. But the day after his primary, he had tacked sharply back to the middle, where he remained ever since. In his two years as governor, he had pursued policies designed to position him as a new kind of Republican: a reasonable, moderate leader who wasn't afraid to wage war against extreme elements in the party.

In the beginning, he relied on symbolic, stylistic measures to signal he wasn't like his predecessor, Jeb Bush. He removed Jeb's appointments to state boards and replaced many of them with Democrats. Soon, however, he began to pursue policies that would mark him as one of the country's most prominent moderates. He wanted to expand dramatically the government's role in the property insurance market. And in the summer of 2007, he hosted a huge climate change summit, following which he issued a series of executive orders on global warming.

The capital press corps considered Crist one of the more masterful politicians in Florida's history, a gifted retail politician who could charm anyone. They loved to cover the Crist-as-the-antithesis-of-Jeb angle. And they especially enjoyed it when Crist took on Republican legislators, which he did quite often during his first two years in office. He liked to make a production out of phone calls and meetings with Democrats in the house of representatives. He was clearly trying to create the perception he was a courageous, fighting centrist who would take the party back from conservative ideologues, which, more often than not, meant house Republicans, and particularly me. He often used me as his foil, playing to the liberals' view that I was an out-of-touch, stuck-in-the-past, right-wing disciple of Jeb Bush.

I never bought into any of it, though. I didn't believe conservatism had vanished in Florida overnight. But even if it had, even if America and the Republican Party were shifting to the left, I wasn't prepared to join them. I believed in what I did.

It might be hard to remember now, but in the early months of 2009 the GOP was somewhat in the wilderness, engaged in a national debate about whether or not the party had to move to the center to stay relevant in American politics. I thought the U.S. Senate was the right platform to take a stand that the country already had a Democratic Party and didn't need another.

While the prospect of fighting for the direction of my party and the nation excited me, there were other considerations that made a Senate campaign a difficult undertaking for me. Broad and Cassel had tolerated my absences when I was speaker, but I doubted they would give me leave to wage a statewide campaign. Even if they did, it would be a risk to run for the Senate while still associated with a law firm. The firm's clients would likely become fodder for my opponents' research.

By late January, I started to raise a little money and travel the state to make my case to voters that the country needed to return to the principles of limited government and the American free-enterprise system. I thought the Republican Party needed to make that argument and counter the president's policies. If I was right, I thought I would pick up support quickly. If I was wrong, I would run out of steam immediately, and realize this was not the time.

I spoke to virtually every Republican club or executive committee in the state that would have me. I usually drove myself to the engagements, and often returned home after midnight. On more than one occasion, I felt myself starting to drift into sleep at the wheel, the darkness and hum of the engine lulling me to sleep. I would turn up the air-conditioning as cold as it could get and roll down all the windows. Then I'd turn on the radio and blast it. If that didn't work, I'd call someone on my cell phone, usually Jeanette, and talk until I pulled into my driveway.

I didn't know it at the time, but these early speaking events were the seeds that would blossom into a hundred flowers. Each one led to invitations to address another group. I felt like a preacher on the circuit, delivering the Republican sermon on small government and free enterprise. My audiences were enthusiastic, and started spreading the word about the young conservative with the right message, who was running for the right reasons.

There were still many questions I needed to answer before I could take the plunge. But I had made a good start. I had found a good message that resonated with the Republican base. My wife was supportive, and sometimes even excited about the campaign. Most polls showed I was barely an afterthought for most voters, but I was experienced enough not to worry about early polls. Most voters didn't know who I was, but if my message created a little enthusiasm and momentum, I would raise enough money to tell them who I was.

I wasn't the front-runner, and I didn't think I would have a clear path to the nomination. But I thought it was at least a fifty-fifty proposition. By February, I was pleased with my progress. That would change in just a few days.

CHAPTER 24

A Hug and a Wait

THE NEWS ON THE MORNING OF FEBRUARY 4 WAS HARD TO believe. Charlie Crist was considering the Senate race now that Jeb Bush had announced he wasn't running. There had been rumors to that effect earlier, but no one had taken them seriously. Everyone close to him had laughed them off. It made little sense to anyone. Crist was an immensely popular governor who stood a good chance of running unopposed for reelection. It was an open secret that he harbored presidential ambitions, and a landslide reelection as governor in 2010 would ensure he was a serious contender for the presidential nomination in 2012. It was still unlikely he would run for the Senate, but his flirtation with the idea would freeze the field and make it very hard for any other candidate to get traction until he made a decision after the legislature adjourned in May.

I'm not proud of my initial reaction to the news. If Crist runs for the Senate, I thought to myself, I'll run for governor. It made political sense. I had spent nine years in state government, and I knew Tallahassee politics and state issues very well. But my reaction was strictly grounded in ambition. I missed public service, no matter how hard I tried to convince myself and others that I didn't. All it took was the availability of a high office to expose how intensely my ambition still burned.

I continued to travel the state, giving speeches and raising my profile. I would run for either senator or governor depending on Crist's decision. It didn't matter much to me which office was available—I wanted back into politics. I hadn't made my intentions clear to the partners at Broad and Cassel, and they were understandably annoyed by the frequent news reports about my potential candidacy. They had expected me to focus on our new business venture, and instead I was spending more and more time on the road in what certainly appeared to be a political campaign. I knew by the middle of February that if I decided to run for office I would have to leave the firm.

I contacted my clients and informed them I intended to open a small practice of my own as a sole practitioner, and hoped they would consider retaining my services. To my relief, they all assured me they wanted to continue our association. For the first time in my life, I would be working for myself, and without a guaranteed monthly paycheck. If I couldn't generate enough business or if I failed to collect my fees every month, I wouldn't be able to pay my bills. It wasn't the most opportune moment to strike out on my own, but I didn't believe I had an alternative.

Although I was prepared to switch races and run for governor, I remained focused on national issues in my speeches. With every speaking event, it became clearer to me how agitated the Republican base had become. The conservative faithful were the backbone of the party, and they had been concerned about the party's direction even before the 2008 election. But one month into his term, President Obama had badly overreached his mandate and his miscalculation gave rise to a new political movement that would define the elections of 2010.

In Washington, the passage of the president's economic stimulus bill in February 2009 was greeted as a respectable first success for the new president. Its $800 billion price tag might have been massive in scope, and some of its provisions demanded by the Democratic leaders in Congress were typical pork barrel excesses that wouldn't do anything to encourage economic growth. But circumstances being what they were—a deep economic recession, financial markets in crisis, a president riding a wave of popularity in the wake of his historic election with an ample reservoir of political capital—his first major legislative initiative didn't appear to be an overreach. But to many Americans, already shocked by the unprecedented expense of the banking and insurance industry bailouts, it was one step too many toward an era of big government and potential financial ruin.

I was frequently invited to address a proliferating number of so-called Tea Party rallies. The conservative and libertarian activists who attended the rallies had formed an informal alliance to protest the stimulus bill and the accelerated leftward drift of government policies. They were focused on one thing—government's growing role in the national economy—and they weren't just angry at Democrats. They were mad at Republicans, too.

My experience has been that the vast majority of the people you will meet at a Tea Party event are regular folks from all walks of life. They were dentists, teachers, accountants and construction workers, many of whom had never been part of a political movement before but were genuinely frightened by the country's direction and felt compelled to speak out in opposition.

I don't think their concerns were new to American politics, but their sudden prominence in the national debate was fueled by the confluence of two unique factors. In a single action, the president had monumentally exacerbated concerns about government spending and our massive national debt. And the widespread access to social media gave people the means to communicate those fears and organize their opposition without relying on the convening power of a national political party. With Facebook, Twitter, e-mail and texts, anyone could become a political organizer.

In addition to birthing the Tea Party, the stimulus bill would lead to something else as well: the hug that would come to define Charlie Crist. Shortly before Congress passed his stimulus bill, the president looked for a place to hold a campaign-style rally to promote his plan, and a Republican ally to give it bipartisan legitimacy. He found the place in Florida, and the Republican ally in Charlie Crist. On February 10, President Obama arrived at a rally in Ft. Myers, Florida, a city devastated by the housing crisis and subprime mortgage meltdown. Waiting for him was Charlie Crist, who had already declared his support for the stimulus bill. He had traveled to Washington to lend the White House a hand in the effort to convince Congress to pass it, and had lobbied members of Florida's congressional delegation to vote for it.

Crist introduced the president at the Ft. Myers rally, and when the president made his way to the podium the two men embraced each other. In the months to come, we would use that image to devastating effect.

That embrace reminded Republicans of all the things Crist had done to build his popularity at the expense of the party's. He had run for governor as a self-proclaimed Jeb Bush Republican, and then in office had done everything he could do to distance himself from his predecessor's policies. He had repeatedly left Republicans in the lurch as he announced policy initiatives, without their consultation, that betrayed their principles. He ignored, and often mocked, their views. He misread the times and his party, and believed the path to political prominence as a Republican was to emulate the language and philosophy of Democrats. By endorsing the stimulus bill, he had abandoned Republicans in Florida's congressional delegation and exposed them to greater political risk for opposing it. Had the embrace symbolized only Crist's self-interested political maneuvering, the entire episode wouldn't have amounted to much. But to many Republicans, and especially to the Tea Party movement, it symbolized the Republican Party's fear of the left and its acquiescence to the rise of big-government intervention in the private sphere as the answer to the nation's problems, with all its worrisome implications for America's future.

The embrace was covered by the press, but it didn't garner much notoriety in the immediate aftermath of the event. Republicans in Tallahassee just shrugged their shoulders. They were accustomed to Charlie breaking ranks to do whatever he believed was in his best interest. They didn't believe they could do anything to prevent it.

He had that aura then—the aura of a popular and masterful political tactician, whose charm and charisma gave him the freedom to do as he pleased. He didn't need to demonstrate detailed knowledge of important issues. He could speak on any topic using nothing but clichés. He could poke conservatives in the eye repeatedly. He had a 70 percent approval rating. Nothing could hurt him. Florida had never seen anything like him. He was invincible.

I watched all this and privately seethed. Crist's example symbolized the problem with Republican leaders generally. They were afraid to oppose the president and take a stand against the conventional wisdom that the country had moved left. If he wanted to, Crist would likely become Florida's new senator, and he would go to Washington not to fight for the convictions of conservatives, but to ally himself with the Democratic president who was intent on defeating them.

In my anger, I often complained that someone should run against Crist in a primary and make the argument that America remained a center-right country and conscrvatives deserved to be represented by at least one of the national parties. Charlie Crist's election would be a major setback for conservatives, which ought to motivate them to oppose him. "Then why don't you do it?" responded Jeanette, who was often the audience for my complaints. With that simple question, she exposed me as part of the problem in the Republican Party. At the time, I was just another Republican who worried about the future of my party and country in private, but refused to risk anything to do something about it. I wanted somebody to take on Crist, but I didn't want to do it myself.

Jeanette embarrassed me with the truth, but I tried hard to deceive myself. I accepted that Crist would be impossible to beat. Even if someone managed to make a race of it, Crist would bury his opponent in negative ads. I spent much of my two years as speaker fighting Crist's policies to little avail. I was used to losing to him. And, I rationalized, if he ran for the Senate, I could run for governor. Having a conservative back in the governor's office was important, too. But I couldn't get her question out of my mind. She was right. I was behaving just like the politicians I criticized. I wanted to be someone more than I wanted to do something, and I preferred the path of least resistance to my ambition.

I continued my tour of the speaking circuit, met with donors and began to hire consultants. After every speech, people would tell me they had been waiting to hear someone articulate a conservative message without apology or obfuscation. They told me they were tired of settling for the least bad alternative, tired of being told to vote for less conservative candidates because they were more electable. They wanted to vote for someone who wasn't embarrassed to think and talk like a conservative, and they hoped it would be me. It was heady stuff. I was flattered by their attention. But I still thought taking on Crist in a primary would be a suicide mission. So did every political consultant with whom I discussed the idea. The smart play for me was to run for governor, or to be really safe, for attorney general.

Jeanette accompanied me to Kissimmee, where I was scheduled to address the Osceola County GOP. As I waited to take the podium, I mentioned again that I was leaning toward running for governor if Crist declared for the Senate race. "Oh, I guess all you want is a title," she replied.

I was stung and frustrated by her criticism, and mystified. Jeanette

My maternal grandfather, Pedro Victor Garcia, was a great influence on my life.

My mother, Oriales (Oria), at the top of the stairs, holding my older sister, Barbara, as she arrived in Cuba on a trip in 1960. My father and brother joined them in Cuba on that trip to see if it was possible to move back to the country.

My father and me outside the first home my parents ever bought in Miami, 1972.

Playing with my sister Veronica in the Toledo Plaza apartment complex that my father managed.

My dad, Mario Rubio, worked as a bartender.

My mom, Oria Rubio, worked as a maid.

My love of football started early. Here I am during my first year of Pop Warner in Las Vegas, 1980.

On my way to a Miami Dolphins game with my dad in 1990. My blue Pontiac Firebird is in the background.

Veronica and me posing in our caps and gowns in 1996. I graduated from the University of Miami Law School and Veronica graduated from Florida International University with her bachelor's degree.

With my wife, Jeanette, and my parents on our wedding day, October 17, 1998.

I ran for West Miami city commissioner in 1998. Among my first supporters were (left to right): my wife, Jeanette; Jeanette's sister Adriana Fonseca; David Rivera; and Jose Mallea.

In 2006, Dan Marino came to Tallahassee to lobby on behalf of an autism bill. It would pass during my final session as speaker in 2008.

Jeb Bush, Florida's governor until 2007, was a significant supporter and influence from the beginning of my political career. Here, he gave me a sword on my swearing-in as speaker of the house in 2006.

With my father next to me and family behind me, I officially entered the Florida Senate race as a Republican candidate in April 2010 at Cooper Park in West Miami. This was the last public event that my father was able to attend before his health declined.

Meeting with voters in St. Augustine, Florida, in 2010 during my statewide bus campaign.

Pictured with my opponents Governor Charlie Crist and Representative Kendrick Meek before a debate in October 2010.

The moment the Senate race was called in my favor on November 2, 2010.

My entire family joined me onstage to celebrate my election and thank our supporters. My wife, Jeanette, is holding our son Dominick, as our son Anthony and daughters, Amanda and Daniella, stand next to her.

My mother also joined me in acknowledging the victory. She turned eighty that same night.

With my wife, Jeanette, holding the Bible, I was sworn into office as a senator by Vice President Joe Biden.

My sisters, Veronica and Barbara, and my brother, Mario, were all with me on the night I was sworn in to the U.S. Senate in Washington, D.C., in January 2011.

On a trip to Afghanistan with other Republican senators in 2011, we met with military and government leaders.

really isn't political, and she's well aware of the sacrifices she's had to make to support my political career. I couldn't understand why she felt so strongly about the question. Every political veteran I knew thought Crist would be impossible to defeat, and advised me to run for another office. Why did she have to make me feel so guilty for doing what was the obviously practical thing? Because she was right. She was willing to accept the sacrifices a Senate campaign would impose on her, but not, it became increasingly clear, if I ran for office simply for the prestige of the title. She would bear whatever burden she must if I were acting from conscience, but not if I were fighting for nothing more than my vanity.

Nevertheless, our conversations on the subject as well as my conversations with a small group of friends who agreed with Jeanette always ended when I became angry. How would I raise the money to beat him? How would I defend myself from his attacks? Who would risk making an enemy of the most popular politician in the state by supporting a candidate who couldn't win? How would I find clients and build a business after I lost, if the whole state knew Crist would want to punish me for running against him? Why was this so hard for them to understand?

I started to change my mind in late March, when the Crist people began sending me the message they could reach out and hurt me any time they pleased. I heard from some of my clients, including Florida International University, that they had been approached by the Crist people and informed the governor was disappointed they had hired me. Some of his operatives were openly challenging me to run, telling people they hoped I would run so they could finish me off once and for all.

Had the Republican Party chairman or Crist himself reached out to me personally in the spring of 2009, they could probably have persuaded me not to run. I'm not proud of it now, but I think if they had acknowledged my concern that the party had strayed too far from our conservative principles, I would have walked away from the Senate race. I was looking for a face-saving way out. Instead, out of pride and hubris, they chose to intimidate me. And I, too, reacted out of pride. They didn't respect me, and it made me angry. I became more comfortable with the idea of running for the Senate, whether or not Charlie Crist decided to stand in my way.

Pride, prestige, respect. They drive our ambitions, and sometimes become them. We don't often recognize how they can blind us to their ultimate insignificance to our happiness even though the evidence is often in plain sight. I sat in my home office one warm spring afternoon, making calls to prospective donors. Jeanette was running errands, and our younger son, Dominick, was alone in his playroom next to the office. I heard our home alarm sound to indicate someone had opened a door or window. I assumed Jeanette had returned and so, lost in conversation, I thought nothing of it. But after a few minutes, something stirred my awareness and I hung up the phone to check on Dominick. He wasn't in the playroom. I ran to the back of our house and found the door open. My heart began to race. We have a small pool, only a few feet deep, but big enough for a small child to drown in. That's where I found my little boy, floating facedown.

I jumped in and pulled him out. He was silent for a few seconds—seconds that felt like minutes. Then he began to cry and vomit pool water. I was shaking as I held him, imagining the calamities that might have happened—could have easily happened. I might have been upstairs and not heard the door chime. I might have spent a minute longer on the phone. But I hadn't, and my son was spared. Yet, so close had we come to a tragedy, I saw how slight a thing pride is compared to love—how powerless it is to heal a broken heart or fill a life that has lost a beloved. The campaign and its problems meant nothing to me that afternoon. I held my son in my arms—my breathing, living son—and I wanted nothing else.

The shock of almost losing him and the moment of clarity it gave me subsided. I haven't forgotten it or the lesson it taught me. Yet I went back to the work I had chosen—to politics, to the campaign and its demands. And as before, these pursuits monopolized my time and thoughts. I think I understand now that the restlessness we feel as we make our plans and chase our ambitions is not the effect of their importance to our happiness and our eagerness to attain them. We are restless because deep in our hearts we know now our happiness is found elsewhere, and our work, no matter how valuable it is to us or to others, cannot take its place. But we hurry on anyway and attend to our business because we need to matter, and we don't always realize that we already do.

On Good Friday, a well-known lobbyist, one of Crist's closest supporters, asked to meet me for lunch. I expected another heavy-handed attempt to scare me out of the race. I was surprised when he told me he thought Crist would be crazy to run for the Senate seat, and if I announced I was running, he would probably change his mind and remain in the governor's office. He didn't want a primary, not even one he was confident he could win. To his credit, the lobbyist was transparent about his motives for approaching me. His business depended on his access to the governor, and if Crist left for Washington, there was no guarantee he would have the same kind of access to his successor.

Jeanette had been suspicious of the meeting and urged me not to go. She thought I was relying too much on the opinions of others, as well as on my fears. "Put your trust in God, not other men," she cautioned. Easier said than done, I thought at the time. Did God read polls? In all of the polls, I trailed every other name. I was upside down in some of them—pollster speak for when there are more people who have an unfavorable impression of a candidate than a favorable one.

As Crist's decision drew near, many of my potential rivals began to position themselves to run for an office other than the Senate. Attorney General Bill McCollum, who had lost the previous Senate primary to Mel Martinez, announced he wouldn't run for the Senate, a clear indication he expected Crist to run, but would run to succeed him as governor. Congressman Connie Mack announced he would seek reelection. The Mack family was close to Crist.

McCollum's decision put more pressure on me. He had already started raising money for his reelection as attorney general, which he could easily transfer to a gubernatorial campaign. He was lining up supporters for the campaign, while I was still debating which office to run for. I couldn't wait any longer for Crist to make his decision. I needed to make my own and hope it would influence his. On April 14, in an interview with the *St. Petersburg Times*, I said my decision whether or not to run for the Senate would not be predicated on Charlie Crist's decision. Many people didn't believe me. Most assumed I was bluffing, and I would eventually run for governor or attorney general.

I still harbored illusions I could preserve my options a while longer. But with each passing day, I was drawn more to a Senate campaign. Maybe it was the people I met on the stump who urged me to run or maybe it was Jeanette's surprising calm about the campaign. For whatever reason, I was beginning to feel more at peace with it. I was ready for whatever Charlie Crist decided to do. Or at least I thought I was.

CHAPTER 25

Do Not Be Afraid

I STOPPED WAITING FOR CHARLIE CRIST TO MAKE UP HIS mind. I gave an interview to the local Univision station on May 4, announcing my candidacy. I released a Web video the next day formally launching my campaign, and I told the *Miami Herald* I didn't think my "odds were that long. Races of this magnitude are decided by who presents a clearer picture of the future, and I intend to do that." When asked why I was running, I replied, "I don't agree with the notion that to grow our party we need to become more like Democrats."

I had the field all to myself for the next seven days. No one really thought I could defeat Crist, but I was surprised by how interested the press was in my candidacy. On Mother's Day, May 10, Jeanette and I hosted a lunch for all the mothers in our family. I excused myself from the party several times that afternoon to check the Internet for any news that might have leaked about Crist's plans. That evening, several media outlets reported that Crist would announce his Senate bid on Tuesday.

We released another Web video before Crist announced, framing the race as a choice between more of the same and a leader who will stand up to the establishment.

An election coming into focus. A choice for Florida's future. Some politicians support trillions in reckless spending, borrowed money from China and the Middle East, mountains of debt for our children and a terrible threat to a fragile economy. Today, too many politicians embrace Washington's same old broken ways. [Cue image of Crist embracing Obama.] But this time, there is a leader who won't. Let the debate begin. Marco 2010.

I loved it. When I first saw it, I was excited to do battle, and sent my consultants the following message, not entirely in jest.

> I just ran this on my computer and three things happened. 1. I got chills.
> 2. My wife and children painted themselves up in blue face like Braveheart.
> 3. I went to the closet and got out my costume from Gladiator and I could hear the crowd chant: Maximus! Maximus! Maximus!

I flew to Washington on Monday, where I would have access to the national media when Crist announced. I wanted to appear confident in my long-shot bid. I understood the challenges I faced, but I was, in fact, increasingly confident about my chances. The year 2010 was beginning to feel like a national wave election, in which conservatives frustrated with the party establishment's support for moderate candidates had all the energy and momentum. If I could just plug away, I thought by late summer I could ride the conservative wave to a come-from-behind victory in the Republican primary. I knew Crist would have an enormous financial advantage and the support of Florida's biggest Republican donors. But the contested primary would prevent the state party from weighing in on Crist's behalf, and the National Republican Senatorial Committee (NRSC) would have to remain neutral as well. Or so I thought.

I went to the Capitol with one of my finance consultants, Ann Herberger, for a meeting with John Boehner's chief of staff, Paula Nowakowski, a friend of Ann's for many years. She told us that in a meeting of House and Senate Republican leaders, Senate leaders announced plans to try and invoke Rule 11 in the Florida Senate primary. When a state party chairman and two national committee members signed a Rule 11 letter, the state party and the NRSC could intervene in a contested primary. It was an obscure provision intended to prevent the David Dukes of the world from hijacking Republican nominations. Now it seemed it would be used against me. It was an obvious abuse of the rule, and just as obviously, it would potentially devastate my campaign. If invoked, Rule 11 would allow the Republican Party of Florida and the NRSC to raise and spend vast sums of money for Crist, and the state party and NRSC staff would be at his disposal.

That night I sat in the lobby of the Marriott in downtown D.C. with Ann and another of my consultants, Carmen Spence. Ann received a call on her cell phone, and I could tell by the expression on her face that someone was giving her more bad news. It was Jeb Bush. He had just gotten off the phone with the NRSC chairman, Senator John Cornyn, who informed him that the NRSC would not remain neutral, and would endorse Crist the next day.

Crist declared his candidacy the next day, and within minutes of his announcement, a steady stream of prominent Florida Republicans announced their support for him. For most of that day, it seemed like barely a minute would pass before I received another e-mail, text message or phone call informing me of another Crist endorsement. It was a carefully crafted plan to demoralize me. And it worked.

Publicly, I tried to appear unimpressed and undeterred. But privately, I was shaken. I had had a previously scheduled meeting with Senator Cornyn that day. I didn't see any point in keeping it and told Ann to cancel it. She insisted we go anyway, arguing that they should have to tell me personally why the committee was violating its customary neutrality. We attended the meeting where both Senator Cornyn and his staff explained that the party needed to win the Florida seat without spending a lot of money that was badly needed in other Senate races. They felt Charlie Crist gave them their best chance for an easy victory. The message was pretty clear: they weren't asking me to get out of the race, but they would do everything they could for Charlie. Not only would I be running against a popular sitting governor, but he would now have the full financial and political support of the Republican Party.

As we were leaving the meeting, I got a phone call from another of my consultants, Heath Thompson, who told me Senator Jim DeMint from South Carolina had asked to meet with me. Given the onslaught of state and national Republican endorsement announcements for Crist, the fact that any Republican senator wanted to talk to me was shocking. I went to Senator DeMint's office and was greeted by young staffers who had seen some of my speeches on YouTube and seemed genuinely excited to meet me. I was escorted to the senator's office, where I gave him my standard pitch about how I could win the nomination. Only Republicans could vote in Florida primaries, and they were typically dominated by the most conservative Republicans in the state. Florida conservatives had never been very fond of Crist, and once they realized they had another choice, they would abandon him and vote for me. I didn't need to raise as much money as Charlie. I just needed enough to let Florida Republicans know they had a choice in the primary.

Jim was encouraging but noncommittal. He had started a political action committee, the Senate Conservatives Fund, to support conservatives in contested primaries. My campaign fit the bill. I didn't leave the meeting with his endorsement, but I was a little encouraged by his willingness to discuss the race and consider endorsing me on a day when I felt the entire Republican universe had lined up in opposition to me.

The NRSC endorsement of Charlie Crist would turn out to be a blessing in disguise. It would galvanize conservative support for me, and fury with the Republican establishment for backing Crist. That night, though, I retreated to my hotel room physically and emotionally exhausted. Alone on the road, away from my family, rejected by my party, I was discouraged and depressed. I called Jeanette and we talked for two hours—or, more accurately, I talked while Jeanette listened to me share my disappointment and feel sorry for myself. I wanted to go home.

Had I done so, I think I might have decided to quit the race. Fortunately, I couldn't. I was scheduled to speak to the South Sarasota Republican Club the next morning. A local supporter, Raul Fernandez, met me at the Ft. Myers airport and drove me to the event. I spent most of the drive on my cell phone trying to prevent the state party from invoking Rule 11. I had no doubt the state party chairman, Jim Greer, would sign the letter. He was Crist's close friend and supporter. I called our state national committeeman, Paul Senft, and tried to convince him not to sign. But I could tell from the tone of his voice he already had.

Our national committeewoman, Sharon Day, was my last hope. If she signed the letter, the rule would be invoked and my campaign almost certainly would collapse. Seconds after she took my call, Sharon made it abundantly clear she would refuse to sign the letter, and found the whole effort to force me from the race offensive. I had finally caught a break. I didn't know Sharon all that well at the time and was worried she would eventually cave under pressure from the governor and the party establishment. But she is a formidable person, and she never wavered. Had she signed it, I doubt I would have ever made it to the Senate.

I had dodged a bullet, but the forces arrayed against me were still much on my mind, and demoralizing. As if I needed any further reminders of the odds against me, the steady stream of Crist endorsements continued to dominate the news. I felt besieged by the avalanche of support for Crist—I felt as low as I had ever been in my political career. But I got a bit of a boost at a speech in Venice, Florida. A group of homeschooled kids and their parents met me when I arrived, holding handmade signs supporting me. They had seen a video of my farewell speech to the Florida House and had come to encourage me on their own initiative. They were evidence that there were people out there who were looking for something different in this election. Time would tell if there were enough of them and if I could reach them in time.

After the speech I drove a rental car across the state in time for another event with conservative activists in Ft. Lauderdale. I got home after the kids had gone to bed. It was only Wednesday night, and it had already been a long week. I started early again the next day, leaving home before sunrise to catch a flight to Jacksonville. My brother, Mario, picked me up at the airport and drove me to my lunch with the Republican Women's Club of Duval Federated. Like at other events I had attended that week, my speech was well received, and the crowd enthusiastic. It finally occurred to me how unaffected regular Republicans were by the Crist steamroller. My audiences seemed excited about my message and genuinely pleased to have a conservative candidate to support.

I didn't make it home that night until after ten. The next morning I attended an event at my son Anthony's school. The school year ended before Father's Day, so the school always organized a father's breakfast in May. Before breakfast was served, Anthony and his classmates sang several songs for their fathers. The lyrics of their last song seemed squarely directed at me.

Be brave, be strong, for the Lord our God is with you. Do not be afraid. Do not be afraid. For the Lord our God is with you.

I felt as if God were sending me a message in the sweet voices of three-year-olds. The last five days had been a trial. I had felt forsaken by my party and destined for failure. I had forgotten that I had not been forsaken by the people who mattered—by the family who loved me and the people who believed in me. And I had not been forsaken by my God. I looked down and saw on the table in front of me a laminated paper key chain with a Bible verse.

I've commanded you to be brave and strong, haven't I? Don't be alarmed or terrified, because the LORD your God is with you wherever you go.

—Joshua 1:9

I carried it with me for the rest of the campaign.

I flew to Tampa after the breakfast for meetings with grassroots activists, an interview with Neil Cavuto on Fox News and a keynote address to the Tampa Republican Hispanic Club. I made the five-hour drive home alone. I had a long time to reflect on everything that had happened that week. I had always been on the political inside looking out—as majority whip, majority leader and speaker of the house. People came to me to ask for my support. Now I was on the outside looking in, and I was the one who needed help. How many times had I been told I had a bright political future? Now the same people who had flattered me had endorsed Charlie Crist and were telling me it was not my time. By every conventional standard, I didn't stand a chance of winning. I was comparatively unknown. I didn't have much of a fund-raising network and I was running against a prolific fund-raiser. I had never run a statewide campaign. Crist had won statewide four times in the last ten years. If I lost, I probably wouldn't have a political future of any kind.

Why would God put me in this position? Why had He given Jeanette such peace of mind when she had always been bothered by the time politics took from our family? None of it made sense to me. But I would not be afraid. On that long drive home, I started to believe that something special was about to happen if I had the courage for it.

I devoted the rest of May and all of June to making the case that my candidacy was viable. I didn't spend as much time raising money as I should have. We had a growing Internet fund-raising operation, but I wasn't raising nearly enough money to finance the kind of campaign I needed to run. I didn't have a broad base of longtime financial supporters like Crist did. I did spend a good amount of time with potential donors, which would pay dividends down the road. But at the time, they barely knew me and just wanted to see if I was a serious candidate.

I had hopes of landing an endorsement from the Club for Growth, a well-established organization of fiscal conservatives. The club had a national network of active supporters, who, if motivated, could raise hundreds of thousands of dollars in small and midsized donations for a candidate. Given his spending record in Tallahassee, Crist wouldn't get the club's endorsement. But given the odds against me, I didn't know if I could, either. I met with club leaders in Washington D.C., and our meeting went well, but I could tell they were worried I didn't have a realistic path to victory. I made the case that their endorsement would help me create a path. It would boost my credibility and help me raise money. But in an election year with so many competitive races, and the majority in both houses of Congress at stake, the club was reluctant to waste its resources on a candidate it preferred but didn't think could win. I left the meeting hopeful that I had a decent shot at their endorsement, but knowing it would be a while before they made a decision.

I returned to Miami that night. When I landed, I saw I had an e-mail from one of my consultants informing me that Senator DeMint wanted to speak with me the next day. The first question Jim asked me was if I was going to change my mind and drop out of the Senate race. Crist's people had spread the rumor in Washington that I was only posturing and would soon give up my Senate bid to run for attorney general, and the NRSC had parroted the assertion. I told Jim I had no intention of switching races. He was glad to hear it, and told me he would endorse me and use the resources of the Senate Conservatives Fund to help finance my campaign. It was very welcome news.

I went back to Washington on the morning of June 16 and held an endorsement press conference with Senator DeMint, followed by a telephone press conference with Florida reporters. Because I was running against the candidate chosen by the party leadership, we had a hard time finding a place to stage the endorsement. The senatorial committee would not allow us to use its facilities, of course. Other venues we inquired about using turned us down as well. We eventually decided to hold the event outside on a sidewalk across the street from the Capitol, and hoped it wouldn't rain. It turned out to be the best day of the campaign so far, after weeks of being pummeled with news of endorsements for Crist. Jim was a first-term senator and, at the time, still relatively unknown. But the fact that a sitting Republican senator would break ranks with the senatorial committee and endorse me intrigued reporters, and it was the first sign that I might prove to be a credible challenger.

Crist's people tried to belittle the endorsement and DeMint. A *Miami Herald* reporter asked Jim why anyone in Florida should care if he endorsed me. Crist had called him personally to talk him out of supporting me. When that failed, his people pushed the line that Jim was an extremist and coaxed Florida reporters to question me about him and try to get me to distance myself from him. Jim handled the questions like a real pro and I followed his lead. He told reporters his endorsement didn't mean he and I agreed on every issue. But we agreed on the most important thing: America was in trouble and we needed to change course fast. I didn't know Jim well when he endorsed me, but my respect and admiration for him grew over the course of the campaign and the time we've served together in the Senate. He's genuinely committed to the principles of limited government and the free-enterprise system. He's not a show horse. He's the real deal.

Jim's endorsement was a nice boost, but I immediately returned to the rigors of the campaign: the early-morning flights; the endless interviews, speeches and meetings; beseeching donors; the lonely hotel room at the end of the day. I had to make a living in whatever time I could spare from the campaign and squeeze in time every week to work for my clients. I also made certain I never missed my kids' school events. But most days, I left the house before they woke up and came home after they had gone to bed. I missed them, and Jeanette. It's strange how lonely you feel even when you're constantly in the company of others, if the ones you love the most aren't there.

As the end of the fund-raising quarter approached, we scheduled a few finance events in the hope we could raise enough to make a small impression. We held one in Orlando that was only a modest success, and another at Miami's Biltmore Hotel that did a little better. Neither event reached its stated goal, and the hosts were embarrassed. Every dollar counts, I told them. It took courage to put your name on a fund-raising invitation for me in June 2009, when it would be noticed by the Crist people, and filed away in their long memories.

Meanwhile, the Crist finance machine kicked into high gear. Charlie is a legendary fund-raiser, renowned for his relentless pursuit of every available and not so available dollar. I wondered if I had it in me to be such a prodigious fund-raiser. Everyone told me I would have to be. But I hated putting the hard sell on people for money. If that's what it took to win, I would lose.

Everyone expected Crist would have a record-breaking finance quarter. No one expected me to match him. But I had to show I was on pace to raise enough money to be a viable, if disadvantaged, challenger.

I was proud of our campaign at the end of June. We had survived Crist's early knockout strategy, the onslaught of endorsements and calls for me to get out of his way, and we were still on the field. We had even managed to score an important endorsement. And we were outworking Crist on the campaign trail. I spoke to any group who would have me, and was gaining supporters at all of them. We saw a glimmer of hope in a Mason-Dixon poll at the end of June. Among Florida Republicans who recognized both Charlie's and my name, we were essentially tied. When we released our fund-raising numbers, though, I knew we had a rocky road ahead of us. We fell well short of our goal—so short there was no way we could spin it into a positive.

We had a good message and a great political environment to run in. The idea that the race would be a battle for the heart and soul of the Republican Party intrigued people who followed campaigns closely, and ensured our campaign would have their attention. For now anyway. Candidates can't live on Facebook and Twitter alone. They need money to run ads and, more important, to defend themselves from the attacks that begin the moment they start to rise in the polls. We didn't have the money, and I wasn't very confident we would do much better in the next quarter.

After we reported our numbers, everyone waited anxiously for Crist's report. We knew he would report a big number. We didn't expect the bombshell that awaited us.

CHAPTER 26

Message Received

M Y STAFF ASSUMED I MEANT TO GIVE THEM A PEP TALK, but the e-mail I sent them the morning of July 7, the day we reported we had raised only $340,000 for the quarter, was intended to boost my morale as much as theirs.

> Folks, today is not going to be the best day of this campaign. We are going to get pounded today for our fundraising number. And over the next 7 days CC is going to roll out endorsements, big $$ and work behind the scenes to make our campaign look not so credible. The ultimate goal is to get us to move races. We should even be prepared for some prominent GOP people who are supposedly "neutral" to come out and say that I need to run for AG for the good of the party.
>
> Here is the bottom line. This race is predicated on the idea that the national environment and the GOP environment is ripe for what we are and what we are about. If we are properly organized, eventually the energy we derive from this environment would help monetize our campaign. This is not the only way I can win, it is the only way anyone can beat someone like Crist.
>
> From the beginning the theory that the environment was conducive to this was either true or it is not. A big test of that is going to happen over the next month. If our low fundraising numbers cause movement folks to look

elsewhere then the environment was never strong enough to sustain this race anyway. If we survive this test then we are in better shape than we came in because:

a. We will raise more money next quarter and each quarter after that;

b. We will be inoculated from this issue.

I think we should weather this storm of the numbers and endorsements and then counterpunch with endorsements of our own to show we are still standing and moving forward despite failing the "traditional" political test.

Assuming we can weather this storm, the only permanent harm that can come our way is if we take our eye off the ball of what this campaign is about.

Here is the simple formula

1. MESSAGE=SUPPORT

2. SUPPORT=MONEY

3. MONEY=VOTES

I will keep working hard. I am both anxious and curious to see just how strong this environment really is. If it allows us to keep moving despite what we are about to face then we are sitting on a GOP "storm of the century."

I flew to Orlando two days later for a meeting. When I flew home that afternoon, I had an unwelcome surprise waiting for me when I landed.

The Crist campaign had been setting expectations about his fundraising haul for weeks. They had bragged to reporters they were on track to raise $3 million. They let our low number sink in for a day before they announced theirs. In the seven weeks since he had announced his candidacy, Charlie Crist had raised $4.3 million, or an average of $86,000 a day. "I am humbled by the support that I am receiving from the people of Florida and around the country," Crist wrote in the statement announcing his total.

It was an extraordinary, record-breaking amount of money. The previous quarterly record for a Senate campaign was the $1.7 million Mel Martinez had raised in the first quarter of 2004. Even the mighty Jeb Bush's best quarter was only $2.7 million. There was no way we could spin this. It was just bad news—very bad news.

I kept campaigning over the next few days, but as the magnitude of Crist's haul sank in, I grew increasingly discouraged. That Sunday, in its regular weekly feature, the *St. Petersburg Times* declared the political winner and loser of the week. It was no contest.

> Raising a whopping $4.3 million for his Republican Senate campaign, Crist surely quelled what had been the growing buzz about the threat from Republican Marco Rubio. As much as we relish covering a fight for the soul of the GOP, no candidate can use Twitter to overcome a 30-point deficit in the polls and eight-to-one financial disadvantage.

In one paragraph, the newspaper had perfectly captured the common perception of the race after Crist's announcement, and my own mind-set as well. That weekend I began to contemplate seriously switching races or dropping out altogether.

I met Al Cardenas for breakfast that Saturday. He strongly advised me to quit the Senate race and run for attorney general before I did lasting damage to my career. He reminded me that if Republicans lost the governor's race in this election, the attorney general would become the de facto head of the Florida Republican Party, and the obvious front-runner for the gubernatorial nomination in 2014. I had an opportunity to escape an impossible predicament in better shape politically than I had been in when I entered the race. I would have the entire GOP leadership behind me, including Governor Crist.

On Sunday night, I convened a meeting at our house with some of my closest friends and advisers. I invited State Representative Steve Bovo and his wife, my former aide Viviana; Julio Rebull, a trusted adviser; my former house colleague Ralph Arza; my campaign manager, Brian Seitchik; and my pollster, Dario Moreno. Another friend, Esther Nuhfer; David Rivera; and David's aide, Alina Garcia, joined us on the phone as well. I asked them to come under the pretense that I wanted to discuss my options with them: whether to remain in the Senate race, to switch to the attorney general race or not to run for any office. But after my conversation with Cardenas, I was already leaning strongly toward ending my Senate campaign and running for attorney general. I just wanted my friends to endorse the decision.

I laid out the rationale for ending the campaign. I would never raise enough money in a bad economy and while running against a sitting governor known for keeping score and punishing transgressors. Even if I got a little traction in the polls, it wouldn't be sustainable when Crist unleashed a barrage of negative ads against me that would quite possibly make me unelectable for any office forever. When they were done with me, I said, no one would want to hire me to be their lawyer.

Jeanette led the charge against my decision, and most of the others joined her. The money would come after the legislature adjourned, they argued. If I spent more time making finance calls, I would raise more in the next quarter. From time to time, someone would blurt out the name of a donor I hadn't reached out to yet who might be willing to raise money for me. I pushed back, arguing again and again that no matter what we did or how long we waited I would never raise enough to make the race competitive, and being stubborn could cost me any future political career, and quite possibly my livelihood. But every time I thought they were all on board, one of them would come up with another reason to stay in the race.

I blew up. I needed their affirmation, I told them, and they were torturing me with what-ifs. "Is this what you really want?" I shouted. "For me to stay on the road and away from my family for another year and a half only to be humiliated and destroyed?" There was another office available for the taking, a highly coveted one, state attorney general, the best stepping-stone to running for governor someday. But they wouldn't budge. Eventually, I left the discussion and went upstairs. They left minutes after I walked out, and I faced Jeanette alone.

The family argument didn't work on her. She reminded me how much she disdained politics. But she was at peace with this campaign, and willing to carry the burden at home, because I had convinced her I was fighting for the things we believed in. I became angry again. Why couldn't she see how impossible the situation was? I couldn't win, and staying in the race could cost us everything. I went to sleep angry and confused. I wanted out, but people I trusted wanted me to fight to the bitter end. Their opinions mattered to me, and no one's opinion mattered more than Jeanette's.

The next morning, when I got up to take the kids to school, I found a note Jeanette had left for me, giving me permission to do whatever I thought was right.

> I support you in anything you decide.
> I'm with you in this together with God.
> I love you and believe in you.
> Me.

I had a speech in Port Charlotte that night, and Jeanette decided to go with me in anticipation that it would be my last speech as a candidate for the U.S. Senate. We discussed my decision again as we drove to the event. Whenever she seemed to accept it, however, she would catch herself and ask if we couldn't take more time to think about it. I lost my patience again. "No!" I shouted. "No more waiting." Jeanette countered, "Nothing important in life is easy, and the problem with you, Marco, is that you want it to be easy." I was furious with her.

I called Al Cardenas from the car and told him his analysis of my situation had intrigued me, but I would need leading Republicans in the state to support me publicly if I decided to switch races. I authorized Al to call a few of them and see if he could get them on board.

The audience in Port Charlotte became unexpected allies in Jeanette's appeal to my conscience. I'm not sure why, but somehow I managed to find my voice again in my speech that night. I talked from the heart about the challenges facing our country and the reason why I wanted to serve in the Senate. The response overwhelmed me. One person after another thanked me for running and told me they had waited for years to hear a candidate speak about the things that mattered most to them. I felt guilty as I listened to them, knowing that in a few days' time I might disappoint every one of them.

Jeanette didn't say a word on the drive home. She just listened as I mused aloud about what might have been if only I had enough money, if only the odds weren't so long, if only the risks weren't so great.

The incumbent attorney general and presumptive Republican nominee for governor, Bill McCollum, called me the next day. He didn't push me to switch races, but he did extol the virtues of the AG job and expressed his excitement at the prospect that I would join a united Republican cabinet slate. In truth, I wasn't looking for a deal that would guarantee me the nomination. I knew I would have a primary even if Crist agreed to endorse me for attorney general. Crist's lieutenant governor, my former house colleague Jeff Kottkamp, wanted to run for the office, and I didn't think anyone's endorsement would deter him.

If I ran for attorney general it would be because my fears had gotten the better of me. I was afraid to lose. I was afraid to be embarrassed. I was afraid to fail. I wanted to take the easiest path available to elected office, and I made up all sorts of rationalizations to disguise my cowardice. Hadn't I wanted to run for AG a few years earlier? Wouldn't I have run for it if the opportunity had presented itself when I was leaving the legislature? Wasn't it the right thing to do for my family? With the support of the party establishment, I wouldn't have to begin campaigning in earnest until next year. I could spend more time with my kids. I could make a little money before I had to leave my practice. I wasn't afraid, I tried to convince myself. I was just being practical, and putting my family before myself just like my parents had done.

I had just about made up my mind. I had even written a speech announcing my decision and apologizing for disappointing my supporters. "Our ideas are strong," I intended to say, "but our fund-raising hasn't been." Nevertheless I decided to keep my Senate campaign schedule until I announced my decision, figuring that the events I had scheduled were events I would have to do anyway as an AG candidate. I flew to Tallahassee and met two former aides, Bill Helmich and Evan Power, who drove with me to Pensacola, where I was scheduled to meet with the editorial board of the *Pensacola News Journal* before an eleven o'clock speech to the Gulf Coast Economics Club. Brendan Farrington, the AP political reporter, came along for the ride.

We talked about various issues on the three-hour drive, but Brendan was most curious about how I thought I could win the Senate race considering Crist's enormous financial advantage. Since I was already strongly leaning toward switching races, I had a hard time making a convincing argument for how I would defeat an opponent I didn't believe I would defeat. Then Brendan got a phone call.

I could tell it was about me. After he hung up, he apologized for what he was about to ask me. He had just gotten off the phone with a very reliable source in Tallahassee who had told him in no uncertain terms that I was going to switch races.

If I admitted I was thinking about it, my Senate race would be over right then. If I ruled it out, my campaign for attorney general might be over before it began. Lying wasn't just morally wrong, it would be politically devastating. Once you lie to a reporter, they will never trust anything you tell them again. The press might like you personally, but if they think you're a crook or a liar, you're finished. They'll suspect everything you do and say, and they'll make their suspicions clear in every story they write about you.

I was trapped, and I was angry. I knew what had happened. Crist's people had gotten wind of the calls Al Cardenas was making on my behalf. Rather than wait for me to make an announcement when I was ready to do it, and risk that I would change my mind, they decided they would force my hand that day. They wouldn't give me time to let the people who had risked the most to support me know my decision before it became public. I wouldn't even be able to give Senator DeMint the courtesy of a phone call to explain my reasons.

In my past run-ins with Crist, I had managed to swallow my pride, keep my temper in check and react intelligently, not emotionally, to the provocations. Not this time. I'd had enough of their disrespect. I told Brendan I wasn't going to drop out of the Senate race. I was going to shock the world in August 2010 when I won the Republican Party nomination for the U.S. Senate.

I sent an e-mail to Cardenas telling him Crist's people had jumped the gun after they learned he was making calls. The Crist people were trying to deny me the ability to tell my closest supporters I was quitting the race, after the risks they had taken to back me and the money they had struggled to raise for me. I hadn't even told my wife my final decision. Al acknowledged their bad faith, and sympathized. But it didn't change anything, he told me. I still couldn't win the Senate nomination, and I could still be attorney general. Furthermore, he had put his own credibility on the line by making calls on my behalf. I ended the exchange by telling him that I had not agreed to be treated this way. Crist had overreached. They had put me in a terrible situation. And now they would have to wait for my decision.

I returned to Miami the next day in time for a morning speech to a local Rotary Club. When I finally got home, Jeanette had a surprise waiting for me. She had assembled the same group of friends from the previous night, and this time they had come better prepared to convince me to stay in the Senate race. David Rivera brought a poster-size sticky pad. As each of them suggested something that needed to be done to give me a decent chance to win the Senate nomination, David would post one of the big notes on our family room wall.

I just sulked. After my declaration to Brendan, the idea of switching races was all but dead. I would have to stay in the Senate race or stay in private life. I grew increasingly irritated with every suggestion David posted on the wall.

I wasn't just feeling trapped by Crist's maneuvering. Something else was gnawing at me. I was ashamed. I felt I had been tested by adversity and failed. I had lost my nerve. I was nothing like my grandfather, a disabled man who had lost his job and his status and yet took any work he could find to feed his family. Walking for miles every day, falling down, getting up, walking some more; rejected, humiliated, ignored. He had never quit. He had never given in to self-pity.

I was nothing like my father, motherless and working since he was nine. He had gone to bed hungry many nights. He had lived in the streets and slept on a wooden crate in a storeroom. He had tried and failed and tried and failed again to start a business. He had lost his country. His work as a bartender had him coming home late at night well into his seventies. I had never heard a single complaint escape his lips.

The trials I was facing were nothing compared to theirs. I worried I wouldn't get to be a United States senator because I couldn't raise money and my opponent had embarrassed me. If I decided to see the thing through to the end, it would be only because I had no other choice. It was such a pitifully small test of my strength, and all I wanted was to get out of it.

Why had God allowed me to go further than my father or grandfather had ever had a chance to go? They were better men than me. Why did He give me opportunities they never had? Why had I failed, when my blessings were so much greater than theirs and their trials so much more severe than mine?

Because God uses our failures more than our successes to teach us the most important lessons and to lead us to Him. Maybe I couldn't be a U.S. senator or the attorney general. But I could be something more. I could be more like the better men who raised me and taught me what it takes to be a good man.

God had blessed me with everything I needed to make this race. When I worried I couldn't provide for my family, I found a job and clients. When I worried about the sacrifices my ambitions would force on my wife, He gave her the strength and conviction to support me. That day in Washington, when I left the meeting with Senator Cornyn and his staff feeling dejected and hopeless, hadn't I been bolstered by Senator DeMint? When two party leaders had agreed to invoke Rule 11, didn't a woman I barely knew find the strength to say no? When I came home demoralized and feeling sorry for myself after the worst forty-eight hours of my political career, He opened my ears to the voices of little children, telling me, *Do not be afraid. Do not be afraid.*

This wasn't about the Senate. It wasn't about politics. God didn't endorse candidates. He wanted me to trust Him, to rely on Him, to lean on Him. He didn't want me to believe He would make me a senator. He wanted me to believe that whatever happened He loved me and would give me the strength and peace of mind to endure it.

No matter what I did, I couldn't escape this test. My friends wouldn't give me a pass. My wife wouldn't support me if all I wanted was a job with a title. I wouldn't be able to scheme my way out of a predicament and into an office I didn't have to fight as hard to win. I wouldn't rely on Him if I ran for attorney general. I would have the party establishment behind me. And if I won, I would give myself the credit for being shrewd and calculating.

I believe now God wanted me in a hopeless situation, where my scheming and calculating wouldn't save me. Only the most improbable confluence of events would make it possible for me to win election to the Senate, even to make it just a competitive race. Everything I thought I knew about campaigns would have to be proven false for me to win.

I know all these things now. But I wouldn't admit them then. I was resigned to running and losing the Senate race, not because I wanted to, but because I couldn't think of a face-saving way out of it. Before my friends left my house that night, I asked them if they were happy with my decision. "Is this what you want? To see me destroyed by millions of dollars of negative ads? To watch my political career end in humiliation?"

By now they had gotten used to my self-pity. "We'll see you tomorrow," they said.

CHAPTER 27

A Clear Goal

THE NEXT FUND-RAISING QUARTER WOULD END ON SEP-
tember 30. I had to raise a million dollars by then to have any hope of
being considered a credible candidate, and I would have to pull out all the
stops to do it. I'd have to pass around a basket at my speeches collecting
contributions. I would have to hold dozens of fund-raising events, and no
event could be too small. I would need an aggressive mail solicitation program. And finally, I would need one big finance event that would raise as
much as a quarter of our fund-raising total to prove I could attract support
from big donors.

I needed to tighten up our campaign operation and reduce our overhead. Our "burn rate" was too high, which is campaign speak for spending
too much money. We needed a bare-bones operation that focused on two
things: raising money, and getting me to events to raise money.

Finally, I had to land a few attention-getting endorsements. The one we
wanted the most was the Club for Growth's.

On Monday, July 20, I drove to our small campaign headquarters in
Coral Gables for a meeting with my campaign manager, Brian Seitchik, to
discuss the state of the campaign. Brian was a realist and had reached the
same conclusion every other political professional had reached: I should
run for attorney general. I wasn't going to do that now, and I couldn't have

a campaign manager who didn't think I should be running. We parted ways on good terms.

Once Crist made it clear he might run for the Senate, some of the consultants who had offered to work for my campaign informed me that if Crist did run, they could only work for me if I ran for another office. They didn't want to risk offending Crist or the NRSC. Fortunately, my media team, Heath Thompson; Todd Harris; and Heath's future wife, Malorie Miller, promised to stay no matter what. They introduced to me to Pat Shortridge, a Minnesota-based conservative consultant, who joined the campaign full time in August. My press secretary, Alex Burgos, and Viviana Bovo were committed as well. And Ann Herberger, my finance consultant, agreed to continue working for us as a volunteer. Everyone who worked for my campaign did so at some risk to their own careers. Were I to lose the nomination, which seemed probable at the time, they might find future opportunities quite scarce.

Staff shake-ups are always difficult. They're best handled quickly to minimize the damage. But before I could announce the changes, someone did it for me. I was in Pasco County the following Thursday for a speech when Alex Burgos called to tell me Adam Smith of the St. Petersburg Times had been tipped off about Brian's and Ann's departures, and wanted a comment. Neither Alex nor I wanted to lie to Adam. I had no choice but to confirm it.

"This isn't a purge or anything—quite the contrary," I told Smith. I tried to put a positive spin on what was an unpleasant necessity, but I was worried the news would be perceived as more evidence my campaign was going nowhere. I worried all night about the reaction. The theme of the story was exactly what I feared it would be.

> In a sign of turmoil in Marco Rubio's underdog campaign for U.S. Senate, two of his top campaign staffers are dropping off the campaign.

I was certain that supporters who read it would begin abandoning the campaign. To my surprise, the news had almost no impact. I attended a Republican event in Tampa the next day and another in Ruskin the following day. No one brought it up.

The Crist campaign smelled blood, however, and circled in for the kill. On August 5, Al Cardenas endorsed Charlie Crist. I was caught completely off guard—Al hadn't called to let me know what he was going to do. A week later, two key allies of mine in the legislature, Dean Cannon and Will Weatherford, endorsed Crist. Mario and Lincoln Diaz-Balart, both friends of mine and members of the U.S. House of Representatives, followed suit. None of the endorsements moved votes or made it any harder to raise money. They wanted the endorsements to demoralize me, and for a short time they did.

I set aside the last week of July for a family vacation on Captiva Island, Florida. We rented a vacation home there with Jeanette's family. It would be the last opportunity to spend time with my family for quite a while, and even those few days were interrupted by campaign work. I had to leave Captiva for a day to fly to Washington, where I had a meeting scheduled with Bill Kristol of the *Weekly Standard*, as well as a fundraiser and, if time permitted, a coffee with the editors of the *National Review*.

The coffee, which I'd barely been able to fit into my schedule, would turn out to have the most immediately beneficial impact on my campaign. I flew back to Florida the next day, and on the drive to Captiva, Pat Shortridge called to tell me the editors of the *National Review* were considering putting me on the cover of their next edition. But they wanted an assurance that I wasn't going to switch races. I told Pat to give them the assurance.

I spent the next two days with my family, disconnected from the daily grind of the campaign. It was never far from my thoughts, though. It had been a very difficult month, but I was starting to see a glimmer of hope on the horizon. I had reorganized the campaign and reduced our overhead without paying a political price. Appearing on the cover of the *National Review* would give me a chance to nationalize my campaign—to turn it into a proxy fight for the national battle between conservatives and moderates for the soul of the GOP. If we could do that, we might be able to raise a million dollars before the end of the quarter.

Pat began setting up a direct-mail fund-raising program. It was something I knew very little about. I learned it would cost us more than it raised in the beginning. We would mail solicitation letters to proven donors on lists other Republicans had built over the years. Very few people would send us any money, but those who did would become part of our own list. And because their donations were well below the maximum, we could go back to them for additional donations time and again throughout the campaign.

We hired Esther Nuhfer as our finance consultant. She had little experience raising money statewide, but that didn't really matter. For the most part, the people who would host fund-raisers for me were new donors, many of whom had never before been involved in politics. If they had been, they might have thought twice about crossing a sitting governor. Our fund-raising got off to a slow start in August. It takes time to set up events, and it's hard to schedule any in Florida in August, when many people vacation in a cooler climate. Most of our events that quarter were held after Labor Day.

I spent most of August doing the same things I had been doing all along: speaking to Republican clubs across the state and appearing on conservative radio talk shows. Pat ordered preprinted contribution envelopes, which I took to every speaking engagement. When I finished my remarks, I would make a pitch for donations, and volunteers would pass around the envelopes. Some folks took them home and mailed them to us later. But by the end of the month, more and more people were donating on the spot, and it wasn't unusual to raise $2,000 at the events in $50 and $100 contributions.

I was committed to the Senate race, but that didn't mean that temptation didn't creep into my mind from time to time. In early August, Mel Martinez announced he would leave the Senate early. Someone suggested I ask Crist to appoint me to his seat for the remainder of his term with the understanding I wouldn't run for a full term. I could use the appointment to position myself to run against Bill Nelson in 2012.

A week later, rumors circulated that Crist would appoint Lincoln Diaz-Balart to finish Mel's unexpired term. Some friends suggested that if Lincoln was appointed, I could run in and easily win a special election to fill Lincoln's vacant House seat. I discussed both ideas with Jeanette. She is my best adviser, especially when I'm tempted to do something I know in my heart I shouldn't. She thought they were bad ideas, and after talking with her, I agreed.

Those distractions aside, I remained focused on the clear goal we had set for the campaign. Get the campaign organized and raise a million dollars, and I would live to fight another day. If I failed to do that, I would be finished, quite probably finished for good in politics.

I had a follow-up interview with the editors at the *National Review* scheduled for August 11. If all went well, I would be on the cover of the magazine scheduled for release on August 20. We were laying the groundwork for a major fund-raiser in New York for late September. Dan Senor, who had worked in the Bush administration, had arranged a number of appointments for me with major New York donors on August 17; among them were Paul Singer, a well-known national donor, and Mark Gerson, a young entrepreneur. They both seemed interested in the campaign but had doubts about my viability. They wanted to know how I could plausibly pull off a major upset. An answer would come forty-eight hours later.

I was in Orlando when the *National Review* hit newsstands on a Thursday morning. On the cover was my photograph, taken as I stood at the podium in the Florida House when I was speaker. My arms are crossed, my gaze fixed, and printed across the center of the page in bold white letters, the headline "Yes, HE CAN."

The story was as good as the cover. It read in part:

> On paper, it looks like a mismatch between an unbeatable juggernaut and a doomed also-ran. Yet Crist may be vulnerable. . . . Rubio is one of the brightest young stars on the right. Their contest could become the sleeper race of 2010.

The story included several flattering quotes from Jeb Bush. "He's got all the right tools," Jeb said. "He's charismatic and has the 'right principles.'" It closed with this analysis:

> The good news is that Rubio doesn't have to match Crist dollar for dollar. But he does need to hit a certain mark—enough to lift his name into the consciousness of most Florida Republicans. . . .

The *National Review*'s argument for my viability lent third-party validation to our fund-raising efforts. It was the first of several major turning points in the race. Supporters who were trying to attract donors to our cause now had a flattering article in a respected conservative publication to use to convince their friends to become involved. We used the article in a highly effective direct-mail piece that actually made money—something early prospecting mail rarely does.

A major test of our progress would be the quarterly Florida Republican Party meeting scheduled for the weekend of August 21. I was initially reluctant to go. Crist had handpicked the state party chairman, and although he was required to remain officially neutral in the primary, everyone knew he and the entire apparatus of the state party were doing whatever they could to support Crist's campaign. I argued with staff that it would be a waste of time that would be better spent meeting with voters. In truth, I was worried about how I would be received. I thought party officials would create situations that would make Charlie look popular to the press at my expense. I was afraid to go.

Jeanette, on the other hand, encouraged me to go with the whole family. We should have a major presence there, she said. And we would bring plenty of copies of the *National Review* with us.

David Rivera suggested we host a hospitality suite on the first night. But since the state party was paying for the event that weekend, it had to approve any other events held at the hotel. It refused to let the hotel rent us a hospitality suite or cater any event I hosted. So we had Cuban coffee delivered from a restaurant outside the hotel to David's room, and we hosted a Cuban coffee reception the first night. It was jam-packed. I signed more than two hundred copies of the *National Review* for guests who crowded David's suite.

The next morning we had volunteers stationed outside the conference room where the party was holding its quarterly board meeting. They were supposed to give copies of the *National Review* to people as they entered. But there weren't any magazines there for them to hand out. We had hired a young woman from Gainesville to help coordinate our grassroots campaign, and she was supposed to deliver the magazines that morning. Unbeknownst to us, she had been in contact with friends at the state party, and by extension with the Crist campaign. She had disappeared the night before during the coffee reception, and no one could find her. When she failed to report for duty the next morning, we knew something was up. She came to my room later to tell me she was leaving the campaign. She had been offered a job by the state party. Later that day, Adam Smith of the *St. Petersburg Times* reported another staffer had left my campaign. It was clearly an orchestrated effort by the Crist campaign to embarrass me.

Other than that one small incident, I thought the weekend had been a success. Many Republicans were still apprehensive about openly supporting me. But I had as many attendees wearing my lapel stickers as Crist had. I was well received everywhere I went that weekend. People seemed excited to see me. One of Charlie's consultants told a reporter my campaign was already worthwhile after I got the cover of the *National Review*.

The end of August saw a slight uptick in our fund-raising. We were collecting more envelopes at my speeches. Some of our midsized events were raising as much as $20,000. The mail was starting to make money. The crown jewel of the quarter would be the fund-raiser in New York in late September, hosted by the Fanjul family, a Cuban American family that owns a large sugar and real estate conglomerate. It sounded unbelievable, but if the event hit its target, we stood a good chance of posting a million-dollar quarter.

My kids would often overhear me discussing our fund-raising with Jeanette. In late August, Amanda did something that nearly broke my heart. She had recruited her brothers and sister to help her collect loose change around the house. She added the allowance she had saved and money she had received as gifts to the coins she had found, and presented me with a twenty-three-dollar donation to my campaign. It's a moment I'll never forget.

The Fanjuls suggested I spend Labor Day weekend in the Hamptons, where many of their friends and major Republican donors would spend the holiday. Jeanette and I stayed in Mark Gerson's guesthouse. On Sunday night, Pepe and Emilia Fanjul hosted a dinner for us on their boat, and they invited former New York mayor Rudy Giuliani. Rudy stayed for the entire dinner, and afterward we talked about my campaign. He wasn't ready to endorse me yet, but he was intrigued. There was no love lost between Rudy and Charlie Crist.

Crist had promised to endorse Rudy for president in 2008, and he and Rudy had planned to fly around staging endorsement rallies in various Florida cities. But when Rudy's numbers began to fall, Crist backed out of the commitment and endorsed John McCain just a few days before the

Florida primary. Rudy still held a grudge and was waiting for the right moment to exact maximum retribution.

I kept a punishing schedule of speaking events, interviews and fundraisers. I traveled every day but Sunday. My days began early in the morning and ran late into the evening. We did everything we could to keep our burn rate low. We often drove instead of flying, and we avoided renting cars. As often as possible, I stayed in my supporters' guest rooms rather than in hotels. Many mornings it would take me a few seconds to remember the city I was in and whose guest room I inhabited. I was often hoarse from speaking. I spent so much time talking on my cell phone I developed a sore on my ear. Everyone on the campaign worked to the point of exhaustion.

I began to believe that we would meet our goal. It would all depend on the New York event. On the morning of September 23, Jeanette and I boarded a flight for LaGuardia Airport. We had lunch with Mark Gerson that afternoon, and I made a few more fund-raising calls before we left for the Fanjuls' apartment on the Upper East Side of Manhattan. The event was well attended, and while it didn't appear that many people had brought checks, the total raised that night exceeded our goal. The next day I flew to Washington for a couple of interviews and a meeting with Senator Tom Coburn. Then we returned home to Florida, and I went back out on the road.

More good news arrived on September 25, when conservative columnist George Will wrote a very flattering and encouraging account of our campaign. On a Sunday morning a month later, I was making breakfast for the kids when I thought I heard Will mention my name on ABC's *This Week with George Stephanopoulos*. I turned up the television in the kitchen in time to hear him predict I would win the primary. Jeanette came into the room and I excitedly told her the news. "That's nice," she said, then handed me a bag of garbage and asked me to take it outside.

I worked sixteen to eighteen hours virtually every day. I did Lincoln Day speeches, more interviews, more little fund-raisers. I missed my family. I wanted to wake up in my own bed every morning and have dinner with my wife and kids every night. But whenever I started to feel sorry for myself, I thought of my grandfather and my parents, and the years of thankless toil they had endured. How tired had they been? How often were they discouraged?

In the long and hard days of the summer of 2009, I found the strength to go on by remembering where I had come from. I had done the best I could. With the support of my wife and friends, I had overcome my fears and was fighting for what I believed. Would it be enough to make a difference? I didn't know, but I would find out soon enough.

CHAPTER 28

Winner of the Year

P AT SHORTRIDGE CALLED ME WITH THE NEWS EARLY ON the morning of October 3. They hadn't finished counting yet, but he was confident we had raised over a million dollars for the quarter. When we announced the total on October 6, the impact was immediate.

In his daily blog "The Fix," *Washington Post* reporter Chris Cillizza wrote, "What Rubio did with his fundraising showing over the past three months is ensure that the race he had hoped for will happen. That race? A choice between himself, a conservative, and Crist, a moderate, with national implications for the future of the Republican Party."

Adam Smith of the *St. Petersburg Times* reported, "Charlie Crist has a real race on his hands. . . . The hefty fundraising quarter establishes Rubio's viability and is likely to spur more interest in the 38-year-old Cuban-American from Miami." The executive director of the Club for Growth told Smith, "We're certainly going to take a closer look at getting involved in this race." A few days later, they would announce their endorsement of my campaign.

To borrow a phrase used too often in politics, our million-dollar quarter was a game changer.

The Crist campaign released its total two days later. He had raised $2.4 million, with now more than $6 million on hand. He still held a signifi-cant advantage, but we had every reason to be optimistic. Our strong quarter ensured we would continue to receive media attention. It would be months before we raised enough money to buy television spots to introduce me to voters. In the meantime, we had to rely on earned media, the free press, to get out our message. If I had had another poor quarter, the press would have ignored me, concluding I wasn't a legitimate challenger.

We encouraged people who liked me but were worried about getting involved in the race. Time and again, I met with prospective donors and conservative leaders who expressed their frustration with Crist. But a consultant or lobbyist had whispered in their ear that I couldn't win. Now there was a glimmer of hope that I might.

We had always expected our fund-raising would trail Crist's. We just wanted to have enough money on hand near the end of the campaign to finance a last-minute surge that could overtake him. And we didn't expect my poll numbers to improve until we raised enough to buy advertising. We were wrong. Two weeks after we announced our fund-raising numbers, two polls showed we had made significant gains on Crist without spending a cent on television. In August a Quinnipiac poll had Crist beating me by almost 30 percent. Quinnipiac's most recent survey showed his lead cut in half. A Rasmussen poll released the same day gave Crist a fourteen-point lead, down from twenty points in August.

Alex Burgos, my press secretary, released a statement that summed up my mind-set perfectly.

> We're not breaking out champagne. We expect to remain behind for some time. We understand that with Marco Rubio's growing momentum, the target on his candidacy will only get bigger.

We had turned a corner. Twelve weeks earlier, I feared I couldn't mount a credible challenge to Crist and had to be talked out of quitting the race to avoid embarrassment. There was still a long fight ahead of us, but we were clearly in the game.

I was enjoying our recent success, but I still had to work three times harder than Crist to raise a fraction of what he raised. I had to meet with more voters than he did. I had to give more speeches, and give them well, day after day. It was starting to take a physical and emotional toll. I wasn't sleeping enough. I didn't get any exercise. I wasn't eating properly. Dinner was usually something that came on a cardboard plate, eaten in the car as we drove from one event to the next. I usually went to bed after midnight and woke up before six the next morning for the first call of the day.

But we were moving. I had buzz, and I didn't want to lose it. Our improved poll numbers and fund-raising were attracting interest from the national press and from others. Mitt Romney called me just to check in, he said. He wasn't ready to endorse me, and I didn't ask him to. But I knew he was reaching out because he thought he might soon want to endorse me. National cable interview requests started to increase. Even the BBC covered a campaign swing through the Panhandle. Everywhere we went local TV crews were waiting. Local newspaper reporters followed us to every event. My higher profile made it easier to schedule more fund-raisers and attract more people to them.

By the middle of November conventional wisdom believed the race had been transformed. Whispers were now heard from the Crist world that they realized they had waited too long to take the threat seriously and were now in free fall. They had hoped to score an early knockout, and almost had. Now they found themselves in a proxy fight for the soul of the Republican Party. They were confident their financial advantage would overwhelm me. Now they accepted I would have enough money to compete to the end. They decided they couldn't wait any longer. It was time to attack.

On November 17, the *National Journal* blog "Hotline On Call" reported the Crist decision.

> Buffeted by weeks of negative press and a newly threatening rival from the right, FL Gov. Charlie Crist's (R) campaign will step up direct engagements with his opponent, insiders tell On Call. Crist will attack former FL House Speaker Marco Rubio (R), citing his rival's failure to advance some conservative causes while leading the State House, for spending excessively while in the Speaker's office and for dragging his feet on immigration legislation that many Republicans favored.

Thanksgiving couldn't come soon enough. I was exhausted, physically and mentally, and needed the four-day weekend to rest. The first volley of Crist's attack would launch just after the holiday.

Moments before I took the stage on December 2 for a speech to Florida TaxWatch, an organization of fiscal conservatives, Crist's communications director released a statement accusing me of hiding my real record of supporting "the largest tax increase in Florida history" and squandering "hundreds of thousands . . . in taxpayer dollars" and implying I had "tucked away" in the state budget $800,000 "for artificial turfs on Miami-Dade fields where he played flag football."

I had never been in political combat like this, and his attacks stung me. But my campaign did a good job of pushing back and discrediting them. The largest tax increase the Crist release criticized was the consumption tax I had proposed to replace property taxes as part of our property tax reform. It was a false charge because the plan would have reduced taxes overall. I had nothing to do with the artificial turf earmark—by their own admission, two other legislators had put it in the budget. Crist's spokeswoman had also alleged I had presided over a banquet of pork for Miami when I was speaker. But as Florida's most populous county, Miami-Dade always receives the largest share of the state budget. It has the biggest delegation in the Florida House and Senate, and many of the appropriations were sought by other members of the delegation, not me. State spending for Miami didn't increase appreciably when I was speaker.

It takes a while to get accustomed to attacks when you haven't been a target of them before. And I didn't have to wait long for the next one to appear. The *St. Petersburg Times* ran a story detailing my involvement with Florida International University. The gist of it was an allegation that I had steered money to the school when I was speaker and, in return, they hired me after I left office. In truth, the school's share of the funding was in proportion to what it had received in past years, and what it has received since. Furthermore, all of the projects had been vetted and approved by the board of governors. None of them were linked to anything I had planned to do in the future. In fact, at one point the school had felt as if they had not gotten enough.

During the last days of my last session as speaker, FIU's director of legislative affairs, my former aide, Michelle Palacios, came to my office to complain about how the school was being treated in the budget. I thought this was unfair and it led to a pointed argument between us in front of Jeanette and David Rivera. I felt bad about it afterward. It had been a tradition in Florida for presiding officers to shower their hometown university with new projects. Given that I was the first presiding officer from Miami in many years, she was under tremendous pressure to deliver for the school.

Because they were hurting me personally, I was certain these attacks were hurting my campaign. I was sure they would blunt our momentum.

Our biggest fund-raising event in December was hosted by Senator DeMint on the fifteenth. I was having my picture taken with major donors when I received a text message from Scott Plakon, a freshman state legislator who had been one of the few to endorse me publicly:

Congratulations on the new Rasmussen poll!

I had no idea what poll he was referring to, but I immediately searched on my iPhone for an answer. On the Rasmussen Web site there was a satellite image of a hurricane bearing down on Florida, and in bold, a subject title I will never forget: "43–43." According to Rasmussen, the race was now tied. I shared it with the D.C. crowd, who appreciated hearing the news but didn't seem to grasp its importance. In Florida, the impact was immediate. Adam Smith, at the *St. Petersburg Times*, explained it succinctly: "Whether or not you believe the Rasmussen poll showing Charlie Crist tied with Marco Rubio, the governor's inevitability argument is gone."

After weeks of attacks and intense press scrutiny, we were still gaining on him. The attacks weren't working, at least not yet. Voters were worried about big things, and our plan was to keep our campaign focused on big things.

Stung by the events of the last three months and especially the troubling trend in the polls, the Crist campaign had to reassure its supporters and donors. They released a memo about the state of the race that closed with an attack: I was "a typical double-talking politician" and "not the conservative he has painted himself to be. . . . On everything from taxes and spending to gun rights and cap and trade, his campaign rhetoric is very different from the reality of his record."

We had certainly gotten his attention. We held a Christmas party for the staff at our home the day Crist released his state-of-the-race memo. It was a much bigger group than had sat in my family room the previous July and tried to persuade me to stay in the race.

On December 31, we released our own state-of-the-race memo. I think it more accurately reflected our state of mind than Charlie's had reflected his.

> A lot of wild punches. And early negative advertising. And mud-slinging mail. And anonymous websites. All repeated ad nauseam. So be forewarned. It's coming. Very, very soon.

Pat went on to describe the stakes of the campaign, which I believed had become more important than who won and who lost.

> The outcome of this election will, in many respects, help determine the future of the United States—whether your children and mine will have the same opportunities we had, and our parents before us had. Again, remember: this is not about us. It is about our country and our future.

When I began the campaign, I just wanted to win. I just wanted back in politics. I wanted back in politics so bad that I had considered quitting the race to run for a different office. I had stayed in the race partly because I wanted to, but partly because I felt I didn't have another choice.

Months later, though, I had fallen in love with it. Maybe some of that had to do with the gains we had made and the national attention that was now focused on our race. But I think it had more to do with the people who responded to our message, who believed in me not because I was the front-runner, but because I believed the same things as they did. They were worried about the direction of the country, and they could see that I was, too. People who had never contributed to campaigns contributed to mine—people who couldn't even afford to gave me a little. They didn't do it because they liked me more than they liked Charlie Crist. They did it because they felt I would stand for the principles they stood for, and I could be trusted with their concerns about the country.

We had expected a long, hard slog. We had assumed we would trail Crist until the last few weeks, and maybe never catch him. Yet as 2009 came to an end, we were tied and maybe even ahead a little.

For more than two generations, my family had never achieved their ambitions. Their talents were unappreciated and unused. They deserved better. They hadn't done anything wrong; they just had some bad breaks. Why was I succeeding? Why was I living my dreams? I wasn't more deserving than they were. I wasn't smarter or a better person. What was the difference between us that allowed me to attain so much in such a short time?

America. America was the difference. I had been born a citizen of the greatest nation in all of human history. I was an American son. I was born privileged. And I was born, as all Americans are, with responsibilities, too. America's greatness isn't self-perpetuating. Each generation is responsible for the America we leave our children, for ensuring we are not America's last privileged generation.

I was on the verge of receiving a truly special privilege. The son and grandson of immigrants and exiles, I was entrusted with the hopes of my fellow citizens, with the dreams they had for their children. That was what this campaign had become to me. I carried the stories of the people who had come to believe in me, who didn't care how far behind I was in the polls, who didn't think I was crazy to run against a popular and powerful incumbent governor, who didn't believe anything was inevitable in America. They wanted me to make a difference—to go to Washington and stand up for them, and offer a clear alternative to the direction that worried them. They believed in me, and I believed in them.

On January 2, Adam Smith picked his "Winner of the Year" in Florida politics: Marco Rubio.

> Eight months ago even some of his biggest admirers were calling him crazy and shortsighted. Why in the world would the promising former Florida House Speaker launch a futile U.S. Senate campaign against an immensely popular sitting governor sure to raise vast amounts of money? . . . Today, Marco Rubio vs. Charlie Crist is among the marquee races across the country and Rubio is a star.

I had "stuck to it," Smith wrote. Yes, I had. But only because of the people who had stuck with me. Win or lose, I had been privileged, and I will never forget it.

CHAPTER 29

It Could Happen, but I Wouldn't Bet the Ranch

I DID MY FIRST INTERVIEW WITH NEW YORK TIMES RE-
porter Mark Leibovich in November, and a second one in early December. I had been cautious and expected the worst. The *New York Times* is
reviled in conservative circles as the official newspaper of the American
left. But Mark's questions were fair, and his interest in the campaign and
the Tea Party movement seemed genuine and without bias. I felt the same
way after I read the *Times*'s Sunday magazine cover story on January 6,
"The First Senator from the Tea Party?"

Some of my advisers believed the magazine's editors had tried to hurt
me by linking me to the Tea Party. But even if that had been their purpose,
and I don't know that it was, I wasn't upset by the identification with the
Tea Party. I was pleased with it, and considered it an advantage in a closed
Republican primary. And however one feels about the *New York Times*, it
has a reach few other publications have and influences the national media,
including the television and radio news producers, as much as any other
newspaper in the country. The week after the story appeared, we were del-
uged with media requests, all of which increased awareness of my campaign among Florida voters, and conservatives around the country, who
were increasingly willing to donate to the campaign of the "First Senator
from the Tea Party."

We had the wind at our back. Throughout the fall, more than a dozen county GOP executive committees had held Senate primary straw polls. I had won every one of them. Some reporters were skeptical about the relevance of straw poll victories since the committees were mostly comprised of the most active and conservative elements of the party. But those were the people most likely to turn out in the primary, and I was encouraged by their results.

We used the straw polls to build our momentum and encourage our supporters. When you're thirty points behind in the polls, you use any piece of good news to generate enthusiasm. Maybe the straw polls didn't mean that much. Maybe conservatives were just sending the state party a message that they didn't want to be ignored and, having made their point, would ultimately decide to vote for the front-runner in the August primary. A January straw poll in Pinellas County would give a clearer indication of where the race was heading, and its results would be difficult for anyone to ignore. Pinellas is Charlie Crist's home county. A defeat there would be devastating to Crist, and his campaign worked very hard to ensure that didn't happen.

I was at home the night of January 11 when the state committeeman from Pinellas, Tony DiMatteo, called me. A native New Yorker, Tony D (as everyone calls him) was one of my strongest supporters and had encouraged me to stay in the race. He had been a longtime Crist supporter who had been turned off by the governor's pivot to the left. He had also been Rudy Giuliani's county chairman when Crist had used the Pinellas Lincoln Day dinner to announce his support for John McCain days before the Florida presidential primary.

"I have some bad news for you," Tony said in his thick New York accent. "You only got 67 percent of the vote." I had won the GOP straw poll in Crist's hometown 106 to 52. There was no way to spin the result. Charlie had had a very bad night. Later that month, Senator DeMint and the Senate Conservatives Fund made an online "money bomb" fund-raising appeal for me, hoping to raise $100,000 for my campaign. It raised $400,000.

In late January Quinnipiac released its latest poll. For the first time in the race, I held a narrow lead. Later that same day, the Crist campaign announced its fund-raising total for the last quarter, and we announced ours. Crist had raised $2 million. We came close to matching him, with $1.75 million. Most of his donors had given the maximum donation, which meant they couldn't give him any more. Malorie Miller predicted he would start to run out of donors and his fund-raising totals would decline every month. The great majority of our donors gave well below the maximum and could continue to donate to us throughout the campaign. Crist still had a four-to-one advantage in money on hand, but the trend was strongly in our favor.

For the first time since I got into the race, I would rather be us than them, I thought. I was feeling pretty good about myself and my chances when I was brought swiftly back to earth the next day. I attended a candidates forum in Tallahassee before an Associated Press editors meeting, where a collection of editors and reporters from all of the state's newspapers were waiting to give me the front-runner's treatment. They grilled me mercilessly for a solid hour. My press secretary, Alex Burgos, no rookie in dealing with the press, was shocked by the level of hostility in the room. Most of the questions were tough, but fair. Some of my interrogators, however, were openly antagonistic, framing their questions in an almost dismissive way. The editorial page editor of the *Palm Beach Post*, Randy Schultz, practically shouted his questions. It was not my favorite memory of the campaign, and I'm sure it knocked me off my game a little.

That weekend, Tim Nickens, an editor at the *St. Petersburg Times*, wrote an editorial, "The Week Crist Got Back on Track." Nickens began by calling me "the darling of the windbag Washington conservatives" and he praised Crist's performance at the editors meeting as "particularly sharp." He called my performance "pitiful" and argued that Crist would make up any ground he had lost come August. Of the possibility of my winning the race, he concluded, "It could happen, but I wouldn't bet the ranch."

If Crist had in fact begun a comeback, it wasn't showing up in the polls yet. A new Rasmussen poll was released on February 1 that gave me a twelve-point lead over Crist. The poll was taken before Nickens's editorial, however. Once voters read the editorial, maybe they would change their minds. It could have happened, I suppose, but I wouldn't have bet the ranch on it.

Another poll was released that day by Republican pollster Tony Fabrizio. Based on its results, Fabrizio had some surprising advice for Crist. He should quit the race for the Republican nomination and run for the Senate as an independent. It was a provocative suggestion, but no one took it very seriously at the time. It was clear the race was starting to spiral out of Crist's control. We expected his campaign would begin punching wildly in the hope of landing a hard hit that could reverse our momentum. State senator Mike Fasano, a big Crist supporter and someone I had considered a mentor, struck first. In a *Miami Herald* interview, he called me a "slick package from Miami." "Miami" is code for a lot of things in Florida insider politics, among them the perception of Miami as the home of corrupt Cuban American politicians. We cried foul to the press, but reporters dismissed it as whining. I told myself and my staff we would just have to drop it and learn to live with it.

We kept the campaign focused on the things we could control. We commemorated the first anniversary of the now infamous stimulus bill rally where Crist and President Obama had embraced by staging our own event at the same place. We did a joint event with a national conservative fund-raising organization, FreedomWorks, in Ft. Myers. We broadcast it over the Internet and did several national television interviews to draw attention to it. We used the event to anchor what we called a "stimulus bomb," an all-out Internet fund-raising appeal on the anniversary of "the hug."

On February 17, Jeanette and I flew to Washington for a speech at the annual CPAC conference of conservative activists. I was receiving a great deal of national press coverage by now, but the CPAC speech was my first chance to showcase my message before almost the entire Washington press corps. I was unusually nervous about it. Normally, I am a confident public speaker, but this one gave me the jitters. I was worried expectations for my speech were too high and I would fall short of them, disappointing conservatives from around the country and leading reporters to wonder what all the hype was about. The speech went very well, and was well received. You always worry that your impression might be different from the press's, but every press account acknowledged that, in my Washington D.C. debut, I had done what I had to do.

There were minor bumps here and there, but we had won all but a few days over the last four months. Our fund-raising was outpacing our every projection. We were ahead in the polls. After months of hounding Crist for debates, he had finally agreed to one, scheduled for late March on Chris Wallace's *Fox News Sunday* show.

By late February, we started to hear rumors Crist was seriously considering running as an independent. It still seemed implausible to me. Crist had spent his entire political career in the Republican Party. His financial base was in the party. He couldn't walk away from that, could he? Jim DeMint had heard the same rumors. His Senate Conservatives Fund launched another fund-raising appeal for me in a Web ad couched as a poll. "Will Charlie switch parties?" it asked.

Everything was going our way, and nothing was going right for Crist. Another Rasmussen poll gave me an eighteen-point lead. Our fund-raising for the first two months of the quarter had exceeded our total for all of 2009. It was clear Crist was becoming desperate. His political director and new media consultant left his campaign. And his attacks became sharper and more personal.

Until now, Crist had left the attacks to his staff and supporters. Desperate now, he began to attack me directly. He gave an interview on February 24 in which he began by asserting his confidence he would win the primary, and then he went on the offensive. "You really want to judge the character of somebody, give them power and then you'll see what they'll do," he observed, then accused me of failing that character test.

> He comes here to Tallahassee . . . he hires twenty people at $100,000 a piece. He spends . . . a half million dollars to make the place where the house members eat nicer. . . . This is a fiscal conservative? Not by any definition I have seen. . . . You carve in for a buddy of yours the opportunity to sell food on the turnpike, and who has to veto it? The governor—who he calls the moderate. Who's the real fiscal conservative here? His first budget that he presents to me as speaker of the house when he had power—almost $500 million of earmarks. I've got to pull out my pen and veto it.

The statement was filled with absurd lies, but Crist was in a lot of trouble and he needed to do something dramatic and do it quickly to stop my momentum before I couldn't be stopped. He needed a game changer. We realized this. And we knew he would need to use his most effective attack against me soon. We didn't know what it would be. But when I landed in Jacksonville on a late February afternoon, I found out.

CHAPTER 30

March Madness

W HEN I USED THE AMERICAN EXPRESS CARD ISSUED BY the Florida GOP, I reviewed the statement every month and paid for unofficial purchases directly. The Florida GOP didn't pay for any of them. But I always knew that if those statements ever became public, they could be made to appear as if I had used party funds to pay for my private expenses.

The state party chairman was a close ally of Governor Crist. We knew he had access to the records of my American Express charges, and we suspected he would eventually leak them to the press. When I landed in Jacksonville, I had a voice mail message waiting from Beth Reinhard at the *Miami Herald*. Someone had given her copies of my American Express statements.

We spent the next forty-eight hours trying to answer a long list of questions she sent us. The bulk of the charges were for airline tickets, mostly flights between Miami and Tallahassee. They were easily explained. I had billed the party for the flights because I often mixed political business with official travel as speaker, and couldn't charge the taxpayers for them.

There were various other charges that were legitimate but still harder to explain. For example, there were a number of charges to a wine store called Happy Wines. What Beth didn't know was that Happy Wines has a sandwich counter. It's located just two blocks from my district office, and I had used the card to buy sandwiches for working lunches in my office, a legitimate expense. There were grocery charges as well, which she assumed were purchased for my family. In fact, they were for coffee and soft drinks for visitors to my office. State law prohibits the use of state funds for refreshments, so I had used the American Express card to purchase them.

There were some personal charges as well. The largest single expenditure concerned the Melhana Plantation in Georgia, where my family had held a Thanksgiving Day reunion shortly after I had been sworn in as speaker. My travel agent, who had the party card on file, had inadvertently given the plantation the wrong credit card. I caught the mistake at the time and we paid the charges directly to American Express. Not a single cent from the state GOP was used. Complicating the matter, Richard Corcoran, my chief of staff, had charged expenses at the Melhana to his card as well. There was an innocent explanation for that, too. We had planned to have a dinner the night of my swearing in at Melhana for my leadership team and their spouses. We reserved it with his GOP card. But after talking to some of them, we decided to cancel the dinner. The holiday was approaching and most of them wanted to go straight home after the session. The dinner and rooms we had reserved were then credited to my family reunion. We paid that directly to American Express as well. We gave Beth proof we had sent checks to American Express to pay the Melhana bill. She mentioned it near the bottom of her story.

Further complicating all of this was the fact that the Florida GOP had been embroiled for months in disputes over the party's spending. Alleged overspending was one of the reasons Jim Greer had been forced to resign as party chairman in early 2010. The party's expenses had interested the Tallahassee press corps for years. Now the veil was partially lifted on how the party spent money. A feeding frenzy ensued.

The same story ran in both the *Miami Herald* and the *St. Petersburg Times*. Then television stations picked it up, some of them inaccurately reporting that the party had paid for my personal expenses. We spent the next two days playing whack-a-mole with the press, trying to correct the record. For his part, Crist said his campaign had nothing to do with the story. He said he found the whole episode "pretty disturbing," but voters would have to come to their own conclusions.

Making matters worse was my absence from Florida. I was on a national fund-raising tour with stops in Chicago, Arizona and California. Meanwhile, the story was leading a number of television newscasts in Florida, especially in Miami. Jeanette would later admit to me how hard it had been for her those few days I was traveling. She encountered friends and supporters who were too polite to say what was on their minds, but she could tell they believed I was in trouble.

My supporters wanted to hear from me. They still supported me, but they needed to hear my side of the story. For two days and nights the story had been reported on local television without a direct response from me. I finally finished the fund-raising tour and boarded an early-afternoon flight to Miami to face the music.

I had a speech the next morning to the Christian Family Network of Miami. Crist and I were both scheduled to appear. I didn't want to go—I knew it would be a media circus. But I had to face them and the voters.

Crist spoke first. He had a swagger about him that morning, as if he believed he had finally found the magic bullet that would rid him of his rival. He was confident and it showed. During his speech he used the word "trust" fifteen times. Two candidates are asking for your vote, he told the audience. "Who do you trust with your vote?" he asked. They could trust him, he assured them. He had a record of doing what was right, a record that showed his good character. And character, he reminded them, is what someone did "when they think no one is looking." Everyone in the room knew exactly who he was talking about.

I, on the other hand, had no swagger. I was shaken, and I'm sure it showed. I had survived other attacks, but this was different. I was embarrassed by how the story made me look and I was worried. I was convinced this attack would work.

After my speech, I came down from the dais and faced the press for forty minutes. I answered every question they asked and didn't end the press conference until they ran out of things to ask me about. There was nothing more I could do. I had explained my side of the story. Now I would have to wait to see what the impact would be.

The *Herald* had a hot story on its hands: an underdog makes an improbable climb to the top only to be undone by his own mistakes. They wrote a series of follow-up stories and blog posts raising any number of questions about my future. Would the state attorney prosecute me for inadvertently using the party's charge card to pay for personal flights? Would prominent conservatives they had called back off their support for me? What about the $133.35 charge to the barbershop? What was that for? A haircut? Mani-pedi? Moisturizing treatment? They were items purchased for a raffle at a local GOP event, but that fact hardly deterred the wild speculation.

Things got even stranger when Crist appeared on Fox News and claimed he had heard the barbershop charge was for a back wax. He repeated the claim the next day. The reporters who covered it wrote the governor appeared "animated" and "excited" to talk about the subject. "The issue is trust," Crist told the *St. Petersburg Times*. "The issue is whether or not people can trust the speaker to spend their money wisely. I mean, clearly they can't."

On March 9, Crist's campaign opened yet another line of attack. The *Herald* reported that while I campaigned as a fiscal conservative, internal documents from the governor's office linked me to $250 million in "earmarks."

This was less than accurate as well. The majority of the spending items the article referred to had been sponsored by other legislators. My name appeared on documents linking me to them because when called by the governor's office during the veto review process, I had expressed support for them. But there is a big difference between being a supporter of a project and the actual sponsor of a request, a distinction the article never tried to make. However, nuanced defenses don't do well during a time of frenzied reporting and the *Herald*'s headline read, "Rubio's Campaign Image Belies History of $250 Million in Pork Requests."

"Sounds like Porkus Rubio to me," Crist helpfully added. He had me on defense for the first time in months, and he wasn't about to let up. His campaign spent the rest of the month making one related attack after another.

The *St. Petersburg Times* ran a story titled "Marco Rubio's Lavish Rise to the Top," examining the spending of my own political committees and insinuating I had used them for personal gain.

An editorial in the *St. Petersburg Times* said, "These disclosures are just the latest to show how Rubio exploited the perks of political office and subsidized his lifestyle as he climbed to power." Beth Reinhard asked for my tax returns, to see if I had amended them to reflect the illicit charges Crist had alleged. Then Reinhard and Adam Smith at the *Times* teamed up on a story about my former chief of staff's use of his party American Express card. Their main allegation was that we had hired a car service when we attended a GOPAC conference in Washington D.C. in 2006 and had spent $5,000 on rooms at the Mandarin Oriental luxury hotel. There was a good answer for that, too, of course. We had stayed at the hotel because that's where the conference was held. And we had hired a car service because we had a large group of people with us, and it was more convenient and no more expensive than hiring cabs for all of us.

March seemed like one long, brutal beating. We were stuck in a daily cycle: Crist leaks an attack to the newspapers, the papers write a story, television picks it up, Crist attacks me for it. I was convinced we had been seriously hurt, possibly irreparably. I was incredibly embarrassed. For the first time, people were mentioning the attacks at my events. Sometimes a supporter or donor would ask me to explain one or another of them. Other times, someone in the crowd would ask me about them. And a day didn't pass when a reporter didn't ask me about a back wax or some other frivolous allegation.

My mood changed. I sure wasn't upbeat. When I was home, my mind was elsewhere, lost in my thoughts and worries. It was frustrating to Jeanette, and rightly so. The campaign was important, but my kids still needed a father and she needed a husband. I was constantly on the road, and I wasted what little time I spent with my family by obsessing over my problems.

I tried to brace myself and my staff for the next round of polls, which I was certain would show a Crist resurgence. But I was wrong. On March 10, an Insider Advantage poll gave me a thirty-six-point advantage. On the eighteenth, a Daily Kos poll had me ahead 58 to 30. Five days later, another Rasmussen poll had the race 56 to 34 in my favor. I hadn't lost my lead. I had widened it.

I had been on defense every day for a month. It had been a miserable time. Yet our lead had grown. I was shocked. I imagine Charlie was even more surprised.

There was growing chatter that if after all these attacks Crist couldn't turn the race around, he would have to give up on the Republican nomination and run as an independent. He consistently denied it. I still didn't believe the rumors. But that didn't stop us from raising money off the speculation.

The end of the month was now in sight and with it the end of my personal March madness. One major event remained: the *Fox News Sunday* debate scheduled for Sunday, March 28. Unless one of the candidates makes a major gaffe, most debates make little impact on a race. But as Jeanette and I boarded our flight to Washington, we had a feeling this debate would matter more than most.

CHAPTER 31

You Just Don't Get It

I T WOULD BE THE FIRST TIME I FACED AN OPPONENT IN AN organized debate, and it would be before a national audience. I had a tendency to become emotional in my speeches and in informal debates with colleagues on the floor of the Florida House, when I would speak quickly and appear excited. On television, that would come across as angry or shaken, and I knew I would be judged in this debate as much for my tone and composure as I would be for the substance of my arguments.

I suppose from the experience of working with me in Tallahassee, Crist and his team believed I was easily angered and flustered. I knew they thought if Crist pushed the right buttons, I would lose my cool and appear unprepared for the national stage. After the miserable experience of the last few weeks, they had good reason to believe it, along with a treasure trove of material to use to provoke me. I was still sensitive and angry about the false accusations made against my character. It wasn't hard to get me worked up about them. I would have to exercise much greater restraint than I was known to possess if I were to avoid coming off as bitter and overwrought.

Most of our debate preparation was intended to prepare not just my responses to the attacks Crist would make, but my demeanor when I responded. We held numerous and elaborate prep sessions for all the de-bates. We tried to imagine every conceivable question and line of attack, and rehearsed repeatedly until I not only had effective responses, but could deliver them calmly, without rushing them. We tried to replicate the experience of the debate, even some of the smallest details. Todd Harris led the debate prep and did an excellent job of posing questions in the style of whoever was moderating the debate. His questions were often tougher than any of the questions I was actually asked in the debates. We would play the intro music and impersonate the moderator's welcome for whichever news show was hosting the debate. We always held a final, brief prep session on the day of the debate, and to break the tension, we would watch clips from the movie *This Is Spinal Tap*, a favorite of mine.

My friend and former colleague Gaston Cantens played Crist in our mock debates. He did a very good job. He hit me with every conceivable attack. Some were over the top; others were more deftly delivered and harder to rebut. They all pissed me off. But hearing the attacks and responding to them over and over again conditioned me to them, and helped me control my emotions. Had I responded in an actual debate the way I responded in our first mock debate, it would have been a disastrous performance.

I knew my challenge was to diminish the impact of Crist's provocations by responding to them calmly and effectively. Over the course of many hours of preparation, I came to believe that if I could govern my emotions and not appear shaken by his attacks, Crist might overplay his hand and hurt himself. Charlie's strength was never his policy acumen. More than anything else, it was his personal likability that made him popular with voters. He had a real knack for making people like him even when they disagreed with him. But, now trailing in the polls, he had become increasingly harsh and heated in his attacks. If I could remain cool under attack, the focus would turn to his aggressiveness. The more he attacked me, the more he would chip away at his best asset, his likability.

I was a nervous wreck when we arrived at the Fox studios, although I was careful not to show it. Months before, when I was badly trailing Crist, it would have been hard to make me nervous. When I didn't have anything to lose, I didn't have anything to be nervous about. But that had changed now. I was ahead. I believed I would win, and I had become afraid to lose.

Jeanette, David Rivera, Esther Nuhfer and my media consultant, Todd Harris, waited with me in the small greenroom. I had the same feeling you get while pacing in a hospital waiting room while a loved one is in surgery.

Twenty minutes before nine o'clock, there was a knock on the door. It was time to go.

I made my way to the studio, where I found Crist already seated at the table. We exchanged pleasantries while a microphone was attached to my lapel. I was immediately struck by the smell of Red Bull. I don't know how much of the beverage Charlie had consumed, but it was enough to notice— he reeked of it. Plus he had a mug in front of him filled with coffee. I'm in for quite a ride, I thought to myself.

They counted us down, the camera's red light came on and we were on air.

As expected, Crist came out swinging. He repeatedly referred to my political committee as a "slush fund." He accused me of using my public office for "personal enrichment." He frequently called me a "lobbyist." Chris Wallace didn't ask a question that Crist didn't use as another opportunity to attack me. I don't know if it was a Red Bull overdose or a sense of desperation that drove him, but Charlie's aggressiveness was almost frenetic.

Just as in football games, once the debate started my jitters disappeared. I had a clear strategy and I'd been well prepared to execute it. I needed to calmly dismiss each of his attacks, and pivot back to the core of my message: that the campaign was about sending someone to Washington who would stand up to Barack Obama and offer clear alternatives to his policies. Our plan was to let him attack me for a while before responding. If I struck back too quickly, I might appear defensive and prickly. I had to play rope-a-dope for a while, and then counterpunch.

After he had made a series of allegations, he accused me of double billing flights to Tallahassee. It was time to respond. As composed as I could be, I looked him in the eye and said, "Governor, you just don't get it."

The crux of my response was to dismiss his attacks as irrelevant to Floridians. At a time when our nation faced so many challenges, I explained, all Crist wanted to talk about were my American Express card, political committee and airline flights. We were running in a Republican primary, I reminded him, and Republicans are looking for a fighter to take on the Obama, Reid and Pelosi agenda, not for the candidate who makes the most personal attacks.

Nothing is more important in a campaign than to be in sync with the voters' priorities. I had spent a year listening to Republican voters in every county in Florida. I doubt there was another politician in Florida at that time who was more in touch with the mind-set and emotions of Republican voters than I was. I knew they were in no mood to credit a campaign that was based on personal attacks. They wanted an assurance that their nominee for the Senate would fight for the people of Florida, not for themselves.

Wallace ran a clip of Jeb Bush criticizing Crist's support for the stimulus package as a "mistake." Jeb was the gold standard to Florida Republicans, and his criticism was difficult for Crist to brush off. But when Wallace followed up by asking Crist if he would have voted for the stimulus had he been in the Senate at the time, Crist's response was yes, he would have voted for it. It was devastating. Given the mood of Florida Republicans, there was no way Crist could win the primary after reaffirming his support for legislation they abhorred.

After a break for commercials, it was my turn in the hot seat. Wallace asked me about several state immigration enforcement bills that Crist and others had accused me of blocking. I've always believed immigration is a federal issue, best left to the federal government. Our immigration system is a big enough mess as it is. Adding fifty different sets of state immigration laws would only make it worse. I believe border security and immigration policy are federal responsibilities, and as speaker I had said as much. But I had never blocked immigration bills introduced in the house. Most house members hadn't wanted to deal with them, especially since they knew there was no chance the Florida Senate would pass them.

Crist attempted several other attacks, including denouncing my tax swap proposal as the largest tax increase in Florida history, but they were ineffective. Then Wallace turned to him and asked him to rule out running as an independent, which he did, unequivocally. He said he was a Republican and he wasn't going anywhere. That wasn't true even at the time he said it, which we would soon learn.

Months later, the Florida Department of Law Enforcement released the transcript of a telephone conversation between Jim Greer, the Florida GOP chairman, and his executive director, who was cooperating with authorities in their investigation of Greer. The conversation had taken place a few days before the Fox News debate, and in it Greer told his aide that if Crist couldn't turn things around soon, he was seriously thinking about running as an independent.

The debate was reaching the end. The hour had flown by. I needed to deliver my central message concisely in my closing statement. I pointed out that Florida was worse off now than it had been when Crist was elected governor, and then I asked Florida Republicans a simple question: "Who do you trust to stand up to Barack Obama and offer a clear alternative? I'm running for the U.S. Senate because I will stand up to [him]. We can't trust you, Governor, to stand up to Barack Obama." It was a simple equation. If Republicans didn't trust Crist to oppose the president's policies, they wouldn't nominate him.

Crist used his closing statement to launch another attack. He called me a "$300,000 lobbyist-lawyer," and asked, "Whose interest was he really looking out for? We have a very fundamentally different view about public service. I think it is to serve the public. That's why I took the stimulus money—because I put people above politics."

Attacking me personally wasn't an end in itself. Crist needed to provoke an angry reaction from me. He and his campaign viewed me as an immature hothead and wanted to goad me into appearing as such. They hadn't managed to do it yet, and this was his last shot. Not getting a reaction to his last attempt, he went off script and overreached. He said he wanted to know why I hadn't released my tax returns yet. "We asked you to do it three days ago, and you still haven't done it. Is it because you're doctoring them?"

An accusation of filing fraudulent tax returns is a pretty serious allegation, and Chris Wallace felt I deserved an opportunity to respond. Mustering all the calm I could summon, I called the charge "outrageous."

"This campaign is eleven months old, and this debate is now forty minutes old, and we have yet to hear a single, significant public policy proposal from Charlie Crist."

Crist tried to get in the last word. "Oh, yes, we have," he shouted. But Wallace interjected and ended the debate. In my final observation, I had reminded voters that Crist had spent the entire debate attacking me. The sunny, optimistic Charlie Crist, the self-described "happy warrior," was now a shrill attack dog.

We got up to leave. Charlie was polite but in no mood for small talk. We shook hands, and he quickly disappeared into the hallway. Todd Harris came to get me. As we walked down the hall, he whispered to me, "You kicked his ass." My toughest critic was waiting for me in the greenroom. As soon as I walked into the room, Jeanette gave me her verdict. "That was awesome," she said. Over the years, I have come to marvel at how uncanny a barometer Jeanette is of how other people perceive things. She's not a political expert. And yet I am constantly amazed by her ability to spot and predict political trends before they're apparent. In the fall of 2007, after watching the Republican presidential candidates debate, she predicted Mike Huckabee's rise months before it occurred. In the spring of 2011, she predicted Rick Santorum would emerge as a leading candidate when he was still in single digits in the polls. She has an instinct for how voters will view someone or something, and is almost never wrong. If she was happy about my performance, I had a good reason to feel very good about it.

Almost immediately after the debate, the Crist campaign focused on one of my answers to Wallace and insisted it had been a major gaffe. Wallace had asked me whether I would change the cost-of-living adjustment for Social Security. I had answered him honestly, saying that "all these issues have to be on the table," including "the way we index increases in the cost of living."

The Florida press said I had handed Crist his next line of attack. In retiree-rich Florida, talking about any changes to Social Security was political suicide, they insisted. But after talking to thousands of Republican voters, I knew this election would be different. People were worried about the dire fiscal situation the country was facing. For a long time, Americans had felt that government was spending too much money, but believed the consequences wouldn't be experienced until well into the future. The sheer scope and size of the stimulus bill coupled with the massive spike in the national debt had convinced most people that the chickens might soon come home to roost. For the first time, people began worrying they might actually live to see America become insolvent.

Some Republicans had gotten into trouble in the past by questioning the necessity of Social Security and Medicare. That debate was over. Americans had paid into the entitlement programs all their working lives, and they expected a return on their investment when they retired. We need to focus on saving Social Security and Medicare, both of which, but especially Medicare, are headed for bankruptcy. That was the point I had made to voters. I didn't want to abolish Social Security. I wanted to save it. But to do that, I had to accept that my Social Security benefits would be less generous than my parents' benefits.

We had cleared another hurdle. After a miserable month of sharp attacks and tough scrutiny, I had performed well in my first debate. In preparing for it, I had been forced to recognize my deficiencies and try to become a better candidate and person. I learned to listen to tough criticism and take it in stride without losing my temper. Our rough campaign was making me a better candidate, and if I won, it would have prepared me to be a better leader. It began to occur to me that God might be using the campaign to make me aware of my weaknesses and more humble because of them.

More important, the trials of the last month had tested whether I really trusted God. All the planning, all the talking points, all the pushback didn't spare me the humiliation of all those negative stories. We might have blunted them a little here and there, but for the most part they were reported in the most damaging way possible. I was left with no choice but to accept I had no control over their impact.

Would my supporters abandon me? Would donors leave me? Would my poll numbers sink? I didn't know for certain, but I expected they would. I was suffering a wave of terrible publicity, and there was very little I could do about it. Every day that went by, I worried it would be the day it all fell apart. I felt the way I had in the summer of 2009, essentially powerless to control my own destiny. I tried everything else before I accepted I had no choice but to trust in God. Whatever happened to me would be for my own good.

I had gone toe-to-toe with Crist for an hour before three million viewers. He had hit me with everything he had, and I was still standing. I might be wrong, but, looking back at the debate, I think the experience convinced Crist to run as an independent. His advisers had assured him that if he attacked me, I would come undone. He did, and I didn't. There really wasn't anything else he could do. If the primary was about what I believed it was about—nominating a candidate who would stand up to the president— Crist couldn't win. I think he knew that. He had become the angry campaigner, not me. I could tell he didn't like me and resented having to fight me for the nomination. Maybe that had made it easier for him to attack me.

I don't think he enjoyed it, though. It wasn't the image of the happy warrior he had cultivated for years.

As March gave way to April, we survived and kept moving forward. The future looked bright. I didn't know that a stunning turn of events was waiting just around the corner, as was a great personal loss that I would struggle to accept.

CHAPTER 32

The Big Switch

L IFE WAS GETTING HARDER FOR GOVERNOR CRIST. HALF-
way through the legislative session, he was starting to lose his influence. His once immense popularity that he had used to intimidate the
legislature had waned, as poll after poll showed him trailing me by twenty
points. He was a lame duck, and Republican legislators began to assert
themselves, knowing he would be out of the governor's office next year.
They passed a series of conservative bills on issues ranging from merit pay
for teachers to property insurance reforms to mandatory ultrasound tests
for women seeking an abortion—all these would present a challenge to the
governor. If he signed them, the press would conclude he was trying to
shore up his appeal to conservative primary voters. If he vetoed them, it
would be taken as a sign he was going to run as an independent despite his
denials to the contrary.

I was feeling more confident that the worst of the attacks were behind
me. I took Easter Sunday off and spent the day with my family at Veronica's
house. I noticed my father was out of breath after he got up from his chair
to get a glass of water. I asked him about it, and he admitted he had been
experiencing shortness of breath for a while. He had seen the doctor, who
suspected bronchitis and prescribed a cough suppressant.

I had an event the next day with Rudy Giuliani, who had decided to
endorse me. He was still very popular in Miami, especially among Cuban

Americans. We unveiled his endorsement in Little Havana. I think Rudy believed I was the better candidate, but there was no mistaking he was also intent on settling his unfinished business with Charlie. He never mentioned Charlie by name, but when he told the crowd, "When Marco gives you his word, he keeps it," everyone knew what he was talking about.

My parents came to the endorsement and got a kick out of meeting Rudy. My dad struggled to catch his breath as he walked from the car to the event. I was increasingly worried about him. He was never one to complain, and he didn't let on that he wasn't feeling well. But there was no hiding it. He was plainly in ill health.

The next milepost on the campaign would be our financial report for the first quarter of 2010. Expectations were now reversed. I was assumed to have raised more money than Crist, and Crist's people were busy inflating expectations in the hope I would fall short of them, which they would attribute to the negative stories about me that had dominated the news in March. I sent an e-mail to my supporters on April 7, announcing that we had raised $3.6 million. The figure stunned observers, even those who had believed the Crist campaign's exaggerations. Most impressively, over 95 percent of my donors hadn't maxed out their contributions. We now had fifty thousand donors, and almost all of them could still donate more.

If anyone had any doubts that we were in control of the race, they were erased when Crist tried to release his totals quietly on a Friday afternoon, the preferred time for announcing bad news. He had raised $1.1 million. We had outraised him three to one.

Rumors were rampant now that he would leave the Republican Party and run as an independent. He issued another obligatory denial. Then his campaign announced they were spending a million dollars on television ads in Orlando and Tampa. Crist had hoarded his money in past campaigns, waiting for the last few weeks of the election to exploit his advantage. To spend such a sum on ads this early indicated to me that he was planning one last attempt to improve his support with Republican voters before the qualifying date for the Republican primary. If it didn't work, he would run as an independent. Either way, we weren't taking any chances. We scheduled a three-day bus tour across the state for the middle of April, around the same time his ads would be on the air. We would kick it off in Orlando.

I had just dropped the kids off at school on the morning of April 12, the day before the bus tour, when my cell phone rang. It was my father. He was very short of breath, and asked me if I would take him to the hospital. I was shocked. He never admitted to being sick and dismissed every illness as little more than an inconvenience. He had to be very ill and very frightened to ask me to take him to the hospital.

I drove immediately to his house and found him waiting on a bench outside. Fifteen minutes later we were sitting in the waiting room at Baptist Hospital. They ran a battery of tests, and later that afternoon the pulmonologist came into my father's room and asked to speak with the family. My sisters and I stepped into the hallway, where he delivered the bad news. My dad's lung cancer had returned, and his emphysema had progressed considerably. There were no surgical options, he told us. He advised us to meet with an oncologist, but in his opinion, considering my father's age and the advanced stage of his emphysema, chemotherapy wasn't a good option, either. Barbara and I were still probing him for treatment options, when Veronica asked the question neither of us wanted to ask: "How long does he have?"

"With treatment, maybe eight to twelve months," he said. "With no treatment, considerably less."

Just as the news my father wouldn't survive the year was sinking in, staff called to tell me Crist had just gone on air with a brutal attack ad. He e-mailed it to me. In a small waiting room at Baptist Hospital, just minutes after I'd been told my father was terminally ill, I watched a thirty-second spot linking me to my successor as speaker, Ray Sansom, who had been forced to resign from office. The ad captioned the word "indicted" under Sansom's picture, and "subpoenaed" under mine.

All my life my dad had taken care of me. He had driven me to two hospitals when I had a bad stomachache until he found a doctor who would diagnose my problem. When I had injured my knee playing football, my father went with me every day to rehabilitate it. When I came home rather than stay in Gainesville waiting for my last final exam, he had driven me back to school and sat for hours in a Burger King waiting for me to finish my exam. Even when I was grown and married, my dad took me to the hospital when I suffered from stomach flu on Easter Sunday in 1999. He had always been there for me—always—and had never asked for anything from the rest of us. I wanted to be there for him.

We decided to go ahead with the first part of the bus trip, but announced that my father's cancer had returned and we had to cut the trip short so I could make arrangements for his care. I did an interview with Sean Hannity on the evening of April 13, from The Villages in north-central Florida. At the end of the interview I asked Sean if I could say hello to my dad in Miami. I knew he was watching. He always was.

I returned to Miami and cleared my calendar for the next few days. We had him discharged from the hospital and moved him to Barbara's house, which was just a few blocks from my house. I spent much of the first day making certain he had oxygen there. The next day, I took him to get a PET scan to determine whether his cancer had spread. It hadn't, and his oncologist thought it was worth a shot to see if he could tolerate chemotherapy. My sisters believed that, given his age and emphysema, chemotherapy would only debilitate him more rapidly and make his last few months of life unbearable. But, like me, they couldn't accept the idea of letting his cancer grow if there was a chance we could arrest it. I pushed for the chemo, and my dad consented.

I drove him to his first chemo treatment and got him situated in the chair where he would receive the chemo over the next several hours, leaving him with a portable radio tuned to a baseball game and a sandwich from Subway. I went home reflecting on the end of the cycle of life, when the child takes care of the parent.

Encouraging my father to undergo chemotherapy proved to be a terrible mistake. He didn't respond well to it. He lost a lot of weight and all his hair. He stopped after three treatments. I had made a very bad call, and my dad had suffered for it.

It took me a while to get back into a frame of mind to continue the campaign. My heart wasn't in it. I knew my father wanted to see me win. Even in his suffering, he watched Fox News all day long, waiting for news about my campaign. Back I went, into the thick of it, and soon the campaign's rhythm, its highs and lows, the good and the bad news, began to preoccupy me again.

On April 15, Quinnipiac released another poll that gave me a huge lead. By now, another poll with me ahead wasn't really news. But this poll got my attention because it also found that, were Crist to run as an independent, he would have a narrow lead. As soon as I saw it, I knew it would get Charlie's attention, too.

Until then, we had asked ourselves whether Crist would leave the Republican Party to become an independent. But that was the wrong question. In Florida, you can retain your party affiliation and still run in a general election under the designation of "no party affiliation." In other words, Crist didn't have to leave the GOP to run in a three-way race in the fall. He just had to qualify as a "no party" candidate by filling out the appropriate paperwork and paying the filing fee.

No one had asked Crist that question. So one of my consultants, Alberto Martinez, pitched it to several reporters. *Miami Herald* reporter Marc Caputo asked Crist on April 15, "Will you withdraw from the Republican primary?" Crist responded, "That's the last thing on my mind right now." It was an obvious evasion. By now, we all knew that was exactly what he was considering.

Just as he had done a year earlier when he had dragged out his decision to run for the Senate, Crist again became the constant object of speculation about his intentions. Whether or not he would run as an independent was the hottest political question in the news. Suddenly, he wasn't the struggling former front-runner in the GOP primary anymore. He had once again become Charlie Crist, man of intrigue. He milked it for all it was worth, and then fate gave him the perfect issue to potentially change the direction of the race.

Republicans in the Florida legislature had worked the entire session on a bill instituting teacher tenure and merit pay—the reforms that conservatives love and teachers' unions hate. The debate had become very heated. The teachers' unions used social media and protest rallies to build opposition to the legislation. It was an impressive, well-executed, grassroots effort that caught the bill's supporters off guard. The legislature passed it anyway, and sent it to the governor. He could either sign it and please conservatives who had deserted him for me, or he could veto it and please the teachers' unions, many parents and a growing number of voters who had rallied to the teachers' unions' side. I never had any doubt which course he would choose.

He vetoed the bill on the afternoon of April 15, and the next day he was greeted as a conquering hero at a celebration rally held at Alonzo and Tracy Mourning Senior High School in Miami. Suddenly Facebook and other social media were inundated with teachers and even union officials thanking Crist, and urging support for his Senate bid as a reward for vetoing the bill.

Some people in my campaign began to panic. They believed Crist had seized a rare and perfectly timed opportunity to transcend traditional politics and win the election in a three-way race. They thought he would be able to put together a coalition of moderate Republicans, centrist Democrats, independents and teachers' unions. I was less worried about it. I recognized he had managed in a single stroke to generate enthusiasm for his campaign and open a path to victory in the fall. But I knew, too, he would have to sustain the new enthusiasm over an entire summer and the beginning of the new school year until the general election. That was a steep hill to climb. Furthermore, if anyone should have been worried, it was Kendrick Meek, the expected Democratic nominee. The teachers' unions were part of his base, not mine.

Over the weekend there were more signs Crist was getting ready to run as an independent. He pulled his ads comparing me to Sansom off the air, and rather than replace them with another ad, he asked that his money be returned. He was saving his money again.

On the afternoon of April 19, Rob Jesmer, the executive director of the National Republican Senatorial Committee, sent an e-mail to Republican donors, affirming his view that Crist would not run in the Republican primary. He concluded, "Whether or not you supported our endorsement of Governor Crist, we all share the same goal of keeping the seat in Republican hands. To that end, if the Governor decides to run independent . . . we will support Marco Rubio in any way possible."

That same evening, for the first time, Crist admitted what everyone already knew: he was seriously thinking about running as an independent. "I'm getting all kinds of advice," he told the press corps with a chuckle. "I take my cues from people in Florida. That's what I care about. . . . This is a decision that has to be made by the thirtieth, and I want to do what's right for the people of our state."

The next week was dominated by speculation about Crist's intentions. It was clear to me what he was going to do. Meanwhile, far offshore in the Gulf of Mexico, the oil rig Deepwater Horizon was about to explode, a disaster that would soon have an impact on the campaign.

The rest of April was fairly uneventful until it was time to qualify for the ballot at the end of the month. We held a filing announcement in West Miami on the twenty-seventh. We chose as the site a small city park just a few blocks from my house. The park had sentimental value to me. I had played there as a kid after we returned from Las Vegas. I had taken pictures of Jeanette and my parents there that I included in a mail piece in my first campaign for West Miami commissioner. We held Amanda's first birthday party there.

My father's breathing had become so labored that we had to drive him in a car right up to the stage. After I made brief remarks in English and Spanish, I sat down at a table and signed the qualifying documents. My father sat to my left. He was nearing the end of his life—a life that had begun over eight decades earlier in Havana, a life that had known pain, hunger, suffering and more than six decades of hard work. Now his younger son might be elected to the U.S. Senate in seven months—an achievement that seemed unlikely to me just a year before, an achievement that would have been unimaginable to him when he arrived penniless in his new country over half a century before. It was the last time he would appear at any of my public events.

Later that evening, word spread that Crist had scheduled a major event in his hometown, St. Petersburg, for the evening of April 29. There wasn't any doubt or drama anymore about what he intended to do. He would run for the Senate as an independent. At 9:07 on the morning of April 29, I received a text message from Al Cardenas regarding news he had just received from Crist's campaign manager Eric Eikenberg.

> Eric Eikenberg just called me to let me know that he gave cc his 2 week notice yesterday—confirmed cc is running as an npo. Keep this to yourself for now.

Alex Leary of the *St. Petersburg Times* wrote an article a few days later that described the factors that had influenced Crist's decision. Leary had spent the entire day before the announcement with Crist. He wrote about people who had called to encourage the governor. According to Crist, Donald Trump, Arnold Schwarzenegger and tennis great Chris Evert had all urged him to run as an independent. So had a good many teachers and school superintendents. So had people in the street he had met that day, who expressed to him their frustration with partisan gridlock. But the most telling incident included in the article had occurred at 11:12 a.m. that day, when Crist's pollster told him he was winning a three-way race for the Senate by twelve points.

I listened to his announcement on the radio as I drove Anthony to his T-ball game. Crist decried partisan politics and condemned Republicans in the legislature as recalcitrant. He didn't want to work for a political party, he said. He wanted to work for the people of Florida. He wanted to do this for them. That might have all been true. But as Alex Leary's article made clear, most of all he wanted to win. And so did I.

CHAPTER 33

Behind Again

IT HAD BEEN QUITE A RIDE ALREADY. I HAD GONE FROM A
sure loser without a viable way to quit the race to the surging front-
runner. Now the stars had aligned again for Crist. The bickering Florida
legislature and an unpopular bill had given him the opportunity to wear
the mantle of a postpartisan populist. He made the most of his opportunity and reclaimed the lead in the race for the U.S. Senate. A Rasmussen
poll released on May 4 confirmed he had retaken a lead, though by a smaller
margin than Crist's pollster had given him. Making matters worse, a new
issue loomed that gave him the perfect platform from which to take command of the race.

The explosion on the Deepwater Horizon had resulted in an uncon-
tainable oil gusher that was pouring fifty-three thousand gallons of oil a
day into the Gulf of Mexico, threatening Florida's coastline. Predictably,
support among Floridians for offshore drilling dropped dramatically. I was
asked by a reporter on May 4 if I still supported offshore drilling. I responded by acknowledging the horrible threat from the oil spill, and confirmed I still supported offshore drilling. I didn't believe we could become
energy independent without it. Crist saw his opportunity and pounced.
Although he had supported drilling in 2008, he was now 100 percent
against it. It was a smart political move.

I knew that as long as oil was spewing uncontrolled into the Gulf, offshore drilling would be unpopular. But when the well was capped and the spill contained, over time support for offshore drilling would increase. People understood the country needed all its energy resources. But in the present crisis, support for drilling, like support for Social Security and Medicare reform, would be a test of principle over politics. My only hope was that voters would give me credit for being serious about the issue and not opportunistic. Time would tell.

Another issue that had come to the fore began to hurt us as well. I was troubled when the Arizona legislature passed an immigration bill that allowed law enforcement officers to demand proof of legal residence from anyone they had lawfully detained and suspected of being in the country illegally. I thought the law would lead to racial profiling. As I started to hear more about Arizona's illegal immigration problem, I recognized that Arizona's situation was different and more severe than Florida's. Florida doesn't share a porous border with a neighboring country. It's surrounded by ocean. We certainly have an illegal immigration problem, but it is mostly caused by people overstaying their visas.

The Tucson border sector in Arizona is the scene of rampant illegal crossings, drug smuggling, gunrunning and human trafficking. An all-out drug war in Mexico was starting to export violence to Arizona cities. Arizonans were fed up. They wanted something done immediately to address the crisis, and state legislators had answered by passing the new immigration law.

When I was first asked about it, I strongly criticized the law and said it raised the specter of a police state. But as I learned more about the situation in Arizona, the provisions of the law and the modifications that had been made to it, I softened my opinion. I still didn't support state immigration laws, and I didn't want a law like Arizona's enacted in Florida. But I understood why Arizonans supported it. If I had been in their shoes and my state had been overrun by cross-border violence, I probably would have voted for it, too.

Now I was getting it from all sides. The anti-illegal-immigrant crowd was upset with me because I didn't think Florida should pass a similar law. Pro-immigrant groups denounced me for supporting the law in Arizona. I had managed to unite both sides against me.

For a time, the Arizona law became a litmus test issue in the national debate on immigration. You were either for it or against it. Like the debate itself, there seemed to be only two acceptable positions: you were either for strictly enforcing immigration law and expelling all people who were in the country illegally or you were in favor of letting them all stay. But it's always been hard for me to see the issue in such black-and-white terms.

The anti-illegal-immigration side often loses perspective on the issue. But the pro-immigration crowd is also guilty of a maximalist approach. They ignore how illegal immigration unfairly affects immigrants who live here legally or are trying to immigrate here legally.

Every year my Senate office is approached by hundreds of people who request our assistance in expediting changes to their immigration status. They've followed the rules, paid the necessary fees and patiently waited. It isn't fair to them to permit millions of people to remain here who didn't follow their example and apply for legal status. What message does that send to aspiring immigrants? It tells them they can immigrate to our country a lot quicker if they do so illegally.

Immigration advocates also allow themselves to be manipulated politically, which is something Cuban Americans have experienced in every election. Many candidates have campaigned in Miami's Cuban communities promising to get tough on Castro. "Cuba Libre," they shout, and then, after they're elected, they ignore the issue. Today, it's common for Democratic candidates to make all sorts of unrealistic promises about immigration reform to Latinos in the hope of mobilizing their support, and once in office they fail to keep them. President Obama was elected with a substantial majority of Latino support even though John McCain was one of the most outspoken immigration reform advocates in the Republican Party. The president promised he would pass comprehensive immigration reform in his first year in office. He didn't. He didn't even propose a comprehensive bill despite having Democratic majorities in both houses of Congress. Why? Because the solution is a lot more complicated and harder to put together than Democrats ever concede. Also, immigration is such an effective wedge issue against Republicans, some Democrats would just as soon keep it than make the necessary concessions that could lead to a bipartisan resolution of the issue.

Immigration reform advocates have allowed Democrats to define the debate by insisting on support for specific bills that are unlikely to become law in their current form. For example, the vast majority of Americans and my Republican colleagues support the idea behind the DREAM Act, of making a distinction for and helping undocumented students who are high academic achievers—kids who were brought to the United States when they were very young and have grown up here. They're ready to contribute to the country's future. They're not in compliance with immigration law and, thus, not American citizens. But they are culturally as American as anyone else's children. I'm sure we would find a way to keep them here if they could dunk a basketball. Why would we deport them if they're valedictorian of their high school class?

But the bill is too broad as currently written. It could encourage chain migration, by authorizing the relatives of students covered by the act to come here. A narrower bill would serve the same primary purpose of the DREAM Act, permit undocumented students to remain in the country and go to school without exacerbating the illegal immigration problem. The modifications necessary to assure its passage are not difficult to conceive or write into law. Nor should they trouble people on either side of the debate. But many activists refuse to concede that and denounce any opposition to the current DREAM Act as anti-immigrant. And many Democrats happily urge them on. I don't question that many of my Democratic colleagues are sincere in their desire to help undocumented students. So am I. But I'm not so naive that I don't recognize that some Democrats enjoy the advantage with Latino voters that Republican opposition to the bill gives them.

There is no doubt, either, that the rhetoric and tone used by some Republican opponents of immigration reform have hurt the party with Hispanics. George W. Bush strongly supported comprehensive reform, yet his support among Latinos lagged behind his Democratic opponents'. John McCain was the chief Republican sponsor of comprehensive reform legislation, but he lost Hispanics to President Obama by more than a two-to-one margin. Most Hispanics have long been Democratic voters. But there are growing numbers of them who might be open to supporting Republicans. Many of them are socially conservative, and worried about the influence on their children of our hypersexualized secular pop culture. Republican support for traditional cultural values appeals to them. Many Hispanic voters who lawfully immigrated here did so for the economic opportunities available here and to escape the hardships caused by the government-dominated economies in their countries of origin. The Republican free-enterprise agenda attracts them as well. But it is very difficult to appeal to Hispanic voters for their support when they believe Republicans are trying to deport their loved ones.

I often feel as if I live in two worlds. I get angry when I hear stories of couples from wealthy families who come to Miami from overseas in the last weeks of a pregnancy, deliver their children at Jackson Memorial so their babies are born American citizens and then leave the country and stick the American public with their hospital bills. I appreciate the frustration people have when they feel their country is being overwhelmed by illegal immigration.

On the other hand, when I hear some people accuse immigrants of destroying the American economy and culture and stealing jobs from American citizens, it stirs my anger, too. I can't stand to hear immigrants described in terms more appropriate to a plague of locusts than human beings. And although I believe they are a small minority, I begin to wonder if some of the people who speak so disparagingly about immigrants would be just as worked up if most of them were coming from Canada.

I understand it is a difficult issue. It's a law-and-order issue. But it's also an issue about human dignity and common decency. And when we lose sight of either aspect of the issue, we harm ourselves as well as the people who wish to live here. Many people who come here illegally are doing exactly what we would do if we lived in a country where we couldn't feed our families. If my kids went to sleep hungry every night and my country didn't give me an opportunity to feed them, there isn't a law, no matter how restrictive, that would prevent me from coming here. We should debate our differences on immigration with regard to all the issues that deserve our respect and attention.

The firestorm over the immigration issue slowly died down, but the BP oil spill was an entirely different matter. Crist used his governor's office masterfully and to full effect. It seemed as if he held a press conference every night to highlight his latest effort to save Florida's coastline. He took well-publicized trips to affected beaches. He called for a special session of the legislature to pass an offshore drilling ban.

My campaign was knocked off balance. For over a year, our plan was a simple one. We needed to convince Republican primary voters to send someone to Washington who would stand up to President Obama and the Democratic leadership in Congress. There was no way Charlie Crist could win a primary that was defined by that aspiration. But I no longer had a primary opponent. I had general election opponents. My message had to be broader. And we hadn't yet found one. As Memorial Day neared and another poll showed Crist ahead, some of the campaign staff became seriously worried that we were drifting.

I took my family to the Florida Keys for a few days of rest over the holiday weekend. On Saturday morning I got a call from my sister Barbara. My father was incoherent and barely conscious. Jeanette and I raced home from the Keys and met my family at the hospital. My father's condition looked very grim.

Another battery of tests couldn't confirm what was wrong. He was suffering strokelike symptoms. His mouth was turned down and his speech was slurred. The words we could manage to make out didn't make sense.

He improved slowly over the next few days. I spent the nights sleeping in a cot next to his bed. He kept me awake much of the night as he called out to his brothers, Papo and Emilio. He addressed them as if they were in the room. Is this what you see before you die? I wondered. Do you see your deceased relatives arrive to bring you to the afterlife?

As it turned out, he was hallucinating, probably in reaction to the chemotherapy. He had gotten an infection from the chemo that manifested itself neurologically. We brought him home a few days later. It was clear now there would be no more chemotherapy. All we could do now was make him as comfortable as possible for however many weeks or months he had left.

CHAPTER 34

Dog Days of Summer

At the time, all discipline seems cause not for joy but for pain, yet
later, it brings the peaceful fruit of righteousness to those who are
trained by it.

—Hebrews 12:11

A YEAR BEFORE, I WAS BROKE, TRAILING BADLY IN THE
polls and afraid. The campaign had become a predicament I couldn't
escape. I couldn't find a way to win, or a way out. So I accepted what I believed would be my inevitable humiliation, and God used my despair to
lead me to Him. Then the race turned, and I gained the upper hand. In the
summer of 2010, it had turned once more. I was trailing Charlie Crist again.
He had seized his opportunity and played it well. But now I saw my changing fortunes for what they were: just another test. Whether I won or lost the
election wouldn't matter as much in my life as whether I had learned to put
my trust in Him.

All around me was worry and near despair. My campaign staff, many
of whom had joined the campaign only a few weeks before, complained I
wasn't showing enough leadership on the oil spill. They wanted me to spend
a week in the Panhandle, matching Crist event for event. I needed a broader

message, too, they advised. I couldn't win now by being the more conservative candidate. I had to appeal more to independents.

I wasn't the same person I had been a year before. I wasn't the self-reliant, worldly young man with all the answers anymore. I accepted I wouldn't always know what I should do. But I didn't rattle as easily, either. I still had a long way to go in my walk in faith, but I had come a long way from where I had begun. I tried to turn to God before I relied on myself. And I prayed for wisdom and the strength to accept His will.

I realized I couldn't command as much attention on the oil spill as the governor could. If the election was defined by the oil spill, I would lose, and I accepted it. Traveling the state trying to imitate him would be a waste of time, and counterproductive. We would be playing his game and, in effect, helping him make the election about a debate I couldn't win.

I believed that by Labor Day, when voters refocused on the race, their attention would return to the economy and the direction of the country. If we were ready then to win the argument about which candidate was more committed to changing the country's direction, we would win the election. So I spent most of the summer laying out the policy ideas that would be the foundation of my argument for change in the fall. It wasn't glamorous work. Traveling the state giving policy speeches isn't as exciting as a full-throated battle for the heart and soul of the Republican Party. But it prepared the ground on which I would fight and win in the fall.

We built up our organization as well: our get-out-the-vote infrastructure, our absentee ballot program, our county-level volunteer teams, all the blocking and tackling the press mostly ignores but that make a big difference on Election Day. And we raised money, building up the war chest we would need in the fall. It was tedious work, outside the media spotlight and a letdown for many who had joined us thinking they were enlisting in a nationalized campaign with national media attention. I used my football experiences as a metaphor to encourage them and myself.

You spend the summer months getting ready for the football season by training in the gym and on the field. Before training camp even begins, and months before the first game, you spend long hours lifting weights and running conditioning drills. There are no crowds to inspire you. There are no television cameras recording off-season workouts. It's just you and a few teammates, out on the field in the early-morning hours, grinding it out and getting stronger. That's what we were doing that summer. All the fund-raising and policy speeches and grassroots building was the thankless grunt work that would pay off in the fourth quarter of the championship game that was still months away.

We hit some bumps along the way. Back in 2005, I bought a house in Tallahassee with David Rivera, where I stayed while I was in the legislature and working in the capital. After I left the legislature, I allowed my part of the house to be used by others in exchange for assuming my portion of the monthly payments. Or so I had believed. In fact, complete payments hadn't been made for several months, and there was a dispute about how much was owed each month. As soon as I found out about the problem, I called the bank to discuss it. The bank referred me to a law firm in Ft. Lauderdale that was now handling the file. When I called the law firm, they informed me they had just received the file and would call me back when they had reviewed it. But the next day, before returning my call, they initiated the first steps in the foreclosure process.

The firm would later be sanctioned by the state of Florida for unfair practices. It was a foreclosure mill. Rather than work with home owners to settle disputes, it rushed to file foreclosures so it could collect attorneys' fees and costs. We finally got someone at the firm to talk to me the next day. David went to the firm's office in Broward County and paid the total amount due, including legal fees, with a cashier's check. Disaster averted, or so I thought.

Alex Burgos got a call from the *Palm Beach Post*. They had been tipped off about the filing. Alex explained there had been a dispute about how much we owed, but we had resolved it and were no longer in arrears. The story ran away. "Rubio Faces Foreclosure on Tally Home," the headline blared.

There was more bad news the next day. The Florida Chamber of Commerce released the findings of a new poll it had commissioned. Crist's lead was growing. He was ten points ahead now, and the media was taking notice. Adam Smith posed the question on his blog: "Has Marco Rubio lost his mojo?" The gist of his speculation was that I had lost the energy that had once characterized my campaign. He acknowledged that part of the reason was the publicity Crist received during the oil spill. But he also thought I was struggling to make the transition from a Republican primary candidate to a general election candidate.

There was some truth to the lost-energy speculation. It did feel like we had less energy, but not for the reasons Adam believed. There had been so much anticipation built up in the state for the primary that would help decide the national debate over the direction of the Republican Party, so there was a natural letdown when Crist pulled out of the primary. The general election was four months away. Voters naturally were less engaged. Kids were out of school and families were on vacation. And our campaign was concentrating on the unseen and less exciting work of organization building and fund-raising. But Adam's article reinforced the new narrative of the campaign. Charlie had turned around the race. I was off balance and struggling in a general election environment.

The *Miami Herald* ran a piece that called the oil spill Charlie Crist's "lucky charm." As we headed into the Fourth of July, the conventional wisdom held that Charlie was back in control of the race and we were floundering. The Crist campaign took the opportunity to proclaim the return of the "happy warrior." There would be no more attacks on me or any candidate, he promised.

Behind the scenes, though, his campaign was still pushing story lines that would put me at a disadvantage. They tried to raise expectations for my fund-raising that they didn't believe I could meet. They argued to reporters that since I was now the presumptive Republican nominee, I should be able to beat Crist's record-setting first-quarter fund-raising total. If I couldn't, then the failure was further evidence I was losing steam.

I tried to ignore the distractions and continued raising money, rolling out our policy initiatives and building our get-out-the-vote operation. I was convinced that once voters focused on the race again, my numbers would improve. President Obama's policies were becoming even more unpopular in Florida, and I was the only candidate who opposed them. I still had less name recognition with general election voters than Crist did, and the summer polls reflected that. That would change once I started to buy television time in the fall and introduced myself to them.

These were the dog days of summer. The crowds at my speeches were half as big as they'd been before Crist dropped out of the primary. The press had lost much of its interest in my candidacy. It wasn't easy to see a light at the end of the tunnel. It took patient confidence that I had not always possessed. But I did now. I sincerely believed that, by the fall, if we had done the quiet but important work we needed to do that summer, I would pull ahead again and never look back.

We got a little good news the second week of July. Rasmussen released a new poll that showed I had reclaimed the lead. It was a very small lead, but a lead nonetheless. More good news came four days later, when we announced our fund-raising total for the quarter. We had raised $4.5 million, exceeding Crist's record-breaking total and even the seemingly unrealistic expectations his campaign had tried to set for me.

Other new polls still gave Crist the lead. He had raised $1.8 million for the quarter—less than us but more than he had raised the previous quarter. The press saw it as further evidence he was back in control of the race. But I wasn't worried. Once the Democrats chose their nominee, political gravity would set in. Crist and Kendrick Meek would fight over the half of the Florida electorate that approved of the direction of the country, and I would claim the half that didn't. We budgeted to begin our television advertising right after the Democratic primary.

Even before our TV push, the numbers started to shift. Rasmussen released another poll that had me ahead. So did Mason-Dixon. Others followed. A few still gave Crist a lead, but we were confident momentum was shifting our way again.

Jeanette and I did a quick fly-around of the state the day before the Republican primary on August 24. There wasn't any doubt I would win the nomination. I had only token opposition after Crist pulled out of the primary. But we thought we could use the primary to reengage the media's interest in our campaign and as the launching pad for our final push.

I voted for myself early the next morning, then stopped by the Biltmore Hotel, where my top donors were spending the day making finance calls for me. After lunch I went to my sister's house to check on my father. He had deteriorated over the summer and was now bedridden. My nephew Danny opened the door with a grin on his face. I asked him what was so funny, and he told me to come in and see for myself. I walked to the back of the house and found my father sitting in the living room, fully dressed. It was the first time he had been out of bed in a month. He wanted to attend my victory party that night. A few days before, he had filled out and mailed his absentee ballot. He had voted to send his son to the United States Senate, and now he felt strong enough to celebrate. He would have to go in a wheelchair, and he couldn't stay long. But it was the best news of the day.

I left for an afternoon Mass and then went home to change for the party. We arrived at the Doubletree Miami Hotel at six that evening and waited in a holding room behind the stage, where my nephew informed me that my dad wouldn't be coming. He had become weaker that afternoon and didn't have enough strength to join us. He had wanted to be there. He had wanted to make one final sacrifice for his son—one last selfless act in a lifetime of selfless acts. But it was not to be. And soon it would be time to say good-bye, forever.

CHAPTER 35

Good-bye

A S EXPECTED, KENDRICK MEEK WON THE DEMOCRATIC primary, and he got a short-term bounce in the polls. But he didn't have much money, and few observers believed he could win the general election. Our path to victory required a viable Democratic nominee to compete with Crist for Democratic votes. In a three-way race, I would only need to hold the Republican base and win a decent share of the independent vote. I wouldn't be pressured to move to the left. I could run as who I was: a fiscal and social conservative. But as we began the fall campaign, we worried that a three-way contest might be effectively reduced to two. If Kendrick became irrelevant—he was underfinanced and a distant third in all the polls—Crist would become the de facto Democratic nominee. Democrats would embrace him as their best hope to defeat me. We couldn't let that happen.

We discussed what we could do to help keep Kendrick viable. He didn't have the money to finance an effective television ad campaign. We needed to help him get free airtime. Debates were the best way to do that. And so, two days after the Democratic primary, we agreed to seven televised debates. Some Republican observers questioned why we would agree to so many debates, particularly after we regained a lead in the polls. But they served their purpose. They kept Kendrick in the news and relevant. Thanks in large part to Kendrick's effectiveness as a debater, Crist never had a clear field to court Democratic votes.

The seven debates served as a regular reminder that there was an actual Democrat in the race. Kendrick performed very well in all of them. I thought he won at least two of them. He certainly surpassed the low expectations people had set for him. I never understood why people expected so little of him. He was smart, quick on his feet, an agile campaigner and very likable. Those qualities came across quite well in the debates.

We began our TV ad campaign the same day we agreed to the debates. The first ad was designed to establish who I was and why I believed what I did. It was shot in black and white, purposely designed to look and feel very different from the attack ads voters had been inundated with during the primary. We wanted to assure voters our campaign was about big things, not petty politics.

My parents, especially my father, were featured in the spot. I remember one image in particular: an old photograph of my father bartending on Miami Beach in his crisp white uniform. The ad was very effective, and we saw its impact in our internal tracking polls. Everywhere I went, people mentioned it to me, sometimes with tears in their eyes. They told me my story was their story.

Our first debate was scheduled for Sunday, September 5, on *Meet the Press*. Crist had decided not to participate, but Kendrick was all in, which was the only thing that mattered to us at the time. I had planned to devote as much time to debate prep as I had before the Fox News debate with Crist. We were in the middle of a prep session when I received a phone call from Barbara's mother-in-law, who lived with her. She called to tell me my father was struggling to breathe and had become very agitated.

I left debate prep and drove to Barbara's house, where I found my dad sitting up in bed in a panic. He couldn't catch his breath, and the low dose of morphine drops wasn't helping him. I gave him a nebulizer treatment to open up his lungs, but he yanked off the mask and asked to be taken to the hospital. I argued against it. They'll only do the same thing we're doing here, I told him, and send you right back. But he was insistent, so I gave in and called 911. The paramedics arrived, and within minutes, he was on a gurney. One of the paramedics was Chris Boulos, Veronica's boyfriend and future husband. He hadn't been on call, but rushed to the house when he heard my father's name. As Chris and the other paramedic lifted him into the ambulance, my father said out loud, "*De aquí al cementerio.*" From here to the cemetery.

I followed the ambulance in my car and arrived at the hospital at the same time. They gave him oxygen and several more nebulizer treatments, and then transferred him to a hospital room. My nephew Danny spent the night with him. The next day I kept my schedule, which consisted mostly of debate prep, while Veronica and Barbara took turns staying with my father. When I finished, I went home for dinner and helped put the kids to bed before I headed to the hospital, where I planned to spend the night. When I arrived there, Barbara told me he had eaten his dinner and had had a pretty good day, joking with the nurses who'd come in to check on him. Barbara had been there most of the day, and was tired. I told her to go home, and I settled down on the roll-away bed next to his bed.

I turned on the television, and like we had so many times over the years, my father and I watched a Miami Dolphins game together. As the evening wore on, I noticed a change in my father's behavior. He became increasingly disoriented. He thought we were in a kitchen, and asked me to put the dishes in the cupboard. He started calling me Papo, his brother's name. Soon he became agitated. He tried to climb out of bed, though he didn't have the strength to do it. He began shouting his brother's name, asking him to help him. He begged for air. His eyes became glassy. I finally called for a nurse.

She gave him an injection of antianxiety medication. It worked for a half hour, and then he became agitated again. He asked me to hand him a blanket he thought he saw hanging on the wall. He wanted me to fan him to help him get air. They administered the antianxiety drug several more times, but it didn't calm him. He was overcome by anxiety. He was suffering.

My father was becoming hypoxic. His damaged lungs could no longer process enough oxygen to his brain, causing hallucinations and the terrifying sensation he was running out of air. I had researched my father's condition after he had been diagnosed as terminal, and I knew he would enter the last phase of his life when he became hypoxic. In the early-morning hours of September 3, I knew that moment had arrived.

There was only one way to relieve his suffering and make him comfortable. He would have to be placed on a morphine drip. The nurse advised me that once he was started on the drip, he would slip into a comalike state, from which he would probably never awaken. I worried that it was too soon. We had seen him deteriorate before, only to improve the next day. I worried that if I ordered the morphine that night, my mother and sisters would never have another chance to tell him they loved him, and say good-bye.

I stood in the doorway of his room and watched him. He was twisting and turning in his bed, calling to his brothers, Papo and Emilio, "*Ayúdame! Ayúdame!*" Help me. Help me. I turned to his nurse and told her, "Do it."

He calmed down quickly after the morphine drip began. In a brief moment of lucidity, he told me, "*Yo sé que te estoy molestando mucho*"—I know I'm bothering you a lot. A few minutes later, he fell asleep. I would never see him open his eyes again.

The next morning, I texted my siblings and Jeanette the details of what had occurred overnight, and everyone came to the hospital immediately. I still held out hope he would wake up at some point that morning. But as the morning wore on, it became apparent he would not. We canceled the *Meet the Press* debate. Kendrick Meek called to express his concerns. He was brief but very gracious, and I appreciated it very much. Politics can be an ugly business, though. Some Meek and Crist supporters expressed skepticism on Twitter and Facebook about the family emergency that had caused me to cancel the debate. They claimed I was afraid to debate Kendrick and had made up an excuse to get out of it. I didn't hold Kendrick and Charlie responsible for their behavior. We all have supporters who say unfortunate and sometimes cruel things. But it did show the lengths that some people will go, especially since the advent of the Internet and the social media age, to disparage and even dehumanize their political opponents.

It was a long Friday waiting for my father to die. My mother, my brother and sisters, my nephews, my aunt Georgina, my uncle Alberto and aunt Marta, Jeanette and I kept vigil. We never left his side. We watched for any sign of a change in his condition. We knew it was a matter of time, but how long? Hours? Days? None of us knew.

A steady stream of visitors came to pay their last respects. They all grieved for my father and for my mother. My father held on; his breathing was slow but even paced. Friday night we slept in his room, or tried to.

When Saturday morning arrived, my father was still breathing—but barely. In my mind, I was transported twenty-six years into my past, when I was a teenager keeping vigil at my dying grandfather's bedside. I was afraid to leave my father's side for a minute for fear I would miss his final breath. I was afraid to go downstairs to get something to eat or go home to take a shower. So I stayed and watched the life drain out of my father. Nothing else mattered.

We passed the hours by reminiscing about my father. There were moments of laughter and tears. Everyone had something to add about the man who had meant so much to us. At one point, my mother sat next to his bed, stroked his hand and cried. She kept asking him to wake up. They had been married for sixty-one years. It was more than her heart could bear.

They say people on their deathbed often cling to life to spare their loved ones the pain of their loss. If that is true, my father would have surely been one of those people. Knowing we were hurting would have affected him greatly, but knowing my mother was suffering would have been too much for him to bear. He adored her and protected her fiercely. We believed he wouldn't let go until she let him go, and so we asked her to say good-bye and give him permission to depart this life. She resisted at first. But by the afternoon she relented. She caressed his head, told him how much she loved him, and encouraged him to let go. I think that was the hardest thing she ever had to do. She had spent a lifetime by my father's side, and now, at seventy-nine, she faced her remaining years alone.

Early Saturday evening, he began his final transition from life to death. Within a few hours, my father's breathing pattern began to change, as did his physical appearance. He didn't even look like my father anymore. I don't know if that made it harder or easier. The man lying in that bed was not at all like the man I remembered. His face was gaunt and pale. His frame had withered. His false teeth had been removed.

At nine thirty in the evening we noticed a significant change and slower, more labored breaths. We watched his heartbeat from a pulsing vein on the left side of his neck. I watched it slow and then begin to flutter. Then a long pause, and it pulsed no more. It was 9:43 p.m.

He began his life in a big, happy family. Before he was ten it was all taken from him. He had been on his own from a very young age. In a hard life with many ups and downs, he had built and protected for us the warm and loving family he had lost. And he died where most of us would hope to die, in a room filled with people who loved him.

The next day, I posted a statement on the campaign's Facebook page, paying tribute to the decent, selfless, ordinary man whose hard work and sacrifices had given me the opportunity to do extraordinary things.

I was confused and troubled in the days following my father's death. I knew I would have to resume my campaign soon. But I was torn by so many emotions. I felt guilty for ordering the morphine drip, and self-doubt nagged at me. Had I agreed to it too soon? Would he still be alive if I had just waited with him through the night for his anxiety to subside? I was so sad that he had not lived long enough to do the thing he had been so looking forward to: cast a vote for his son for the last time. He would not see my victory, or share in the success that he, more than anyone, had made possible.

I didn't feel like doing anything. When my grandfather died, I quit Pop Warner and retreated into my home, uninterested in anything for months. I felt the same way now. Except I wasn't a teenager anymore. I had a wife and children. And I was a candidate for the United States Senate. No matter how bad I felt, I had to go back to work, just as my father had gone to work after his mother died four days before his ninth birthday.

My first major campaign event after my father's death was a Republican Party dinner in Orlando on September 10. I didn't want to be there. I just wanted to give my speech, get in my car and drive home. I avoided mingling with the crowd outside the banquet hall and sat in a hotel coffee shop with Jeanette until it was time to take the stage. I spoke for about fifteen minutes, and ended the speech with a reflection:

> Sometimes we take things we have in our life for granted. We don't fully appreciate things until they're gone. We've experienced that with people that we love. And maybe that's what's happening now with our country. Have we reached the point as a people where we've forgotten how special this place truly is?

My father had cared all his life for the people he loved. He had hated to see me suffer. I still remember the look of anguish on his face when the doctor told him his six-year-old son needed surgery. He had helped raise Barbara's boys when her husband was in prison. He watched the movie *King Kong* hundreds of times because it was Landy's favorite. I can still see him carrying Danny, who had whooping cough, racing out of the house in a panic because he thought the little boy had stopped breathing.

At the end of his life his children and grandchildren had cared for him. My nephew had cradled him and carried him to his wheelchair. Barbara had smoothed ointment on his skin to treat a painful infection he had developed. Veronica spent the night watching over him at the hospital. I had made the terrible mistake of urging him to try chemotherapy, and later made the decision to give him morphine. It is a natural part of life when children become their parents' caretakers, though it might not seem natural at the time. It's not easy to become accustomed to such a poignant role reversal. It's harder still to become accustomed to the loss of someone you had so long depended on, who had loved you without limit.

It was hard to believe he was gone. I caught myself many times that fall about to call him to let him know I would be on the news that night. I still do sometimes.

CHAPTER 36

Front-Runner Again

A REPUTABLE POLL, RELEASED ON SEPTEMBER 9, RE-
vealed a sudden surge of support. Several other polls confirmed I now led a three-way race by double digits. We attributed the good news to my first television ad, which had prominently featured my parents. The ad had nearly run its course, and had been very effective. Had we waited a few days more before we started advertising, the ad wouldn't have been seen. I wouldn't have allowed it on the air after my father's death. It would have felt like I was exploiting his death for political gain. But we had launched it before my father entered the hospital. It was his final contribution to my success.

The first debate with all three candidates was scheduled for September 17 on Univision. I was more nervous about that debate than any of the others. The debate would be broadcast to a Spanish-language audience. The moderator would ask questions in Spanish, which would be translated for the candidates. We would respond in English, and our answers would be translated back into Spanish. The format posed an interesting dilemma for me. Obviously, I didn't need a translator—I speak Spanish fluently. But both Meek and Crist objected to the request that I be allowed to give my answers in Spanish. In the art of persuasion, it's not just what you say, but how you say it, and I would have preferred the audience heard my voice and not a translator's. My opponents recognized it would give me an advantage and refused to allow it. I worried about how the audience would react. They knew I was Cuban and spoke Spanish, and they might think I was speaking in English to downplay my Hispanic heritage.

The dominant issue in the debate would also be a challenge. Univision executives made no secret of their support for immigration reform, and they used the network to advocate for it. Of all the candidates, my position on immigration was most in conflict with Univision's, and I suspected the debate would turn into a one-hour argument about immigration.

The debate was held at the Univision affiliate's studio in Doral. I knew the place well. I had worked there as a political commentator in the 2008 election. I knew all the people who worked there, and considered many of them friends. When we arrived, we were taken to a small greenroom just off the main studio. I was nervous but well prepared. We were brought into the studio for a quick microphone check, and then returned to the greenroom until it was time for the debate to begin.

There was a delay. The Meek campaign had complained about a small portable fan that had been placed behind Crist's podium. Crist usually had a fan at his feet when he spoke in public. The few times he spoke without one, he perspired profusely. Meek claimed the fan was distracting. Furthermore, he insisted that if Crist had a fan, all the candidates should have one. The dispute was nothing more than a head game, of course, and I found it mildly amusing. If Crist and Meek wanted to fight about a fan, that was fine with me. Crist threatened to walk out if he wasn't allowed to keep his fan. Meek's people finally relented, and it was time to take our places in the studio.

As I stepped up to the podium, I could feel my heart pounding in my chest. I spotted Jeanette sitting in the front row of the audience. She gave me a big smile to remind me to smile. Her mother sat on one side of her while my mother sat on her other side, and gave me a look of motherly pride I had seen many times before. The intro music started and our first three-candidate debate was under way.

The immigration issue certainly played a prominent role in the debate. I was asked why I didn't support comprehensive reform and the DREAM Act. I began by reminding the audience that immigration wasn't just an issue I had studied and debated. It was an experience I had lived. My parents and grandparents were immigrants. My brother was an immigrant.

My aunts and uncles were immigrants. My wife's family are immigrants. I lived in a neighborhood of immigrants. I know how important legal immigration is and how problematic illegal immigration could be. I simply believed the immigration reforms that Congress had considered went too far and would create incentives for others to come here illegally.

I agreed that we needed to do something to help children whose parents had immigrated illegally, who had grown up here and were American in every way except legally, and were at risk of deportation. But the DREAM Act had been written too broadly. We needed more targeted legislation if we were to address the issue without exacerbating our illegal immigration problem.

I was also asked whether I supported making English the official language of the United States, one of the most misunderstood issues of our time. Virtually every important document in the United States is written in English. Our Constitution, our federal and state laws, private contracts and the tests that are administered in our schools are all written in English. English has been the predominant language of Americans since we were thirteen separate colonies. It is our de facto official language, and I don't think there is anything wrong with recognizing that fact. Some people argue that declaring English to be our official language would prohibit other languages from being spoken in this country. But the government can't tell you what language to speak at home. It can't tell a restaurant owner what language to use on his menus.

I think everyone should learn other languages. Knowledge of foreign languages is economically empowering and culturally rewarding. But English is our unifying language. We can all speak whatever language we like here. But we should have one language in common, and given our history, it's obvious it should be English. Some critics argue that it's nativist or racist to support English as our official language. I think that's absurd. Learning to speak English is more than a sign of respect from immigrants for their new country. Knowledge of English is necessary to the economic progress and social assimilation of every American citizen.

On almost every issue we discussed in the debate, Crist managed to take a position to my left—a position he hadn't taken when he was running as a Republican and trying to appeal to conservative primary voters. Near the end of the debate, I decided to call attention to his wholesale reinvention as a postpartisan statesman. "Everyone sees what you're doing," I told him. "Everyone gets it. For twenty years, you ran as a Republican on the same things you're now criticizing me for." I thought it was an effective reminder of what everyone in the audience already knew. Unfortunately, the effect was lost in translation.

The debate was for the most part uneventful. No one scored a knockout or made a major gaffe. However, some reporters thought my positions on English as our official language, the DREAM Act and Arizona's immigration law would hurt me with Hispanic voters. The general consensus, though, which I agreed with, was there had been no clear winner. Further lessening its impact, Univision's Florida affiliates broadcast the debate at eleven o'clock on Friday night.

Crist had shaken up the race in the summer when he withdrew from the Republican primary, and breathed new life into his campaign during the oil spill. But we had been patient, and had faith in our campaign plan. We were confident we could take back the initiative when we began running our television ads. We believed Democrats would rally to the Democratic candidate in the fall. And we knew the race would again become primarily a debate over the direction of the country. It was hard to see that in the summer, when many felt we were letting the race get away from us. But we had stuck to our course.

Now I was the front-runner again. The polls consistently gave me a double-digit lead. We were exactly where we wanted to be. There was much work left to do. But off in the distance, for the first time, I could see the finish line.

When he began his campaign as an independent, Crist had promised the return of the happy warrior, vowing he wouldn't run any more negative ads. As summer gave way to fall and his lead in the polls vanished, he changed his mind again.

In late September, he ran a TV ad criticizing my spending record as speaker and claiming he had vetoed $500 million I had "tried to sneak" into the budget, including $1.5 million for a rowing center and $800,000 to renovate the fields where I played flag football. The ad backfired on him. It was blatantly misleading. The spending had been proposed and promoted by others. I had nothing to do with their inclusion in the budget. But the ad's real damage was to Crist's new image as postpartisan statesman.

Rather than use a narrator's voice in the ad, Crist looked directly into the camera and attacked me himself. Nothing could have contradicted his happy warrior image more than the image of Crist as an attack dog, broadcast across the state at his expense.

Crist's allies opened a 527, a tax-exempt political fund, to promote Crist's candidacy. They sent a mail piece titled "The Real Rubio" to Republican voters across the state. The front of the piece had an image of what appeared to be militant student protesters, along with a picture of Che Guevara over my left shoulder. On the back, it identified several bills that would have given children of undocumented immigrants in-state tuition rates and health insurance. The mailer was designed to tamp down Republican enthusiasm for me by raising doubts about my positions on illegal immigration.

The use of Che Guevara's image was particularly galling. Guevara was a cold-blooded killer, and he's reviled by the Cuban exile community. The use of his image in American pop culture is a pet peeve of exiles everywhere. But it was only a mailer. And as angry as it made me and others, it would have been counterproductive to have overreacted to it. Had we howled in protest, we would have brought it to the attention of thousands of voters who hadn't received the mailer or who had thrown it away without noticing it. Charlie's campaign would have been very pleased if we had helped them make the race about immigration rather than the direction of the country.

So we stayed focused on our message and paid as little attention as possible to the attacks. It wasn't easy. But having the discipline to stick with our message was the main reason we had retaken the lead. Everything seemed to be going according to plan. A new Mason-Dixon poll showed Kendrick was gaining ground on Charlie. The race was becoming a fight for second place.

I appeared on CBS's *Face the Nation* on the last Sunday in September. As I expected, the show's host, Bob Schieffer, asked me to address the attacks the Crist campaign had been making all year long. For months, his allies in Washington had been spreading unfounded rumors about me, urging senators against endorsing me because "the other shoe was going to drop." Later, they explicitly warned that I was under investigation and would be indicted before Election Day. When I met with Senate Minority

Leader Mitch McConnell for the first time, I could tell some of this was clearly on his mind. And it was clearly on Bob Schieffer's mind as well.

Bob asked me about the American Express charges, and I explained again that the party had never paid the charges; I had paid them myself, which by now was a well-documented fact. The *St. Petersburg Times* and *Miami Herald*, which felt they had ownership of the issue, called it a "nuanced" response. But it wasn't. It was a simple assertion of fact. The claim that I had charged personal items to an American Express card I obtained through my association with the Florida GOP was accurate. It was also accurate that the party hadn't paid them. I had.

Bob also asked me about my personal finances. There existed then and even now a false notion in the press, promoted first by Crist, that I was campaigning as an antidebt fiscal conservative while I accumulated an irresponsible amount of personal debt. Yes, I have debts. But my debts are not some exotic instruments contrived to support my extravagant lifestyle. They consist almost entirely of two things: my mortgages on my two homes and my student loan from law school. I'm not in arrears on any of my debts. And I'm not the only person my age who still has payments left on his student loan. Sadly, with tuition costs as high as they are today, large student loan debt is a fact of life for people who aren't wealthy. President Obama was still paying off his when he was elected to the Senate.

One of the lessons I learned in the campaign is not to fixate as much as some reporters do on the attacks, rumormongering and hyped controversies that political campaigns manufacture. Political reporters are attracted to them because their editors believe such stories drive ratings and attract readers. Voters have different interests. That's not to say voters don't care about questions of public and private integrity, or that they hold politicians in higher esteem than the press does. But they won't credit attacks on a candidate's character, no matter how much attention reporters pay them, if there isn't evidence to support it or assertions the candidate cannot persuasively refute. The primary purpose of attacks is not simply to stain an opponent's character but to knock the opponent off message, particularly if the message is a winning one. And in Florida, where over half the voters opposed President Obama's agenda, our message was certainly winning. We were courting voters, not reporters. As long as I stuck to my message, I was certain I would win.

We had more money than my opponents to spend on television ads. Several third-party groups were running ads criticizing Charlie. Ours was also the only campaign that had even a semblance of a grassroots operation. The signs of our success were everywhere. My crowds were bigger, my supporters more enthusiastic. We had begun our own internal tracking poll, a rolling three-day average that showed I had a solid lead with some room to improve.

As we entered the last month of the campaign, victory was in sight. If I stayed on message and we concentrated on executing our plan, I would be elected to the United States Senate. There were only three things that could derail us: a genuine scandal, a race-altering gaffe on my part or a last-minute October surprise. We avoided the first two, but only narrowly averted the third.

CHAPTER 37

Journey's End

T HE BIG SURPRISE IN EARLY OCTOBER WASN'T THAT WE were ahead, but rather that Kendrick Meek had a chance to overtake Charlie Crist for second place. His primary victory and a few effective TV spots had given him momentum that was showing up in the public polls. Our tracking poll confirmed it. It was encouraging news for him and even better news for us.

The only way Charlie could win the election is if Kendrick's support collapsed or Kendrick was somehow persuaded to drop out of the race. There wasn't any evidence he was collapsing in the polls. Quite the contrary. But we knew he would need to raise more money to stay on the air, and to do that, he would need to turn in solid performances in the debates. We had agreed to six televised debates in the fall because they would give him exposure and remind Democratic voters there was a genuine Democrat in the race.

The next debate was scheduled for October 6. As the clear front-runner, I expected to be on the receiving end of attacks from both Charlie and Kendrick. The Crist campaign fired the first salvo the day before the debate, when they launched a television ad attacking my position on Social Security. Political observers believed I had made myself vulnerable to attack when I stated my honest views on the subject in the Fox News debate, and I knew they might be right. They don't call Social Security and Medicare the third rail of politics because voters are disinterested in the programs. Even conservative voters are apprehensive when a candidate talks about changing Social Security or Medicare.

We knew the attack was coming and had taped a rebuttal ad weeks earlier. My gut told me to go up with our rebuttal immediately in the same markets where Crist's ad was running. But to do that we would have to take down a very effective spot that hadn't run its full course. "Burn in" is consultant terminology for the number of times viewers see an ad before they remember it. The minimum burn-in rate is one thousand gross rating points, which means viewers on average will see the spot ten times. If we replaced our current ad with our Social Security rebuttal, the former would have been a waste of money since most viewers wouldn't have seen it enough times to remember it. Fortunately, we didn't have to rely on my gut instincts to make the decision. We closely monitored our tracking polls to see if Crist's attack was hurting us. We saw no change in our numbers for the first three nights, and after six nights we actually improved slightly with seniors. So we left our current ad up until it ran its course, and then ran the Social Security ad for a few days to be on the safe side.

We announced our fund-raising total for the quarter before the debate. We had raised $5 million in the third quarter, an eye-popping number. Had anyone suggested a year earlier that I would raise $5 million in total for 2010, I would have thought they were out of their mind. But our small donors were contributing again and again. Washington political action committees that had previously given to Crist were now donating to us. And our fund-raising events in Florida were now on par with the biggest candidate events in the country.

The debate was held at the ABC affiliate in Orlando, with George Stephanopoulos moderating. It got off to a lively start, as Crist tried to land a few punches by delivering a few well-rehearsed lines. He said I wasn't drinking too much Kool-Aid, I was "drinking too much tea," a clear allusion to my ties to the Tea Party movement. But the surprise of the night to most observers was Kendrick Meek. He was trailing in the polls and short on money, but he was energized and focused throughout the debate.

He took a few good shots at me. In particular, he criticized my opposition to the president's health care bill. I countered by calling the health care bill a massive failure. After we finished our back-and-forth, Crist pointed at both of us as an example of the kind of partisan bickering he wanted to change.

Crist had somehow managed to get himself seated in the middle, to my left and Meek's right. It was a visual metaphor for the position he wanted to occupy in the race. I expected him to say something to draw attention to the fortuitous seating arrangement—something like, "Marco is on my right and Kendrick is on my left, and I'm right in the middle, where most Floridians are." But to my surprise he never seized the opportunity.

Kendrick took a few shots at Charlie, but for the most part the debate was a confrontation between me and an energized Kendrick, which pleased both of us. I thought I did fine, but the best news of the night was that Kendrick did very well. The better he did, the happier we were. I attacked him for being a left-wing, consistent liberal Democrat. To some observers, that sounded like a boilerplate partisan attack. But its purpose was to rally Democrats to Kendrick's defense. There is nothing that motivates the base of either party like seeing one of their own under attack from the other side. The more I went after him, the more Democratic voters would see him as their guy.

After the debate we began a three-day bus tour, and Jeanette and the kids came with me. So did my mother. She had had an awfully rough month trying to get used to life without my father. We thought the trip would do her good. She enjoyed the crowds and the energy of the campaign. And I enjoyed having her with me.

Jeanette and the kids and my mother boarded the bus right after the debate, while I did a few postdebate interviews. When I joined them, I found my mother quietly crying. One of the kids had picked up my iPad, which I had left on the bus. My screen saver was a picture of my father. My mother had seen it and started to cry. I told her it was a reminder he was still with us, coming along on the bus tour, just where he would have wanted to be were he still alive.

The next few days are among my fondest memories of the campaign. The crowds were large and enthusiastic and the events well organized. I was able to introduce my wife and children to thousands of people who had supported me for so many months, and they were able to witness the excitement of the campaign. My mother cried at every event. We had a heckler at one of them, a libertarian who was upset with me about something. He was far away from the stage, but he had a bullhorn, which made it hard for me to be heard. My mother cried because he disrupted the event.

An enormous crowd greeted us at a rally near The Villages in north-central Florida. My mother wept because she couldn't believe so many people had turned out to see her son. And at each event, I would talk about how my parents had inspired me and shaped my character and beliefs. My mother cried every time I mentioned them. She couldn't understand how her quiet, anonymous, itinerant life could inspire anyone. She had just wanted us to have a better chance to make something of ourselves than she had.

Now she saw with her own eyes the significance and scale of the undertaking. This wasn't a West Miami City Commission race. It was a high-profile race in one of the biggest states in the most important nation in the world. This was her son, on the verge of accomplishing something she had never dreamed I might do. Later, she told me how overwhelmed Papá would have been to witness it, and how proud my father was of me before he died. If I hadn't been so tired she would have made me cry.

The race had now entered its last phase. Absentee ballots were being mailed and early voting would commence in less than two weeks. Each passing day brought new polls that confirmed my lead. And each poll was a reminder to my opponents that time was running out. American political history is full of exciting stories of last-minute come-from-behind victories. But with nearly half the voters now casting their ballots before Election Day, the chances of that happening again, at least in Florida, are less likely.

I was aware of all this. Our own polls gave us a bigger lead than the public polls showed. My consultant Heath Thompson, who has a brilliant strategic mind but is not known for his optimism, warned me every day that the polls were bound to tighten in the final days. And every day I braced for it. But by mid-October, it still hadn't happened. What had been clear to me since late September was now clear to the Crist campaign. The race could become competitive only if I made a major gaffe or if Kendrick Meek's campaign collapsed.

Four debates were still on the schedule and each of them posed the risk of a self-inflicted wound. I began questioning my advisers about the wisdom of agreeing to so many debates when we were so far ahead in the polls. They kept reminding me the debates helped keep Kendrick afloat. I understood that, but I still wanted to get out of at least one of the debates. All we were doing, I argued, was giving my opponents a free forum to attack me. Finally, Jeanette got tired of my complaining and told me to suck it up and stick with the plan.

An unforced error on my part was outside the control of the Crist campaign. But they could try to get Meek out of the race. By the middle of October, the press was reporting rumors that Crist and Meek were discussing a deal. Nothing in Kendrick's history or personality led me to believe he would seriously contemplate withdrawing from the race. Everything I knew about him after a decade of dealing with him told me quitting wasn't in his DNA. But the chatter continued and grew stronger, and we began to worry that Crist might manage to make it a two-man race after all.

The Crist campaign began aggressively pushing the narrative that I was an outside-the-mainstream radical and that every vote for Meek was a vote for me. They got Democratic activists and even a few Meek volunteers to make the same case to the *Times* and *Herald*. Crist met with an influential Palm Beach Democratic club, which formally called on Meek to drop out of the race. They had planned to ambush Kendrick and urge him to withdraw at a meeting they'd scheduled with him, but Kendrick got wind of their agenda and canceled the meeting. On October 13, the *Times* and *Herald* political bureau reported the growing speculation and went into considerable detail about how Meek's withdrawal would shake up the race.

The temptation to become overly cautious when you're ahead is, I'm convinced, hardwired in the human brain. I had seen it many times on the football field. But, as the old adage goes, "the only thing a prevent defense prevents is a win." No matter how much I wished I could have canceled the debates, I had no intention of playing prevent defense, and was intent on giving a spirited performance.

Crist came out with guns blazing in our debate on October 15. He leveled many of the same charges he had been making for months, and continued to present himself as the reasonable centrist running against a liberal Democrat and an "extremist" right-winger. I was ready for it, and delivered the counterpunch I had been preparing for days.

This notion, Governor, that you switched to become an independent because you're some kind of centrist who's looking out for the betterment of the country, quite frankly, is a fairy tale that only you believe. You're running as an independent not because you took a principled stand on the issues; you're running as an independent because you took a poll.

Crist unveiled one attack that I hadn't prepared for, citing a local left-leaning Hispanic newspaper to argue I had turned my back on my "Hispanic family." I used the attack to reintroduce my family's story.

We're all used to hard-knuckle politics in these debates, but that's . . . offensive and outrageous for you to talk about me turning my back on my Hispanic family. Let me tell you about my family. My family worked very hard so that I could have opportunities they didn't have. My father worked thirty, forty, sixty, seventy hours a week as a bartender. My mother was a cashier, she was a stock clerk.

He went after me again on Social Security, too, but I managed to turn the attack on him. I called it shameful. "You know my mom's a beneficiary of Social Security—you've met her. And you know why I know it's shameful, Governor? You can't even look at me as I tell you these things." In another year and with another messenger, the attack might have hurt. But in 2010, voters were concerned with President Obama's agenda, and Crist, having reversed his positions on so many issues, didn't have the credibility to attack mine.

I felt pretty good about my performance, although I worried a little that I had been too heated in my exchanges with Charlie. But the most encouraging response of the debate wasn't mine, it was Kendrick's. "I will not drop out of this race for any reason," he insisted when asked directly about his intentions. "I am nominated by the Democrats of the state of Florida. I am in this race to run to be the next United States senator. And no, I am not running for second." That was exactly what I had hoped to hear from him.

Our next debate was scheduled for a few days later. The day before the debate, President Clinton had appeared at a rally for Kendrick and gave a rousing testimonial to Kendrick's virtues and his chances to win the election. Behind the scenes, however, he might have been delivering a very different message. Ten days later, a detailed report in *Politico* described Clinton's efforts to persuade Kendrick to drop out of the race and endorse Charlie. Using his aide, the Florida native Doug Band, as an intermediary, Clinton argued that Kendrick could be a hero to the Democratic Party, credited with stopping my election to the Senate by clearing the field for Crist. If the report was true, we had come dangerously close to a genuine October surprise. Stephen Moore, writing in the *Wall Street Journal*, also reported Meek was on the verge of dropping out, and the speculation began to alarm us.

Kendrick later admitted Clinton had discussed the subject with him, but denied he had agreed to drop out. *Politico's* sources insisted that he had, however. They said an actual date had been set for a withdrawal announcement, October 26, and Kendrick had twice agreed to it. The deal had fallen apart only after Kendrick's wife insisted he still had a chance to win.

I don't know how close Kendrick came to quitting. No one would have blamed him if he had. I had once been the candidate with no chance to win who was seen as an impediment to my party's plans to retain Mel Martinez's Senate seat. I remember how discouraged I had been in the summer of 2009, how hard it had been to get up in the morning and campaign for a nomination I had no chance of winning, how close I came to quitting. Kendrick was working as hard or harder than I was, and he had little to show for it. He was out of money. He didn't have any ads on the air or polls to encourage him. He didn't have a realistic path to victory.

I gained a tremendous amount of respect for Kendrick Meek in the final weeks of the campaign. I thought he was often the best candidate on the stage in our debates. He kept his chin up, and fought as hard as he could despite the long odds he faced. I didn't agree with him on many issues, but I knew one thing about Kendrick Meek. He was a man of character and dignity.

I think I would have still won had Kendrick withdrawn from the race. We had ads ready to air in the event he did. I think we would have made a compelling argument that Kendrick's endorsement of Crist was an example of the backroom deals that were ruining American politics. I think it would have nationalized our race even more and triggered an enormous spike in our fund-raising. Many thousands of votes would have already been cast by then, and I think we would have hung on to win. But it would have made it a much closer race, and been one heck of a final twist in a race that had already had more than its fair share of surprises.

In the midst of all this speculation, Kendrick turned in another spirited performance in the October 16 debate. Crist delivered more of the same attacks on me, and added a new one, asserting I had changed my position on personal injury insurance legislation after the mother of my neighbor, a chiropractor, purchased our former home. The attack fell flat—first, because it was an obvious overreach; and second, because the press had already investigated the charge and found no evidence to support it. Finally, by the end of the campaign, after all his policy reversals and reinventions, Crist didn't have enough credibility left with voters to make any attack stick. He continued to call me an extremist, but the charge fell on deaf ears. Voters knew me by now. The best decision we made was to introduce voters to my personal story before Crist could transform me into someone I wasn't. They had heard my family story many times, in my own voice as I looked into the camera and told them who had made me the man I was.

I was comfortably ahead. We had more money and a better organization. I was going to win. At that point, it was very unlikely that anything Charlie or I said could change the outcome. I didn't need to deliver a knockout punch in our next debate. But I went for one anyway.

Our fifth debate began on the morning of October 24, and was something of a home game for Crist. It was jointly sponsored by CNN and the *St. Petersburg Times*, and was held on the campus of the University of South Florida in Tampa, Charlie Crist territory. Candy Crowley of CNN moderated it, and the *Times*'s Adam Smith was also on the panel, so we expected to be asked again about the American Express card and my spending record.

We had our fair share of supporters in the audience, but Crist had many more, and he was visibly buoyed by them. The debate had the feeling of a last stand, and Crist's body language suggested he had one last trick up his sleeve. I was unnerved.

He was very aggressive throughout the debate—maybe too aggressive. He repeatedly interrupted me. He used all of his time, and much of mine, to make sweeping allegations against my character. As the debate entered its final minutes, I was trying to answer a question from Candy when Crist interrupted me again and tried to fit in all his attacks in one exchange. The exchange is best captured by the transcript of the debate:

Crowley: Mr. Rubio, do you see Mr. Crist as a person who's able to change the play when he had to, and that you're an ideologue, or how do you—?

Rubio: Well, two separate questions . . . He changes positions on issues because he wants to win the election. I mean, it's been documented by the *St. Petersburg Times*, the newspaper Adam works in—

Crist: That is so untrue and so unfair for you to interpret what's in my heart.

Rubio: Can I finish the— There's an article. I didn't write it. The article was in the *St. Petersburg Times*, and it said that, basically, on the day he switched parties, he was sitting across the table from a reporter—

Crist: Well, let's talk about another article that was in the *St. Petersburg Times*—

Rubio:—and picked up the phone—

Crist:—about the job you got—

[Cross talk]

Rubio:—and called the pollster, and the pollster told him you have a better chance of running as an independent.

Crist: You traded tax money to get two jobs at a university and a hospital—

Rubio: Can I—can I—

Crist:—by steering millions of dollars to—

Rubio: That's categorically false. . . .

[Cross talk]

Crist: If people at home make $165,000—I don't, and I'm the governor of Florida. But he traded money to get it. That was in the *St. Petersburg Times*, too.

[Cross talk]

Rubio: That is a false accusation. Not only is that a false accusation but it's been a trend in this campaign. Any time we get into the issues, the governor wants to turn it into something else because he's wrong on the issues.

[Cross talk]

Crist: Why won't you release your RPOF [Republican Party of Florida] credit card and clear this up?

Rubio: On the ideologue issue, as of today I have now been—

Crist: And why is there a federal investigation into your reporting income?

Rubio: This is just one litany of falsehoods after another.

Crowley: Well, why don't you—maybe he would let you—why don't you—Can you answer this question, and then we'll—

Crist:—across the state of Florida for the past year.

At the mention of the American Express card, Adam Smith jumped in:

Smith: Why not release the full IRS records, the full credit card statements from what you charged on the card?

Rubio: Adam, these questions have been answered now since February. My tax returns are public. I've gone well beyond the point of disclosure. The bottom line is people want to focus on these issues because they're wrong on the important issues. This country has a $13.5 trillion debt.

Crist: He doesn't want to release them because he doesn't believe in transparency. I created the Office of Open Government in the governor's office for the first time in the history of our state.

That was it. I'd had enough, and out came a line I hadn't rehearsed or prepared:

Rubio: I've never had a heckler at the debate. I've always had them in the audience.

Upon hearing the heckler line, the panel, the audience and even Kendrick broke out into laughter. Crist appeared as if the frustrations of the entire campaign had finally gotten the best of him and erupted in one singular moment.

In the middle of the laughter, Crist tried to recover, using a line he had used against me in the spring, when I had complained about his attacks:

Crist: That's the way it is. Welcome to the NFL.

Finally the laughter died down and Adam interjected:

Smith: Go ahead. Let him finish.

I gathered myself and pivoted to what the race was all about:

Rubio: I apologize. I mean, I've had this heckler going on for two minutes now.

Here's what I'd like to be able to tell you about ideology and all this talk about— This is a national talking point now that the Democrats have adopted across the country.

Here's the reality. I have now received the endorsement of six separate major newspapers in Florida, not exactly the place conservatives go to hang out, at editorial boards.

And the reason why they are supporting me is because I'm the only candidate in this race that's proposing serious answers to the serious issues that face America. And that's what this election is about at the end of the day.

It's not about you, Governor. It's not about your ability to deliver the lines you've been planning for two weeks. It's not about you, Congressman. And it isn't even about me.

Crist: It's about—

Rubio: This election is about the people watching whose country is going in the wrong direction, who understand that, if we keep doing what we are doing now, we are going to be the first Americans in history to leave our children worse off than ourselves. That's what this election is about. I was hoping that's what this debate would be about. And I hope that's what the next eight days is about.

The debate ended a few minutes later. The race was over and everyone in the room knew it. As I watched Crist leave the debate site, I felt, for the first time in a while, sympathy for him. I knew how great his disappointment must be to find himself involuntarily out of office, after enjoying such acclaim only a year before. And I felt for his parents who were in the audience that morning. They were surely as proud of him as my parents were of me.

The final debate occurred a few days later, moderated by David Gregory of NBC. Compared to the preceding debate, it was mostly uneventful. Kendrick looked tired, which he had every reason to be. I was exhausted, but I had the encouragement of knowing I was going to win. I don't know how he kept walking his long, hard road, but he did. He saw it through to the end, and I respected him for it. Charlie seemed dispirited, as if finally resigned to losing. He took a few shots at me, but they were tamer now. I don't think he wanted the last impression voters would have of him to be the image of an angry, negative politician. Charlie had always been a charmer, a likable and adept politician who loved what he did for a living. I respect that, too. And I think he wanted voters to remember him that way.

We had finished the last of six debates. Five of them had been very spirited affairs. I had been campaigning for a year and a half in a race that had more twists and turns than I could ever have imagined possible. I had experienced every emotion. I'd been discouraged and angry, thrilled and proud. I'd been defiant and embarrassed, saddened and overjoyed. And now I was tired and ready for it to be over.

The day after the last debate, we boarded our campaign bus for the final leg of a statewide tour. The crowds were even larger now, and their excitement greater. Anything could happen, I reminded myself, but it was hard to find anything to be discouraged about. The early voting and absentee turnout figures showed clear signs of a Republican wave. Our closing ads were receiving rave reviews. Our internal polls gave me a solid and stable lead. And at every stop we made, people brought up the heckler line. Even the eternal pessimist Heath Thompson could find nothing to be pessimistic about.

I still hadn't won anything, but at night, after the day's events were over, I allowed myself to reflect a little on my journey. I reflected not just on the campaign that was nearing its end, but on my entire life and the family that had made my journey possible. In moments of triumph, we are advised to find humility. All worldly success is fleeting. I needed only recall my own family's story to be reminded.

Five decades earlier, my parents had arrived in America with nothing. They were younger then than I was now, and had none of my advantages. They didn't speak the language. They didn't have a formal education. They didn't have connections to help establish them in their strange new country.

My grandfather had an even harder life. He struggled to the very limit of his physical ability to feed his wife and daughters, and had to leave the country he loved so much and whose history he felt so personally.

I thought I had it rough when, early in my career, I had despaired over my finances and the fact that my family had to live month to month. For much of their lives, my parents had lived week to week. They lived with the constant worry that they would fail to give their children the chance to live better lives. My grandfather had lived day to day, uncertain he could afford his family's next meal. They had once had dreams. All young people have dreams. But their lives weren't the stuff of dreams. They worked to get by, and to keep their children safe and well provided for.

What adversity had I faced? Bad polls? Lackluster fund-raising? Embarrassing questions about my finances, my credit card, the sale of my house? My father had known the humiliation of failed business ventures. He had known the fear of suddenly losing a job. He had walked a picket line while his meager savings disappeared, and gone back to work to feed his children only to have me insult him for doing it. My grandfather knew the anguish of being refused work because he was disabled, and he had suffered losses I would never experience.

If I failed, I would lose an election. I would still earn a good living. I would still have a future. If my mother and father failed, the rent wouldn't be paid. If my grandfather failed, his daughters wouldn't eat. But the rent was always paid. And my mother and her sisters never went to bed hungry, even though her parents often had.

Two generations of my family had struggled, suffered and survived. They vowed their children and grandchildren would never have to make the choices they had made and have to acquiesce to a reality that refused their dreams. My parents didn't have any specific ambitions for me. They wanted me to be happy, and do whatever my heart was set on doing. And now I had. I had taken the chance they had given me, and was on the cusp of winning an important public office. I would receive public acclaim for my success, but I knew who truly deserved the credit. I am the son of immigrants, exiles from a troubled country. They gave me everything it was in their power to give. And I am proof their lives mattered, their existence had a purpose.

In the last nights of a long campaign, I remembered where my journey began. It began long ago, in the hardships and struggles of ordinary people with extraordinary strength and courage and love, on an island I have never seen.

Why had my dreams come true? Because God had blessed me with a strong and stable family and parents who cherished my dreams more than their own, and with a wise and loving wife who supported me. And He blessed me with America, the only country in the world where dreams like mine would stand a chance of coming true.

CHAPTER 38

The Junior Senator from Florida

T HE WEEKS AFTER THE ELECTION WERE A BLUR OF FRE-
netic activity. I had to close my law firm, set up my Senate offices and
organize my private affairs. I needed to step off the national stage for a
while. So we held a press conference the day after the election, and then we
went dark. I still did occasional interviews with the Florida press, but we
decided to turn down all national media requests for several months.

Every organization I have ever been associated with develops a culture
that reflects the personality and priorities of whoever is at the top of the
organization. If I had started my Senate career by focusing my attention on
press opportunities, my staff would conclude that our office's highest priority was to keep me in the national spotlight. I didn't want to make the
wrong first impression on my new staff.

I had learned as speaker that the decisions you make in the early days
often haunt your entire time in an office. I took extra care to make sure I
made the right decisions. Our first priority was to emphasize constituent
services, which involved getting our phone and mail operations up and
running, setting up casework procedures and identifying staff we would
keep and new staff we would hire for our Florida offices. I wanted our constituent services to be operational on my first day on the job.

I wanted a strong, experienced policy team in my Washington office
that would help me identify emerging issues and engage in national debates

in a constructive way. I also wanted to leave room for younger, less experienced but eager staffers who would be part of a strong farm team system. As senior staff moved on in the coming years, I wanted to promote from within my organization.

The Thanksgiving and Christmas holidays were bittersweet that year. For almost two years, my campaign had been the central focus of our lives. Now I had an opportunity to relax and celebrate the holidays as something more than a brief distraction from the campaign. I played in two flag football tournaments, my team finishing first and second, respectively. I enjoyed the company of my family and friends, and spent more time with my kids than I had been able to in quite a while. I wasn't the distant, preoccupied father they had become accustomed to—a blessing I was especially thankful for that holiday season.

But they were also the first holidays without my father. Every Thanksgiving, my father would make the same comment, *"A mí el pavo no me llama la atención"*—or, roughly translated, "I don't really care for turkey that much." It had become a running joke in the family, and I had often made the same comment to poke fun at him. No one joked about it that Thanksgiving. Christmas, too, recalled happier ones, when he had been with us. I remembered a Christmas years before, when Jeanette and I had been newlyweds. We had spent much of our savings on our wedding and honeymoon. We didn't have money our first Christmas together to spend on a tree and decorations. But to our delight, our holiday was rescued one afternoon when my father pulled into our driveway in his little Toyota Corolla with a tree tied to the roof.

Before I knew it, it was time for us to go to Washington for my swearing in. Both Jeanette's and my family made the trip with us the last week of December. We spent several days taking in the sights of the nation's capital. One experience in particular stood out.

We toured Mount Vernon the second day of the new year. It was the first visit to George Washington's home for all of us. Somewhere along the tour, I became separated from the group. I watched them from afar for a minute, laughing and talking in Spanish and English. My first thought was how different my family was, how different I was, from the men and women who had lived in this place, and from the Americans who had founded our nation. We came to this country or were brought here by our parents from

Cuba and Colombia. But on further reflection, I began to recognize the similarities in our stories.

Our language and customs were obviously different than the language and customs of America's founding fathers. But we were dreamers, too, just like the Americans who had dreamed of a nation where all people would be considered equal, and willed it into existence. They had made a nation where you could be whatever your talents and industry allowed you to be, no matter the circumstances of your birth or whether or not your parents were socially and financially established. I looked at the little assembly of my family and friends, and observed there wasn't a millionaire among them. There were no Ivy Leaguers present, no one who could trace their lineage to the *Mayflower*. In most societies in human history, a family like mine wouldn't have had the opportunities we've had. We might have been employees at a national monument, but we wouldn't have visited it while we were in town to see one of our own take his seat in the national legislature. But here we were. A collection of working-class immigrants from Latin America and their children, who enjoyed a standard of living our parents and grandparents had never known, with opportunities they might have dreamed of but never expected to have. We looked and sounded different from the descendants of George Washington's generation. But we embodied everything America's founding generation had hoped America would become.

I had the same feeling a few days later at the Capitol. At the appointed hour, I walked down the center aisle of the Senate and made my way to where the vice president of the United States was waiting to administer my oath of office. I looked up at the gallery to see Jeanette and the kids, but I couldn't find them. So I glanced at the Senate's ornate ceiling for a brief moment. I wondered how my father would have felt had he sat in the Senate gallery that day. Would he have remembered the exhausting late nights in his seventies, tending bar at a banquet and bragging to anyone who would listen that his son was going to be a lawyer? Would he have remarked to himself how far he had traveled from his destitute and lonely childhood? I hope so. And I hope he would have recognized that he was responsible for the honor his son received that day.

I wondered how my grandfather would have felt, too. Would he have felt he had helped make it possible by planting the seeds of my dreams in those long afternoons on our porch in Las Vegas? Would he have realized I had kept the promise I made to him on his deathbed?

I looked down again and prepared to take the oath. I didn't know whether or not my father and grandfather were watching me. Does God allow our loved ones in the afterlife to share in our successes? Can you see from heaven the triumphs and trials of the family you've left behind? I'll have to wait to find out. In the meantime, I must act as if they are watching me always, and I am and always will be accountable to them.

The rest of the day was filled with festivities and fun. We restaged my swearing in with my wife and children at my side in the old Senate chamber so we could take a picture to remember it by. We had a reception in the Hart Senate Office Building for friends and supporters who had made the trip from Florida. The next day friends and family began leaving for home, and by that night only Jeanette and the kids and I were left. It was a reminder to us that our family was embarking on a new life, with new challenges and opportunities.

CHAPTER 39

Life in the Senate

THE TWO QUESTIONS PEOPLE ASK ME MOST OFTEN ABOUT my job are "Was it what you expected?" and "What surprised you the most?" My answer is the same to both questions. What has surprised me the most is that life as a U. S. senator is pretty much what I expected it to be.

My background as a state legislative leader prepared me fairly well for my experience in the Senate, although the place certainly has a few unique attributes. The U.S. Senate is one of the few legislative bodies, if not the only legislative body, where a simple majority can't accomplish anything. Without the agreement of every single senator—what is referred to as "unanimous consent"—even basic, mundane tasks can be difficult to complete.

In a legislative body with only a hundred members, everyone knows everyone else. It's easier for personal animosities to flare in the House of Representatives, which has 435 members. Many of them have never met each other and have only encountered some of their colleagues in debates over legislation. Many members are strangers to each other, and it's easier to dislike a stranger. There are no strangers in the Senate. Eventually, our paths all cross.

When you debate with colleagues in the Senate, you've met them, have come to know them and, often, have worked with them on other legislation. And you're going to need their cooperation in the future, if only to get unanimous consent for a minor request. When the lights are off and the cameras aren't watching, senators interact and socialize with each other like people everywhere do, even if they have political differences. They talk about their families, sports and the normal stuff of life. Of course, we talk shop, too. Senators are always looking to join with one or more members of the opposite party to sponsor legislation. The rules of the Senate make it impossible for most legislation to pass without some bipartisan support.

But there are other motivations for bipartisan cooperation as well. First, your constituents appreciate it. Most Americans want to see Republicans and Democrats working together for the good of the country. It's refreshing, too, to be able to break free from the usual constraints of partisanship and work with colleagues on the other side of the aisle. Even on issues where there isn't bipartisan agreement, most senators respect opposing points of view, especially if those views rest on principle and not politics.

Building good relationships with your colleagues, based on mutual respect, and working cooperatively to address the country's challenges is an important and honorable undertaking. But that shouldn't come at the expense of the convictions that brought you to office. Setting aside our differences cannot mean setting aside our principles. I campaigned on one central theme: the country faced immense challenges; the election should be about the direction of the country; and, if elected, I would not, in small or large ways, shrink from my responsibility to defend the principles of a free people and the great nation they built.

In my first year, I was asked to vote against a rule banning earmarks, which are funds targeted to specific projects that aren't meritorious or, at the least, are a very low priority to all but a relative few, and have in the past been the means of public corruption. I was asked to vote to raise the debt limit and for very short-term budgets that ignored rather than solved our problems. I refused. I promised the people of Florida I would work to find the right long-term solutions to the nation's biggest problems, not evade them by resorting to stopgap measures and special-interest deal making. I intend to keep my promise.

Even with all the challenges America faces, there is still no nation on earth with a brighter future. The fundamental source of our nation's greatness remains our people. And while their government and its leaders might be languishing, the American people have not diminished one bit. We are still as creative, innovative and ambitious as ever. Even as you read these words, the next great American idea is being worked on somewhere in our country. Ultimately, America will remain great because our people are great. The job of our government is to make it easier for our people to do what they do better than any people in the history of the world.

If there is one nagging concern I have after my first year in the Senate it is the lack of urgency in Washington to address the challenges we face. Many in Washington wrongly assume that our spiraling debt, our broken tax code and our regulatory overreach can wait until after the next election to be confronted. I believe that the longer we wait to solve these issues, the harder they will be to solve. With each passing year, the solutions to these challenges become more painful and implementing them potentially more disruptive. I had hoped that my first years in the Senate would be a historic time, a time when the urgency of the moment compelled our leaders to act in bold and decisive ways to protect our nation and its future. Instead, sometimes I feel as if I have joined a theater company where every vote and every statement is calculated for maximum political effect rather than public benefit. And yet I believe with all my heart that America will confront and solve the challenges we face in this new century. We always have and we will again. And the sooner we do it the better.

On an individual level, what gets you in trouble in the Senate with your colleagues is the kind of behavior that will get you in trouble in any other workplace. If you're a showboat who pontificates on every subject the Senate debates. If you mislead or lie to people about your intentions or fail to keep promises you've made. If you try to make yourself look good by making a colleague look bad. Those things will get you into trouble in the Senate, just as they would anywhere else.

That doesn't mean the Senate is the epitome of bipartisan comity. There are plenty of partisan games played all the time there. When a senator is "in cycle"—in other words, up for reelection at the end of the Congress—the other side tries to make life as difficult as possible for him or her. As I write this in 2012, Republican senators Scott Brown and Dean Heller are running for reelection, and the Democratic leadership is constantly trying to force them into making politically difficult votes or deny them opportunities to show leadership on an issue that might help their reelection.

However, I have had mostly positive relations with my colleagues on both sides of the aisle. I have found that senators with whom I disagree very strongly on issues are still hardworking, decent people who are well informed and have done their homework, even if their policy conclusions baffle me. It's a privilege to debate them, and to work with them when we are in agreement.

In my short time in the Senate, I've come to know senators from both parties who have offered me their friendship and counsel. Jim DeMint continues to be a source of sound advice and an inspiration to me. Joe Lieberman encouraged me to get involved in foreign policy issues. I've traveled overseas with him, John McCain and Lindsey Graham, and benefited from their many years of experience in national security. Whether you agree or disagree with them, they are statesmen who put our country's security before all else.

I've enjoyed my friendship with Frank Lautenberg, a Democrat from New Jersey. We have a mutual friend in Florida, and he's taken a personal interest not only in how I'm adapting to life in the Senate but how my family is dealing with the burdens my office imposes on them. You don't often hear that politicians behave in private as decently as most people do, but they do, and I appreciate the kindnesses Frank and others here have shown me.

Chris Coons, a freshman Democrat from Delaware, and I have spent time together fighting for legislation we wrote that incorporates ideas from both parties to stimulate private sector job growth. Even though we have very different political views, both Chris and I feel it's not just possible but necessary that whenever people can agree to serve a public good without violating their principles, we shouldn't let partisanship for the sake of partisanship prevent us from doing so.

I've met impressive people outside the Senate, too, whom I doubtlessly would never have had the chance to meet had I not been elected to the Senate. I met the Dalai Lama, a man of inspiring compassion. I had dinner with Henry Kissinger, and listened to him like a student as he analyzed the world and its problems in a learned and entertaining discussion. I even met Bono, in his capacity as an advocate for AIDS sufferers. I'm not starstruck. But I do admit it takes a little while to get used to rubbing shoulders with internationally admired leaders.

The press scrutiny in Washington takes a little time to get used to as well. I thought it was fairly intense in Tallahassee, but in Washington it reaches another level entirely. Reporters mill around the trains that take senators from their offices to the Capitol, and around the elevators off the Senate floor. At any given moment you can be asked a question about something you haven't given much consideration to and you don't have a ready answer for. It sometimes seems like a game show, and you only have a few seconds to give the right answer before a buzzer sounds and you lose. Veteran senators have no problem ignoring them. I've seen some of them walk right by a reporter who has asked them a question as if they weren't there. I haven't developed that skill yet. The best I've been able to do when I don't have a ready answer is to refer them to my press office to set up an interview.

I have had experience with opponents using the media in an election campaign to advance a negative interpretation of something they think is a vulnerability. But in Washington, that kind of thing isn't limited to election years. It's a fact of life you have to adjust to immediately. Almost as soon as I arrived in the Senate, some so-called "birthers" argued that because neither of my parents were naturalized American citizens when I was born, I wasn't a natural-born citizen. One activist went so far as to gain access to my parents' immigration records and discovered that my parents first arrived in the United States in 1956, before Castro had seized power in Cuba. That's when the trouble began.

On the day when the *St. Petersburg Times* reported the story, a *Washington Post* reporter called my office. He was preparing to post another story that implied I had embellished my family's history for political gain. I had found out that my parents had immigrated in 1956 only a few weeks before, and in an interview with the *Miami Herald* in September of 2011, I had stated my parents had immigrated before the 1959 revolution. And I intended to discuss their journey more fully as part of this book.

Nevertheless, I am the son of Cuban exiles. My parents did arrive in the United States before Castro took power. But they had believed they could return to Cuba if things improved there. After the revolution prevailed, and before Castro's declaration he was a communist and his open embrace of the Soviet Union, my parents had made plans to return because they had grown discouraged with their circumstances in America. But their family in Cuba warned them that Castro was becoming a tyrant and urged them to return to the United States permanently. My grandfather had returned to Cuba, where he intended to remain the rest of his life until the family persuaded him to leave again. I was raised by people who felt a deep pain at the loss of their country. They could never return to Cuba as long as Castro remained in power. That made them exiles in their hearts, and in mine. That's the way the Cuban exile community, with a few rare exceptions, views them as well. I heard from many Cuban Americans who told me the story had prompted them to research their own family histories. And it prompted me to find out everything I could about my parents' experience. I obtained their entire immigration file, which included the background check they underwent in Cuba, their birth certificates and marriage license and other documents. In the pages of their file and old passports, my parents' story, when they were younger than I am, came alive for me—the story of their hopes and disappointments and fears, and the dreams that are a part of their children now.

I thought the *Washington Post* story overreached. It made it sound as if my speeches and campaign ads were filled with accounts of how my parents had fled Cuba in fear of their lives as they were chased by Castro's goons. All I had really said was that my parents were exiles who'd lost their country and made a better life for their children in America. If I had known the exact date of their immigration during the campaign, I would have made the same claim. I would have acknowledged that they came in 1956, that they had wanted to return and couldn't. In the end, theirs is the story of exile. They had lost their country.

Of all the heightened media scrutiny I've experienced in my first year in the Senate, the most distressing experience didn't involve anything I did or said. It wasn't even about an incident in my political career, although it wouldn't have been reported were I not a public figure.

In July 2011, Univision broadcast a story about my brother-in-law, Orlando's, arrest for drug trafficking a quarter century earlier. I was in high school when he was arrested and had nothing to do with the case. Other media outlets knew about it but never reported on it because it had no bearing on my public office. No one in the Democratic Party would touch it. The story wouldn't have any political impact. But I knew how much having their private lives broadcast to the nation would deeply hurt my family and that upset me greatly. My sister and her husband are not public figures. Simply being related to a senator doesn't change that. They are private people who have no role in my political career or my public service. Univision's decision to lead their national newscast with this story about something that happened to two private people over two decades before exposed my sister to public embarrassment. And, sadly, it was also very painful for my mother who was forced to relive the anguish of that difficult time.

The scrutiny of the campaign and of my first year in office has affected me in some positive ways. I pay more careful attention to detail now. Whether it is a question I am asked or some form I need to fill out, I do everything now with an eye toward how it could be viewed, maybe out of context, in the future. For much of my political career I was very young, very busy and very inexperienced, and sometimes I was sloppy in some of my practices. The scrutiny of the last three years has changed that. But I also need to balance this concern. For in our fear of generating negative attention, we can lose the purpose of our service.

In the book of Matthew, Jesus gave us the parable of the talents. It tells of a master who entrusted his three servants with his property according to each of their abilities. One of the servants received five talents. Another received two talents. And a third was given one talent. When he returned from a long absence, the master asked his servants for an accounting of what they did with the money he had left them. The first two servants explained that they each put it to work and doubled its value. Their master was pleased with them and rewarded them. But the third servant was afraid to lose what he was given. So he hid his one talent in a hole in the ground. For that, he was punished by his master.

I need to be careful not to become like the third servant. So worried about what might be said about me that I end up wasting my opportunity to make a difference. So worried about losing this chance I have been given to serve that I end up burying it in a hole in the ground.

CHAPTER 40

The End of the Beginning

I F SERVING IN THE SENATE IS A REMINDER OF ANYTHING, IT is that people come and go. Our desks have the names of those who used them before us carved in them. The hallways are lined with statues of great leaders who served here long ago. Our office buildings are named for men who made their mark here long before we arrived. But they are all gone now. And so it will be for us.

All my life I've been in a hurry to get to my future. Writing a book about my life has forced me to reflect on my past more than I have before. And in my reflection, I realized that time is the one thing I can never reclaim. I will never be a child again. I will never play high school or college football again. I will never watch a Dolphins game with my father again. I will never meet my wife or see my children for the first time again. Those things happened when I was in a hurry, and they will never happen again.

There are things happening in my life today that will not come again. And, slowly, I'm starting to worry that I won't learn how to appreciate my blessings in the fleeting moment of their occurrence before I have run out of time.

By and large, I've adjusted to the politics of the Senate. But the job's effect on my personal life has been more difficult to manage. After giving it considerable thought, Jeanette and I decided that at least for the first year, the family would remain in Miami and I would commute to Washington every week. Our extended family is in Miami, and they are an important support network for Jeanette as she manages, as she has always had to, the greater share of our responsibilities to our children. As our kids have gotten older, they have more activities outside school. When Jeanette needs help managing the family schedule, we have plenty of relatives in Miami who are willing to provide it.

Jeanette has responsibilities in the community, too. Since March 2011, she has worked as a consultant for the family philanthropic foundation established by Norman Braman, the former owner of the Philadelphia Eagles, and for the charitable activities of Norman's South Florida car dealerships. I got to know Norman when I served in the Florida legislature. He occasionally met with me on behalf of the Miami-Dade Jewish Federation, the Braman Breast Cancer Center at the University of Miami and other local community causes, which he helps support. We've become very close friends over the years.

Jeanette and I traveled to Israel with Norman and his wife, Irma, shortly after my election, and visited two charitable projects the Braman family supports there. During the trip, Jeanette talked a lot with Norman and Irma about the causes she's involved in, and their conversations inspired Norman to ask Jeanette to help him organize the family's charitable giving.

The offer gave me pause. I worried Jeanette wouldn't have time to do all the work the job would require. Furthermore, I've always been wary of working with friends. If something goes wrong at work, it can ruin the personal relationship. Also, Norman is not only a generous charitable donor, he has been a generous donor to my campaigns as well. I worried that my political opponents would drag his good name into controversy by accusing him of hiring Jeanette as a favor to me.

On the other hand, there was no doubt in my mind she would do an excellent job. Jeanette has a passion for charitable causes. And the Bramans trust her, perhaps the most important qualification for the job. And since I was making less as a senator than I did as a lawyer, the additional income didn't hurt, either.

In the end, we both decided she should take the job. And she has done exceptionally well in the position. She's helped organize the foundation, and set up a formal application and review process for donation requests.

She meets with the organizations applying for donations, and conducts follow-up visits. She writes the memoranda on the applications and meets with the Braman family to help them decide which causes they will support. When the decisions are made, she writes the award and rejection letters. Her new job has also been good in other ways as well. After years of having to plan her entire life around me, she now has her own professional identity independent from me. She attends community events not as Senator Rubio's wife, but as the representative of the Braman Family Foundation. For the first time in our marriage, I have had to stay home with the kids on the weekends while Jeanette attends a work-related function. I have to coordinate my work schedule with her work schedule. She works hard, and the new job does take time. But she loves the work. And she loves the fact that she is helping the Braman family make a difference in the lives of others. I'm happy for her and proud of her.

The decision for our family to remain in Miami has its disadvantages, though, which I very much regret. I now miss more of my kids' school events and other important occasions than I ever have before. I'm away for three or four days a week most of the year, which puts more intense pressure on Jeanette. I feel guilty about it, which makes missing her and our kids all the harder to bear.

My typical workweek begins Monday morning when I drop off the kids at school. I still teach a class at Florida International University on Mondays, after which I head straight to the airport and catch a flight to Washington early in the afternoon. When I arrive, I go directly to my Senate office, where I have a regularly scheduled foreign policy meeting with my staff before the usual Monday afternoon vote on the Senate floor. I go home after the vote, do some reading and call Jeanette and the kids to say good night before I go to bed.

The next three days of the week are pretty much the same. I work out in the Senate gym in the morning. I try to attend morning Mass, and call Jeanette on the walk to the church. I'm usually back at my desk by eight thirty. The days are filled with calls, meetings, committee hearings and votes. I usually have lunch with the other Republican senators, followed by more meetings, calls and votes.

Most weeks I'm able to fly home late Thursday afternoon or early evening. I teach a class Friday mornings, and usually work in my Miami office the rest of the day or attend meetings in the community. After two years of campaigning, I try to spend Saturdays with my family, although I can't always manage it. With very rare exceptions, I always take Sundays off.

For the first time in my career, my public office is my full-time job. That's better in one way. I can devote all my professional energies to a single job. But it is tougher on my responsibilities as a husband and father. The difficult balancing act between work and home has become common in contemporary American life. We are blessed to have the financial and social resources to help us strike this balance. And yet it's still the biggest challenge I face in the Senate.

To have the right priorities is a sign of maturity and character. And it's generally accepted in our society that family should be your first priority. No matter what career you've chosen, nothing should come before your responsibilities to your loved ones. But that's often easier said than done. For over fourteen years in public life, I have struggled to keep my family my first priority in deed as well as words.

My long hours on the Dole campaign almost cost me my relationship with Jeanette. My dedication earned the notice and praise of people in politics, but I almost lost my girlfriend and future wife. As a West Miami city commissioner, I often went out to late-night dinners with the city clerk and city manager after commission meetings, while my new wife waited home alone.

In Tallahassee, especially in my first year in the legislature, I usually went out after work to socialize with my colleagues, not because I was looking for a good time, but because I wanted to network with prominent politicians and opinion leaders. Jeanette stayed at home, pregnant and alone. When I decided to run for speaker, I traveled the state constantly, and continued traveling after I became speaker. With little children at home, Jeanette saw even less of me.

All of it was important work. It was all a necessary part of the life I had chosen. But its costs are exorbitant. Increasingly, our entire life—family gatherings, vacations, even visits to the doctor—have to be scheduled around my travels. And most nights, Jeanette has had to bathe, feed and put to bed four little children, while her husband sends his regrets and calls them on the phone to say good night.

Now I'm away from home most weeks from Monday morning until

Thursday night. During Senate recesses, I have to travel around one of the biggest and most diverse states in the country because my constituents deserve to hear from their senator on a regular basis. And there is, of course, the never-ending pressure on a politician to spend a lot of time raising money for the next campaign. Even when I'm home, I'm distracted by work. I read and send e-mails. I talk on the phone to staff and colleagues. I think about legislation or a debate or review documents that require my approval. Like too many of us these days, I'm not as attentive as I should be to the people who need me most.

I love my wife and children. They are the most important people in my life. If I were ever presented with an inescapable choice between them and politics, I would choose them, of course. But the truth is I would try to find some way to manage both my public and personal responsibilities. That's my biggest fear. In trying to be both public servant and family man, sometimes I do neither job well enough. It takes singular focus to be very good at anything. How can I have a singular focus for two different jobs? How can I be a great husband and father, if I'm trying to be a great senator?

I often wonder if I entered politics too early in my life, if it wouldn't have been better had I waited until my children were grown. Obviously, it would be better for my kids to have a father who came home for dinner every night, who coached their teams and who left his work at the office when he was home. I worry, too, that it might have been better for the people of Florida to have a senator who didn't refuse speaking invitations or meetings because of a choir recital or a Little League game to attend.

I have sought the counsel of some of my senior colleagues who have walked the road I'm walking now. Some of them got the balance wrong, and privately admit it. Their children grew up in their absence. Most of their kids turned out fine, but they know they missed the most cherished moments in a father's life, and have to live with the nagging remorse they would never have the chance to re-create them. When your children grow up, they stay grown up forever.

Others did better. They turned down opportunities to travel, to join the leadership or run for president. They cherish the memories other colleagues had missed. They were present for the children despite the demands of public office. But they, too, admit they missed other moments, and now live with the nagging wonder of what might have happened had they taken their shot at a bigger ambition, when the opportunity was there.

There was no easy answer for them, and there won't be one for me, either.

I am just one generation removed from my father's destitute childhood, and two generations removed from the tragedies of my grandfather's life.

But our story does not end with me. The first of my children was born sixteen years after my grandfather took his last breath. My older daughter was only ten when my father died. What is the purpose of exceeding two generations of unfulfilled dreams if those dreams end with me? Don't my children deserve what I had: a loving, attentive father whose sole ambition was to make his children's life better than his own? If I'm focused only on my dreams, who will help them pursue theirs?

What's the answer then? Should only childless people serve in high public office? Or only people willing to sacrifice their family's happiness? That can't be true.

I don't really know the answer yet. I'm slowly starting to figure it out, though. By most worldly standards, my father and my grandfather were not successful men. They never made much money. They never achieved social or political prominence. I admired them, I loved them, but I never considered them successful. For me success was what you accomplished in your career. But now that I have achieved what I once believed was the height of success, I am starting to understand that in the end, just like my father and grandfather, the mark I make in this world will not be decided by how much money I make or how many titles I attain. Rather, the greatest mark I can leave is the one I will make as a father and a husband.

I have begun to learn and accept that all experiences in life are fleeting, and in our last days the most fortunate of us will die as my father died: surrounded by people who loved him and whose lives were better for his place in them. Not many people die with the regret they hadn't worked more. What we regret are the T-ball games we missed, the first day of school we didn't make, the simple, ordinary events that taken together create the lasting bond between parent and child. I know the work I do can be a good and honorable thing, especially if I use my office to honor God. But I know its costs, too.

In my first few months in Washington, Senator Patrick Leahy of Vermont sought me out on the Senate floor one day. He wanted to know how I was adjusting to life in the Senate. It was a sincere and kind gesture on his part, and I deeply appreciated it. I told him I loved it except for the fact that I missed my wife and kids terribly. I missed the chaos of getting them ready for school in the morning. I missed the struggle to wind them down every night and put them in bed. And I missed watching a movie alone with Jeanette after they had fallen asleep.

His expression changed from someone engaging in small talk to that of a man who knew something important and wanted to share it. He offered me a simple admonition, straightforward but powerful advice.

Over the years, he said, he had missed his share of family events while he was stuck in Washington casting a critical vote or working on important legislation. Everyone has a job to do, he acknowledged, and this was his. Almost all parents miss something in their children's lives because they had work to do. Your kids will understand.

But once, when his children were still young, the president called him personally to invite him to an important occasion. When he checked his calendar, he found it conflicted with one of his children's events, and he called the president back and respectfully declined his offer. Years later, he couldn't remember the event the president had invited him to, but his children had never forgotten that he had turned down the president of the United States to be with them.

We all have a job to do and we ought to do it well. In my profession, I have all sorts of opportunities to do interesting and exciting things. There are important people I can meet, exciting events I can attend and interesting places I can visit. But if I have to choose them over my children, they're not worth doing.

Just after New Year's of 2012, Jeanette and I had the opportunity to join an official delegation to Africa. It would have been an interesting and valuable experience to witness America's foreign aid programs in action. Over the last few years, the generosity of the American people has saved the lives of four million people in Africa who are suffering with AIDS. I support the program and it has to be reauthorized this year. The trip would have helped me make the argument that it was in our national interest to maintain it.

But as the trip approached, I found out Anthony had a flag football game and Amanda had a cheerleading competition scheduled during the trip. Daniella was distraught that her parents would be away for eight days. They all had homework every night. Amanda had a big science project to finish, and Dominick was having a hard time pronouncing his letters in pre-K reading.

Our kids needed us at home. My job wanted me in Africa. I might not have another opportunity for a while to see how American assistance was helping make the world a better, healthier place. We moved forward with the trip. We got the necessary shots and had started taking malaria pills. We made arrangements for my sister to take the kids to school and pick them up in the afternoon. My mother-in-law would stay with them at night. My nephew Landy had promised to take Anthony to his flag football game and practices. We woke up the morning of the trip with our bags packed and our boarding passes printed. All that remained to do was drop the kids off at school, say our good-byes and drive to the airport.

On the drive to the airport, I was pulled in two directions. With so much going on in our kids' lives, it didn't seem right to be away from home for more than a week. But I didn't feel I should pass up this opportunity, either. It would be hard to back out of the trip at the last minute. Then I remembered Senator Leahy's advice and realized I was choosing a useful experience that I would like to have but didn't need to have over the needs of my children. I thought God was testing me again, and giving me another chance to prove what I often claimed, but didn't always live up to: that being a husband and father was more important than being a senator.

So many times, I have tried to have it both ways. I've tried to be all in as a husband and father and all in as a politician, and I didn't do either job as well as I should have. We all have many chances in our lives to choose wisely and do the right thing. Not only our lives but the lives of our children are a history of our choices. My history began when my grandfather chose to leave Cabaiguán for Havana, where his daughters would have a chance at a better life. My choices were made possible by my parents' decision to come to America, to move us to Las Vegas and then bring us back to Miami, to work into their seventies. They are the beginning of my story, and I am the epilogue of theirs, as my children will be the epilogue of mine.

There will be other trips. But my children will never be this age again. I picked my children up from school that day, and felt joy as I saw their surprised looks as they discovered their father, who they thought was already somewhere in Africa, waiting for them. Years from now, I might remember the trip to Africa I didn't take only because I included it in this book. But I think my children will always remember the day their father chose them over Africa, and waited outside their school to hug them and bring them home.

Epilogue

From just about the moment I arrived in the Senate, I was rumored to be a potential vice-presidential pick by the eventual Republican nominee in the 2012 election.

I never felt comfortable with the concept. I had just been elected to the Senate, and I was passionate about the issues I was able to influence as a member of the Foreign Relations and Intelligence Committees.

I also recalled my experiences dealing with Governor Charlie Crist, himself a presumptive vice-presidential nominee during much of the 2008 election season. Governor Crist spent so much time campaigning for that job that all of his actions were viewed through the prism that he seemed more interested in positioning himself for higher office than he was at focusing on the job he had been elected to do.

Nevertheless, I felt just as strongly that America was on the wrong course and that a limited-government leader was desperately needed in the White House to address all the challenges facing our country. I concluded that if the nominee of our party believed that I could help him put the country back on the right path by agreeing to serve as his running mate, it was something I needed to consider. And so in late April, after a phone call from the presumptive nominee Mitt Romney, I agreed to participate in the campaign's review process. Ultimately, Governor Romney selected Congressman Paul Ryan as his running mate.

Freed from the speculation about my future, I threw myself whole-heartedly into the fall campaign. Despite having endorsed me and campaigned for me during my run for the United States Senate, Governor Romney and I were never particularly close. However, as I campaigned for him, I came to know him as a good and decent man—a role model of how to be successful at the most important jobs any man can ever have: husband and father. The more time I spent with him, the more I became even more convinced that he would make a phenomenal president and that the American people would benefit from the decency and work ethic that those who know Governor Romney personally had witnessed.

While balancing my responsibilities as Florida's junior Senator, an adjunct professor at Florida International University, and my duties as a husband and father, I was able to travel the country extensively as a surrogate for the campaign. I had the honor of introducing Governor Romney at the Republican National Convention, and I even traveled to Boston to address the staff at Romney-Ryan headquarters. These experiences, combined with the stops I made in the summer of 2012 while promoting this book, allowed me to once again reconnect with people from all walks of life all across the country. It's one of the things I enjoy most about public service. As I did on the campaign just two years earlier, I got to hear first-hand about their hopes and their fears.

Ultimately, President Obama was reelected. The pundits and political scientists will spend years explaining the multiple reasons why. I'll leave the formal analysis to them, but as someone who cared about this election because of what it meant for our country, I was extremely disappointed by the results.

In the aftermath of the 2012 elections, a lot has been made about the Republican party needing to moderate its message. But that misses the point. The way forward for Republicans is not to abandon our ideals. Rather, it is to apply the principles of limited government, free enterprise, and strong families to the challenges and the opportunities of the twenty-first century. And to make the connection between what we stand for and the hopes and anxieties people have in their everyday lives.

When my parents immigrated here, they came with few skills, a limited education, and no money. For most of their lives they worked in the service industry. In almost any other nation on Earth, those jobs would barely provide a daily living much less a better future. But in America, my parents made enough money to buy their own home and a car. They felt so confident in the future that in their forties they added two more children to their family—me in 1971 and my sister in 1973.

We didn't have everything we wanted, but we had more than we needed. Most importantly, we had a strong family living in a safe and stable home. Our parents loved each other, made sure we knew they loved us, and encouraged us to dream. They made it very clear that, because we were Americans, we could go as far as our talent and hard work would take us.

My father grew up poor and motherless. My mother, raised by a disabled father who struggled to bring food home every night, lived in rural Cuba in a home with dirt floors. But their children now live lives so far removed from where they came from not so long ago. The four children of an uneducated working-class immigrant couple from Cuba are all college graduates working in professional fields and enjoying a standard of living significantly higher than our parents.

Our story is not rare in America, but it is rare in the world. Had we been born almost anywhere else, at any other time in history, our lives would have been very different. But because I was born and raised in late-twentieth-century America, I was granted seemingly endless opportunities. Our economy produced jobs for relatively low-skilled workers like my parents. Those jobs paid enough for them to make it into the middle class. The government helped me and my siblings pay for college. And today all four of us live lives much better than our parents'.

Because of where and by whom I was raised, I know that what we have in America is special. It's the exception rather than the rule. And if we lose this intrinsic quality of possibility, there is nothing to take its place. If America declines, so will the world.

I realize that the journey my parents made from poor immigrants to the working middle class is harder today than it was in their time. The world has changed, the economy has changed, and our society has changed. But whether the journey my parents made is still possible to all who are willing to work for it will decide whether America will decline or remain this special place.

As I look forward to the years ahead, perhaps no cause is more important to me than growing and sustaining a broad and vibrant middle class.

One of the fundamental promises of America is the opportunity to make it to the middle class. But today there is a growing opportunity gap developing. In my travels across Florida and the country, I have found that many people are worried that they may never achieve middle-class prosperity and stability, and they fear that their children will be trapped as well, with the same life and the same problems.

For those of us blessed with the opportunity to serve our country in government, one of the fundamental challenges before us is to find an appropriate and sustainable role for government in closing this gap between the dreams of millions of Americans and the opportunities to actually realize them.

The key to a vibrant middle class is an abundance of jobs that pay enough so that workers can provide for themselves and their families, enjoy leisure time, save for retirement, and pay for their children's education so that they can grow up and earn even more than their parents.

Today, too many Americans cannot find jobs like these, and some cannot find any job at all. There are two main reasons for this. First, the weakened American economy is not creating enough jobs of any kind, especially middle-class jobs. Second, we have a "skills shortage." Too many Americans do not have the skills they need to do the new middle-class jobs.

The path to a prosperous and growing American middle class is the combination of a vibrant economy that creates middle-class jobs and people with the skills needed for these new jobs. The federal government can play an important role in encouraging a vibrant economy and in equipping its citizens with the skills they need for twenty-first century middle-class jobs.

Federal policies on the national debt, taxes, and regulations all have a tremendous impact on economic growth and middle-class job creation. Our $16 trillion debt, and the lack of a plan to fix it, scares people from investing money in new or growing businesses. They are afraid of getting hit with massive tax increases in the future to pay off this debt. And the leading cause of our growing debt is the way Medicare is currently designed for the future. That is why we must reform and save Medicare as soon as possible. The sooner we act, the likelier we can do it without making any changes for people who are currently in the system, people like my mother.

Our complicated and uncertain tax code is also hindering the creation of middle-class jobs. You can't open or grow a business if your taxes are too high or too uncertain. The way forward should be to keep rates low on everyone. End the multiple taxation of savings. Simplify our tax code by getting rid of unjustified loopholes. And generate new revenue by creating new taxpayers, not new taxes. Rapid economic growth is the only way to generate the kind of money we need to bring this debt under control. Tax increases do not create new taxpayers. And they do not create rapid economic growth.

Excessive regulations are impeding middle-class job creation, too. Regulation is necessary to protect our natural environment, keep our food and medicine safe, and ensure fair competition and fair treatment of our workers. But following regulations is costly. The more expensive a regulation, the less money a business has left to give raises or hire new people. We have to weigh the benefit of any given regulation against the impact it will have on job creation.

Getting control of our debt and reforming our federal tax code and regulations are critically important, but it is not enough. We will need to do more. For example, we should expand our domestic energy industry. American innovation has now given us access to massive new oil and natural gas deposits, making America the most energy-rich country on the planet. This new energy wealth means all kinds of new middle-class jobs, from the fields and platforms where we drill to the manufacturing plants that will return to the United States with the lower cost of energy. These are just the type of jobs we need most right now: well-paying, middle-class work that doesn't require an expensive advanced degree and that contributes to the strength of our economy.

Sound monetary policy would also encourage middle-class job creation. The arbitrary way in which interest rates and our currency are treated is yet another cause of unpredictability injected into our economy. The Federal Reserve Board should publish and follow a clear monetary rule to provide greater stability about prices and what the value of a dollar will be over time.

Getting control of the debt, reforming taxes, limiting regulations, growing our energy industry, and following a predictable monetary policy are five concrete things the government can do to help our economy create new middle-class jobs. But if the higher wages people make at these jobs are offset by an increase in the cost of living, we are just running in place.

Nothing is taking a bigger chunk out of the budgets of our middle-class households than the cost of health care. We must provide the conditions for people to get the health coverage they need in an affordable way. People should be able to buy a health care plan that fits their needs and budget from any company in America that is willing to sell it to them. And they should be able to buy it with tax-free money, just like their employers buy it for many of them now.

These are just a few of the things we can do at the federal level to create the conditions for middle-class job creation and to stabilize the growth in the cost of living. But no matter how many middle-class jobs are created, you can't grow the middle class if people do not have the skills to get hired for these jobs.

Not so long ago, even if you didn't graduate from high school, if you were willing to work, you could find a job that paid enough for you to buy a home, start a family, and eventually send your kids to college for a better life. Those days are long gone, and they are probably never coming back.

Today, education plays a central role in the twenty-first century knowledge economy. Four-year college graduates earn an average of 70 percent more than those without such a degree. There are a number of things government should be doing in education.

First, our elementary and secondary schools need state-level curriculum reform and new investment in continuing teacher training.

Second, the public school system for millions of disadvantaged American children is a disaster. Many of these schools deny opportunities to those who need them most. We need to allow charter schools and other innovative schools to flourish. The key to that is empowering parents. All parents should be able to send their children to the school of their choice. For parents with special needs children, the freedom to choose their kids' school is especially important.

Third, our tax code should reward investment in education. If you invest in a business by buying a machine, you get a tax credit for the cost. If there is a tax credit for investing in equipment, shouldn't there be a tax credit for investing in people?

Fourth, let's encourage career, technical, and vocational education.

Why can't more of our students graduate with a high school diploma and an industry certification in a trade or career? And we should commit to finding ways for our returning veterans to put the skills they've developed in the armed forces to use in civilian job opportunities.

Fifth, we need to address soaring college costs and encourage skill development that doesn't require the traditional four-year-college route. The groundswell of creativity and technological change in higher education will lead to dramatic reductions in the time and expense of higher education so long as government financial policy doesn't stand in the way. We should make sure our federal aid programs don't discriminate against online course credits and help give parents and students more choices.

And finally, we need to reform our federal college grant and loan programs. College affordability is an issue that is very personal to me. The only reason I was able to go to college was because of federal grants and loans.

On education, the bottom line is we are trying to prepare twenty-first-century students using a twentieth-century education model. Now is the time to be creative, innovative, and daring in reforming the way we provide our people the skills they need to make it to the middle class.

Beyond education, there is another obstacle keeping too many young Americans from moving ahead. Many young Americans do not have the skills they need to get a middle-class job because they grow up in unstable environments. They live in broken and often violent homes in substandard housing in dangerous neighborhoods, with poor nutrition and no access to primary health care. Often, they are being raised by a heroic single parent and sometimes by an elderly family member. And they may not have the chance to participate in after-school activities because their caretakers can't afford the fees or get out of work in time to take them.

Rising above these circumstances is possible. Every day, some amazing parents and caretaker grandparents are overcoming situations like these to give their kids the chance at a better life. I saw my own sister Barbara struggle—and succeed—raising her two sons in the years that her husband Orlando was away. But research on this topic has consistently found that children raised in tough circumstances struggle in comparison with children raised in a more stable family setting. They face higher risks of falling into poverty, failing in school, or suffering emotional and behavioral problems. They have lower scores on standardized tests, lower grades, and a much higher chance of dropping out of high school or failing to attend college.

Widespread societal breakdown is not an issue government can solve, and yet it is one that the government cannot ignore. And the last thing valiant single parents need is an elected official, in some far off capitol, lecturing them or making decisions for them. But we cannot separate the economic well-being of our people from their social well-being. What the federal government can do to confront societal breakdown is limited, yet important. Rather than pretend we know the answer, we should start by engaging those who do important work every day in mentoring young people and leading them on the right path: their teachers, coaches, parents, priests, and pastors. Government leaders should take part in and encourage a national conversation about the importance of civil society institutions and leaders in creating the social infrastructure needed for success.

And I believe that we need to protect our nation's safety net programs. Not as a way of life, but as a way to help those who have failed to stand up and try again, and to help those who cannot help themselves. But these programs must be reformed to enhance family stability, financial opportunity, education, and a culture of work.

But perhaps the most effective thing we in government can do about societal breakdown is acknowledge its impact. At family gatherings, I hear from my sister and my two sister-in-laws—all teachers—how every single day kids bring their home experiences into the classroom. They see firsthand how kids living in dysfunctional homes are going to really struggle to make it. As a people, we cannot build a vibrant and broad-based middle class if we do not solve this problem.

In order to address the big issues our country is facing, we need a limited and effective government. And you can't have one without the other. Big government is not effective government. Big government has never worked. The promise of more government as the answer to all our problems is easy to sell. But when it is put in practice, it fails every time. Big government has never been able to create and sustain a vibrant and stable middle class. We need a limited and effective government whose role is to support those institutions and policies that strengthen the family and community.

If any people on Earth should know that, it is us. Many Americans need to look no further than our own communities to see where the answers to our challenges lie. It starts with strong and stable families. It continues with a vibrant civil society filled with people working together to improve their country and with a thriving free-enterprise economy that creates good-paying jobs and can draw upon people with the skills to do those jobs.

Some have suggested that the reason Barack Obama was reelected was because the American people have changed. That today we have too many people who want things from government and therefore they will vote for whoever promises them more from government. But I still believe that most of the people that depend on government spending for their subsistence would rather have a good-paying job. I am still convinced that the overwhelming majority of our people just want what my parents had: a chance. A real chance to earn a good living and provide even better opportunities for their children.

In October of 2012, the Romney campaign invited me to speak to a gathering of their largest donors at the Waldorf-Astoria hotel in Manhattan. When I arrived at the banquet hall where I was scheduled to give my remarks, I was approached by a group of three uniformed employees from the hotel's catering department. They had seen my speech at the Republican National Convention, where I told the story of my father, the banquet bartender. At events like this, there were usually only two people standing in the banquet hall—the speaker on the podium and my dad, the bartender, behind the bar. He sacrificed all he did so that I could be the other man standing.

That story must have struck a chord because these men had a gift for me. They presented me with a name tag that says "Rubio, Banquet Bartender." I keep that name tag next to my desk in my Senate office as a reminder that today there are millions of men and women all across America just like my dad. They aren't looking for a handout. They just want a job that provides for their families. They want a chance to earn a better life for themselves and a better future for their children. Whether they get that chance will determine whether America remains exceptional or declines.

The dreams my parents had for their children are still out there. They're in the kitchens of our hotels, in the landscaping crews that work in our neighborhoods, in the late-night janitorial shifts that clean our offices. That is where we can still find the dreams America was built on. And that is where we can find the promise of tomorrow.

As it has been throughout our nation's history, these people's journey is also America's destiny. If they can give their children what my parents gave me and my siblings, twenty-first century America will be the single greatest nation that man has ever known. I thank God I will have the opportunity to play a role in ensuring that is exactly how things turn out.

Acknowledgments

One of the first things I learned while writing an account of my life was not to rely entirely on my fallible memory. Luckily, I had a great deal of help reconstructing my family's past, none more valuable than the contributions my sister Veronica made both to recalling our story and then writing it. I am much indebted to her. My brother, Mario, and sister Barbara were very helpful as well, especially in recalling the family's early years in America before I was born. My aunts Georgina and Magda also supplied important recollections as did, of course, my mother, Oriales Rubio.

I was fortunate to be represented and advised by my experienced and wise lawyer Bob Barnett, and to be in the care of an excellent publishing house, Sentinel. I want to thank especially my publisher, Adrian Zackheim, for his encouragement and counsel; associate publisher, Will Weisser; and the indefatigable Niki Papadopoulos, who edited the book with great skill and intelligence. I am grateful to Mark Salter for helping me organize and revise the manuscript on a tight schedule.

Thanks are also due to Allison McLean and Christy D'Agostini for arranging publicity for the book; Natalie Horbachevsky for the interior art and jacket routing and for coordinating the Spanish edition; and everyone in Sentinel's production team, who worked diligently to bring this book to market in record time.

Writing about my Senate campaign reminded me again how much I owe the people who worked so hard to help elect me. Good campaigns make good candidates, and they are the work of many talented, dedicated individuals. I was fortunate to have more than my fair share of some of the best people in the business. In no specific order I want to thank each of you. David Rivera, Alina Garcia, Ralph Arza, Steve and Viviana Bovo, Esther Nuhfer and Gaston Cantens. My campaign chairman, Al Hoffman. My finance chairman, Jay Demetree. My campaign manager, Jose Mallea. Heath Thompson, Todd Harris, Malorie Thompson, Julio Rebull Jr., Albert Martinez, Alex Burgos, Pat Shortridge, Anthony Bustamante, Brandon Patty, Whit Ayres, Zach Burr, Carmen Miller Spence, Ann Herberger, Michael Beach, Dawn Dettling, Patrick Mooney, Eileen Pineiro, JR Sanchez, Luke Marchant, Joe Pounder, Jeff Bechdel, Orlando "Landy" Cicilia, Emily Bouck, Jessica Fernandez, Genessa Casanova, Carlos Fleites, Ashley Beach, Clay Williams, Chris Siercks, Tara Emory, Todd Lewis, Ali Pardo, Lauren Pardo, Tiffany Watkins, John Heffernan, Gina Alonso, Nury Soler, Mike Miller, Alyn Cruz-Higgins, Waldemar Serrano, Luis Hernandez, Javier Correoso, Sharon Day, Robert Fernandez, Deborah Demoss Fonseca, Mario Loyola, Chauncey Goss, Dean Clancy, Andy Laperriere, Sally Canfield, Cesar Conda, Chris Faulkner, Tony Feather, Wendy Grant, Michael Larcher, Nancy McGowan, Tony DiMatteo, Jorge Arrizurieta, Bill Bunting, Jeb Bush, Jr., Chip Case, Larry Cretul, David Custin, Teresa Dailey, Mac McGehee, Bill Diamond, Vivian Diaz, Bob Diener, Sid Dinerstein, Brett Doster, Bertica Cabrera Morris, Gov. Luis Fortuno, Gov. Jeb Bush, Sen. Jim DeMint, Gov. Mike Huckabee, Rudy Giuliani, Erick Erickson, Miguel Fana, Manny Fernandez, Stanley and Gay Gaines, Mark Gerson, Domingo Sanchez, Raul and Betty Fernandez, Marta Flores, Rebeca Sosa, Gerardo Ramos, Dennis Baxley, Nelson Diaz, Larry Godwin, Gary Lee, Tom Lee, Paul Singer, Harlan Crow, David Johnson, Dexter Lehtinen, the Leon family, Lisa Lorenzo, Javier Manjarres, Steve Marin, David McKalip, Tom and Gina Mestre, Dario Moreno, Ana Navarro, Bexie Nobles, Modesto Perez, Ralph Perez, Sergio and Tatiana Pino, Sam Rashid, Chet Renfro, Blaise Ingoglia, Dan Senor, Christian Camera, Amber Stoner, Stanley Tate, Joaquin Urquiola, Steve Wasserstein and Ovi Vento.

I am grateful to all our team leaders, our small-dollar donors who kept us afloat, supporters who attended early Tea Party rallies, the people whose prayers kept us going and the volunteers who may have never met me but worked tirelessly for my election nonetheless. And of course to the people of Florida for the privilege of representing them in the U.S. Senate.

My thanks also to the Fanjul family for believing in me early on when few did.

To my dear friends the Braman family, in particular Norman Braman, whose advice, interest in my growth as a father and husband and pride in my accomplishments remind me of the role my grandfather and father once played.

To my mother-in-law, Maria Giraldo, for helping us keep things together at home, and to my extended family of in-laws, nieces and nephews— the Fonsecas, Guidis, Nereys, Fleites and Tedones—who volunteered their time to help out in the campaign.

The Cuban exile community for reminding me daily of the value of liberty and freedom.

As ever, I am grateful for the counsel, understanding and love of my wife, Jeanette, and our beautiful children, Amanda, Daniella, Anthony and Dominick, who tolerated yet another demand on their father's time that distracted me from my favorite occupation, spending time in their company.

And last but most important, I thank my Lord, Jesus Christ, whose willingness to suffer and die for my sins will allow me to enjoy eternal life.